Happy Cooking!

Betty Groff

BETTY GROFF'S
Pennsylvania Dutch
Cookbook

Also by Betty Groff:

Betty Groff's Up-Home Down-Home Cookbook
Betty Groff's Country Goodness Cookbook
(with José Wilson) Good Earth & Country Cooking

BETTY GROFF'S
Pennsylvania Dutch
Cookbook

With Illustrations by Heather Saunders

Macmillan Publishing Company
New York
Collier Macmillan Publishers
London

Macmillan Publishing Company
866 Third Avenue, New York, N.Y. 10022
Collier Macmillan Canada, Inc.

Library of Congress Cataloging-in-Publication Data
Groff, Betty.
Betty Groff's Pennsylvania Dutch cookbook / Betty Groff.
p.   cm.
ISBN 0-02-545801-9
1. Cookery—Pennsylvania.   2. Cookery, German.   I. Title.
TX721.G65   1989
641.59748—dc20   89-12761   CIP

Macmillan books are available at special discounts for bulk purchases
for sales promotions, premiums, fund-raising, or educational use.
For details, contact:

Special Sales Director
Macmillan Publishing Company
866 Third Avenue
New York, N.Y. 10022

DESIGNED BY ERICH HOBBING

10 9 8 7 6 5 4 3 2 1

Printed in the United States of America

*To the delightful memories of food shared with family
and friends, to the excitement of each new day
and the challenge of the future, knowing
that each one of you will be creating
your own memories*

Acknowledgments

THANK YOU:

Barbara J. Adams, for always being a friend and for the joy of working together on this book. The long hours of research and testing were fun because of your energy and excitement at every turn. Your sensitivity, artistic presentation, and willingness to help in any situation have lightened each responsibility. The mutual enjoyment of rediscovering our roots through the preparation of our regional foods has been so stimulating—it seems we've only scratched the surface. May it open many new doors into the future.

Pam Hoenig, for being a super editor with a keen understanding of my desire to preserve our heritage through food.

Bob and Betty Shirk, for sharing your family cookbooks and insight into other areas of Pennsylvania Dutch foods and folklore.

Saranna Brown Miller, whose illustrations of family heirlooms are the bases of those in this book.

Diane Stoneback, for the many hours of late night inquiries and interviews to search the inner recesses of my mind. The many memories and customs, often taken for granted by all of us, come alive through your ability to ask the right questions. Your sense of humor, warmth, and understanding in writing my story are deeply appreciated.

My husband, Abe, for having faith in me and "pushing" when necessary. Our son, Charlie, and his wife, Cindy, grandsons, Matt and Travis Groff, our son, Bob, and his wife, Janice, and granddaughters, Susan and Sherry, and my Dad and Hazel Herr, for understanding and loving me when the "days were long and patience short." Words cannot express my pride in the strength and commitment of my family.

Contents

BETTY GROFF'S
Pennsylvania Dutch
Cookbook

The Seasons
of the Pennsylvania Dutch

PENNSYLVANIA DUTCH—SPRING

My ancestors, who settled in Lancaster County, Pennsylvania in 1710, thought they'd found paradise. Ten generations later, I can safely say they did, or we wouldn't still be here! Their enthusiasm was evident in a letter they sent back to family members in their homeland: "This is a rich, limestone country, beautifully adorned with sugar maple, hickory and black and white walnut, on the border of a delightful stream, abounding in the finest trout. The water of the creeks is clear and cold; grape vines and clematis intertwining among the lofty branches of the majestic buttonwood form a pleasant retreat from the noon beams of the summer sun."

William Penn was also a convincing salesman when he described the abundance of his land: "Of living creatures, fish, fowl and the beasts of the wood, here are divers sorts, some for food and profit including the elk, as big as a small ox; deer, bigger than ours in England; beaver; raccoon; rabbits; squirrels . . . some eat young bear. Of fowl of the land, there is the turkey (40 or 50 pounds weight) which is very great; pheasants; heath birds; pigeons and partridges in abundance . . . Of fish: sturgeon, herring, shad, catshead, eel, trout and salmon. The fruits which I find in the woods are the black and white mulberry, chestnut, walnut, plums, strawberries, cranberries, burtleberries and grapes of divers sorts."

To this day, the variety of top-quality vegetables, fruits, and flowers grown here annually reaffirms the richness of the soil. And nowhere is it more evident than on the farms of our Amish neighbors here in South Central Pennsylvania. Their vegetable and flower gardens are so lush and immaculate that they could be mistaken for a horticultural college's test plots.

Of course, they are not the only residents to take planting seriously. January and February, the bleakest months on our farm, were brightened largely by the arrival of seed catalogs that offered us a glimmer of hope. Many a spare moment was spent studying the pages for new varieties and totally new crops, though evenings were still given to skating and sledding. The picture brightened considerably a few weeks later when my aunt opened her potting shed and planted the flower and vegetable seeds which sprouted into seedlings on the windowsills of the farmhouse.

April 1 isn't just April Fool's Day in Lancaster County. It's the day farmers begin their new year with the first of the spring planting and yearly contracts.

Because life was slow and easy until spring planting began, we had plenty of energy to expend on the holiday preparations. While New Orleanians celebrate the day before Lent with the Mardi Gras, we observe "Fat Tuesday" as Fastnacht Day. Some say it's the best part of Lent because the day's main event is the making of a special kind of doughnut—the fastnacht. What better way to spend the day before a fast day than gorging on doughnuts?

The doughnut-making custom began as a good way to use up the household's old lard. But if you're picturing Pennsylvania cooks turning out the usual, run-of-the-mill doughnut shop products drizzled with anything from pink icing to chocolate cream and flaked coco-

nut, erase those images. Fastnachts are never round; they're always square. And there are no holes that will become "Munchkins."

To be the real thing, fastnachts have to be made with yeast, eggs, milk, flour, mashed potatoes, and potato water and must be fried in lard. The fried squares are then rolled in powdered or granulated sugar. I'm told that in the days when sugar wasn't as easy to come by, many people simply cut the fastnachts in half and spread them with molasses.

The last person to rise on the morning the fastnachts are made becomes the family "fastnacht" and endures some teasing between bites of rich, moist doughnut.

Our Easter preparations always centered around food and family, with very little emphasis on new spring wardrobes. Whenever my mother had some spare time during the year, she turned hand-blown eggs into bejeweled works of art. We also created molded sugar eggs with cutout scenes, to say nothing of the chocolate-covered fruit, and coconut and peanut butter eggs which were Easter basket highlights.

Often, women would get together and turn candy-making into a social occasion. In our family, however, my father or I did the writing and borders on the eggs while mother did the flowers. That is, that's the way we did it until I took a decorating course and mother and dad eagerly turned all decorating chores over to me.

Easter eggs, the hardboiled ones that the Easter Bunny hid on the lawn, once were colored with golden or red onion skins. But that custom had died out by the time I was a child. We used Hinkle Easter Egg Dyes, made in nearby Columbia. The rich colors that stained our hands (as well as the eggs) and the distinctive aroma of the dyes were as much a part of the holiday as the fresh ham and snowy white coconut cake that were Easter dinner traditions.

Although the Moravians in the eastern part of the state love their saffron cake, the coconut cake is a Lancaster County specialty for Christmas and Easter. The cake trimmed with freshly grated coconut was very special in a day when coconuts weren't so readily available. The round cake has four lofty layers that are piled high with fluffy seven-minute icing. Spread into peaks that resembled whitecaps, the icing always sinks a bit under the heavy layer of freshly-grated coconut that tops off the cake.

Early spring was also the time for suckers (known to early settlers as a form of trout) to spawn in the smaller streams. They came up the runs by the hundreds, to lay their eggs before returning to larger streams. I remember going by the stream on our property at night and shining a flashlight into the water. Hundreds of fish were in one cove—so crowded that I could have reached in and pulled them out with my hands. Although the fish wardens said they shouldn't be caught, many a sucker landed in the frying pan for breakfast.

The Pennsylvania Dutch have a reputation for eating a boring meat and potatoes diet. That's as much of a false stereotype as the idea that Scotsmen are tightfisted with their money. We always ate plenty of fish and more vegetables than some people see in a lifetime. When it came to fish, what we couldn't catch was delivered to the door by a fishman who called at the farm each week. The vegetables we couldn't raise were available at the farmers' market stalls.

Our local streams are full of brown trout—a legacy from old Simon Cameron, former Secretary of War under President Lincoln. A Scotsman, Cameron imported stock from his native land to fill the stream on his estate that's now our Cameron Estate Inn. We keep the stream at the inn, and the pond at our farm, well-stocked with trout as a tribute to him and because there's nothing I like better than a fresh trout cooked with the head and tail intact and then filleted tableside. The flavor is unbeatable.

Each spring, when shad come upstream to spawn, we're responsible for preventing a few from making the trip back downstream. Shad or shad roe, parsleyed new potatoes, and fresh asparagus are a dinner-salute to the season. I always think of my grandfather, Newton, when I have some roe because that delicacy was always reserved for the older men, especially him.

Oysters, expensive and highly coveted, were for special people and special occasions. That's why Lancaster County cooks spent so much time finding substitutes for oysters like salsify or deep-frying blossoms of dandelion, squash, or pumpkins. Although my mother managed to buy oysters weekly when times were good, the large oysters were breaded and pan fried for my father or grandfather. We children were given the broth and ate some of the small ones in stews and casseroles. We never fussed or complained. That's because we realized quickly that while we liked the taste of the broth, we didn't like the mouth-feel of those plump, squishy oysters on our tongues.

Fish and holiday foods helped make spring special, but the season's contributions to the salad bowl made it particularly memorable. While the farmers sterilized the raised beds in the field closest to the house to ready them for their biggest cash crop—the tobacco used for cigars—their wives coaxed them out of a little space in that rich soil for the household's vegetable garden.

It was no different at our farm. The first foods I remember planting were radishes and tender leaf lettuce. Although we can buy all kinds of greens today, I am still partial to the earliest leaf lettuce, tossed with a very light dressing. Even if you live in the city and can't plant a garden, you can raise oak leaf lettuce in a long window box. If you try it, make some of our dressing to go with it. Just combine 2 cups sugar with 1 cup vinegar and 1 cup water, a pinch of salt, and some celery seed. "Fancy it up" with some slices of hardboiled eggs, if you like.

Although it's a well-kept secret, the little town of Mount Joy is the watercress capital of the world. During the peak season four tractor-trailer loads a week are taken out of Donegal Springs which starts near our inn. But I have a personal supply that's closer than that. Whenever I have some freshly baked homemade bread that's still warm, I dash to the pond and cut some watercress. Practically before the kitchen door has closed behind me, I have the bread buttered, sprinkled with salt, spread with cream cheese, and buried under a mound of watercress. Now, that's living!

Spinach and asparagus, two of the earliest vegetables to be planted, were not among my favorites when I was young. (Asparagus and I were on particularly bad terms because one of my jobs as a child was picking the tender asparagus spears each morning. And the reason it was my task—I was the closest to the ground, even when I was standing "tall.") When Abe and I were first married, one of my earliest shocks was learning that these were his favorite vegetables. I looked at him and said, "You must be kidding. I hate both of them." But I've mellowed and have learned to savor them both. My change of heart has a lot to do with making sure they're prepared properly, but it might have something to do with love, too.

At our house, the asparagus is stir-fried quickly and served with a bit of brown butter rather than being cooked to death and then being served in cream and butter over toast points, as my family used to prepare it. Our favorite way to have spinach is the simplest way—in a salad with crumbled bacon and hardboiled egg.

Sugar peas, a delicacy we've enjoyed in Lancaster County since the days of the earliest settlers, are some of the most delicate and most misunderstood vegetables we grow. They look like snow peas but are smaller, sweeter, and more tender. I know of some people who have moved into the area and were given a quart of sugar peas as a welcoming gift. They tried to shell them, thereby throwing the best part away.

As soon as the plants are three inches tall, a fence or some brush is placed along the row to give the vines something to cling to. Accomplished gardeners say that to get the very best crop, the sugar peas should be planted on St. Patrick's Day. But that's sometimes hard to do because we often get an "onion snow" (the last light snow) late in March. It doesn't hurt the young growth, but it often discourages the gardener.

Green onions or scallions were another springtime treat, though consuming them was a bit tricky. Because I grew up in a minister's family, eating onions was only allowed on days when there were no scheduled church events. That ruled out Tuesdays and Wednesdays as well as the weekends. Mondays and Thursdays were my days to hit them hard as a snack with bread and butter or on fried potatoes.

Not all the coveted spring greens here in Pennsylvania are specially planted. One of our favorites is regarded elsewhere as a plague to be obliterated with a bevy of lawn chemicals. In our part of the state, however, dandelions never get out of hand until after they bloom. That's because we love eating the tender young leaves long before the plants ever flower. Even if they get beyond the early stages, we have happier ways of dealing with them than spraying them with poison.

In the old days, thoroughly cooked dandelion was considered a spring tonic. All I know is that it certainly got you going—as fast as you could go in another direction. There's nothing more bitter than dandelion that has been cooked for any length of time. When we make it, the hot bacon dressing that's poured over the uncooked greens wilts the salad without making it mushy or bitter. If you do want to use dandelion in a cooked dish, sauté it very briefly or fold it into the other cooked vegetables. The flavor is pungent but less bitter than endive.

There's a joke we tell on ourselves that will give you an idea of how much we love dandelion greens. It goes like this: "Do you know a simple way to kill a Pennsylvania Dutchman?" When answered "No," deliver this punch line: "Just tell him there's dandelion growing in the center of the nearest interstate highway."

The plants that have escaped the careful eyes of the greens hunters and manage to flower sometimes have their blossoms plucked and batter-fried. I prefer to allow the yellow flowers to ferment with oranges, lemons, and raisins for a smooth, fruity wine. I always say, "Dandelion wine is a sure cure for a cold or cough but even if it isn't, it'll make you forget your troubles while it's going down."

SUMMER

In Lancaster County, we never used a calendar to tell when summer began. That's because our busiest season of the year always began long before the solstice. The date changed from year to year, however, depending on the number of snowstorms we had. Sound strange? It really isn't any more curious than our Pennsylvania custom of depending on a groundhog's shadow to forecast the severity of the remaining winter months or the arrival of an early spring. For us, summer started with the last-day-of-school picnic at our one-room schoolhouse. If severe winter storms forced the closing of school numerous times, the picnic wasn't scheduled until the first week of June. After a mild winter, we could count on the end of May for the picnic. It was a day children looked forward to almost as eagerly as Christmas or Easter. Every last minute was planned to the smallest detail. Although our parents often went to school with us the day of the picnic, there was never any dread. It was a day for games and good eating. Of course, the teacher always had the good sense to wait until the end of the day to distribute our grades.

Today, when I pass an Amish school and see the children tossing a ball over the roof to see how many times they can get it back and forth without the ball falling to the ground, I remember those picnics vividly. Collee-over, as they call it, was one of our favorite games in a repertoire that included other amusements like baseball, rope-jumping matches, and tug-of-war.

Appetites were huge after a morning of play, but the spread of picnic food our parents prepared was even bigger. Crispy fried chicken was stacked on platters with the same kind of precision early settlers used to build log cabins. The bowls of potato salad and light-tasting homemade potato chips must have required at least half the county's potatoes (little did I know how plentiful they were). There were stacks of chicken and ham salad sandwiches and pickled red beet eggs whose bright color matched the day's mood.

Desserts topped the day by providing an ending almost as sweet as a "straight A" report card. Chocolate-covered pretzels, caramel corn, homemade pull taffy, whoopie pies (sweetened whipped cream sandwiched between two chocolate-cakelike cookies), and cupcakes (each with enough icing to cover a small cake) were just a sampling of the temptations that passed among us.

At the end of the day, we headed for home and a season of hard work that still allowed time enough for swimming in the creek, hunting arrowheads, and playing lookout from the top of the silo. In early summer, we watched almost as eagerly for the first bumblebees as our parents did for the first spring robins. That's because my mother and dad always said that when the bumblebees appeared, it was warm enough for us to go barefoot. From then on, of course, it behooved us to watch where we stepped to avoid unwanted encounters with those same bees.

My mother, an avid gardener, tested her skills annually by attempting to have the first new potatoes and garden peas in time for my parents' June 12 anniversary. She succeeded at least 80 percent of the time. The peas, in a day when fat and cholesterol weren't such concerns, were served in cream and butter. And the potatoes had to be scraped rather than peeled. We're fussy about our potatoes and the care we lavish on the new potatoes is just one example. When you're new to the task, scraping enough potatoes for six people will take an hour. But the taste will be worth it because scraping preserves the part of the potato that contains the most nutrients and the bulk of the flavor. After they're scraped and cooked, they crack, providing enough nooks and crannies to retain the brown butter that's poured over them.

Potatoes for mashing are always peeled after they've been boiled because the skins lock in the flavor. Potatoes for homemade chips must never have been stored at a temperature below 52 degrees or they won't stay crisp after they're fried. Potatoes for old-fashioned potato salad are peeled when they're hot and are coated with dressing while they're still warm. Because the dressing permeates the warm potatoes more evenly, less is needed to achieve the final flavor.

When I think about it, however, I guess my family was always rather fanatic about the foods we raised. The garden peas and lima beans were picked when they were young, not when the pods were completely filled. Tomato varieties producing fewer seeds were chosen for planting and each one of the stalks had to be staked so there would be no ugly spots on the tomatoes. Straw was carefully placed in the strawberry beds to keep the berries and the pickers clean.

Those luscious strawberries, the first real treats of the summer, sent our kitchen into full-scale production. We savored plenty of them plain or in the thick fresh cream we always had on the farm. But as the season progressed, we raced to keep ahead of the crop with such treats as shortcakes and pies as well as whole berry jams for special occasions and crushed berry jams for everyday use.

Berry picking wasn't over when the last of the strawberries were picked. We often made a party out of our searches along meadow fence rows or in the woods for wineberries, blackberries, blueberries, raspberries, and mulberries. Naturally, we asked permission to pick if we found any of these treasures on someone else's property. And we always went on these expeditions armed with an ample supply of bug spray and bee-sting medicine because we know we weren't the only creatures who liked the berries' sweetness.

A friend raised in north central Pennsylvania mentioned another precaution her family took on forays to mountainside patches of wild huckleberries. Before women and children started picking the tiny blue berries from the low bushes, several men in the crowd beat on the ground with walking sticks to scare rattlesnakes away. She was never certain, however, if the rattlesnake ritual served any real purpose other than displaying a bit of bravado.

The summer berries, particularly the strawberries and raspberries, were grand atop dishes of our homemade vanilla ice cream—a summer treat we had at least three times a week. For the ultimate splurge, we sometimes were allowed to spoon on the fresh berries as well as some of my mother's homemade chocolate syrup. The ice cream was an evening treat, particularly if other families came to visit or to buy some of our special Persian melons. My brother or cousin would crank the eight-quart freezer until the batch was smooth and creamy. When the ice cream was ready, my mother or aunt always counted noses before deciding on the size serving bowls to use. Naturally, we children always hoped for fewer visitors and bigger bowls.

Close to the Fourth of July, Mother Nature stages her own fireworks display in certain parts of Pennsylvania. That's when lightning bugs or "fire bugs," as we call them, appear and add a special sparkle to lazy summer evenings. When the first frontiersmen settled the area, they were amazed to see something flashing in the air above the meadows at dusk or even later. They wondered if those twinkling lights were the sparks from Indian campfires or were they the woods fairies? Today, we know the lightning bugs are the adult stage of the "glowworm"—beneficial insects that feed on other small pests. Interestingly, no one has been able to breed these insects in captivity so they can't be brought and established in areas where they don't exist. They're so highly treasured that they were made Pennsylvania's state insect in 1974!

We'd even hurry to finish our ice cream so we could catch a few lightning bugs. Our "captives" were put in jars with breathing holes poked in the lids. For a few fleeting minutes before we released them again, the lightning bugs made splendid lanterns. It was a good thing the lightning bugs came out at night because there wasn't time for such frivolousness during the days of mid and late summer. That's when we spent much of our time working with all the fruits and vegetables the fertile soil produced. Although my husband, Abe, has always liked eating tomatoes while they're still in the field and warm from the sun, my family spent a lot of time making something more out of them. We made zesty tomato juice by adding watercress to it. We cooked up stewed tomatoes and served them over mashed potatoes. Green and red tomato slices, first dipped in flour, were pan-fried in a mix of butter and lard, then glazed with sugar. They didn't look great but the flavor was unbelievable. We also turned green tomatoes into pies and green tomato relish. Just before the first frost, my mother always wrapped the prettiest green tomatoes she could find in tissue paper and put them in the basement to ripen so there would be a few for the holidays. Corn on the cob picked fresh in the morning before the sun was too high, was a staple at our noontime dinner, as long as it was in season. Chicken-corn soup, corn pie, and corn fritters used up still more of the crop. What we couldn't eat fresh was cut off the cobs and dried. The operation was something of a culinary ritual conducted carefully by my grandmother, mother, and aunt. As the corn dried on the stove in the corner of the farm kitchen, they took turns staying awake all night to make sure it didn't burn or get too brown. When done properly it turns golden and has a caramel flavor. I loved the taste of newly dried corn more than the taste of candy.

I've chuckled to myself as chefs have "discovered" cold fruit soups in recent years. My family was enjoying that summer treat more than forty years ago. In the days when milk had cream on it, my mother kept handy a pretty old crystal pitcher of sweetened milk. For dessert, we'd toss some of the season's first freshly sliced cling peaches with bread cubes and pour the sweetened milk over the top.

When the freestone peach crop ripened, we canned peaches of every variety we could buy. There were the big white Champion peaches as well as the smaller bright orange peaches with red centers. Because my hands were small, it was my job to arrange the peaches in the canning jars. Their centers had to be turned toward the outside of the jar so they'd look their prettiest. My mother-in-law also taught me to put one peach pit in each jar to help the peaches retain their color and give them a slight almond flavor. The peaches we didn't can became peach pies, peach sundae toppings, and peach ice cream. Still more of the fruit became peach wine.

Toward the end of the summer, my thoughts always turn to smoking meats. It's the result of spending hot summer days playing with my dolls on the second floor of my family's smokehouse. Because we only smoked meats in the winter, the building was cool in summer and wonderfully scented with the aroma of hickory smoke. Though I'll never be able to re-create the scent that took years to impart, I get out my smoker and spend several late summer weekends working to impart a hint of the flavor I remember into turkeys, roasting chickens, pork, and fish.

Although the availability of fresh fruits and vegetables all year round means it's no longer essential to can some of everything, I can't help myself. I still can some fruits and make pickles and relishes every year. When I look at the finished array of bright colors and shapes in the jars, I know what my mother meant when she said that food preparation and preservation is an art.

One evening when guests at the Groff's Farm Restaurant included an Amish neighbor, I said, "I hope you will come down to the basement and see my canned fruits and taste our homemade wines because I'm very interested in keeping the tradition." After dinner, when she and her friends descended the basement stairs, she commented as she surveyed my handiwork, "For you, it is a matter of preserving a tradition. For us, it is still a matter of survival."

FALL

The harvest of colors in the canning jars, from the scarlet red tomatoes and peppers and maroon beets and cherries, to the green beans, yellow corn, and golden peaches and apricots, painted the shelves of country fair exhibit halls with a brilliance that nearly matched nature's outdoor display of changing leaves. Each autumn, these country fairs marked the beginning of a social season that lasted at least until everyone had his good luck dinner of pork and sauerkraut on New Year's Day. Sometimes it lasted even longer if the family calendar included a visit to the grandest fair of them all, the Pennsylvania Farm Show in Harrisburg. Pennsylvania's answer to the state fair, the farm show has always been a test of the participants' ingenuity. After all, it's far easier to come up with fresh vegetables and canned goods in August than it is in midwinter.

Farm families planned and prepared for the fairs all summer long—putting aside the best-looking of the canned goods for possible blue ribbons. When we were at work, we remembered the subtle touches that made the preserved food look top notch—such as making sure the jars of Queen Anne cherries had no more than an inch of liquid at the top so the

jars looked as if they were absolutely brimming with perfect fruit and arranging the plump, round apricots so their creases faced the outsides of the jars. The fair competition was intense. On the line were culinary reputations, including some established by earlier generations and carefully defended by later descendants.

In the week or two before the fair, my mother, aunt, and I sorted through our canned goods for our entries. Our kitchen went into full production a day or two before the fair to produce the cakes, pies, cookies, and candy that would be entered in the baking competition.

On opening day, while the men spent their time ogling the farm animals and new harvesting equipment and the children did their best to eat their way along midways lined with stands selling everything from french fries, caramel corn, and red candy apples to funnel cakes, the women sized up their competition in the exhibit halls. They studied the jars of jellies and jams, relishes, vegetables, and fruits with the precision of quality-control inspectors. They were their own judges as they decided whose canned and baked goods looked the best. Of course, the fun was seeing if the real judges had the good sense to make the right choices when it came time for the blue ribbons and their accompanying two-dollar cash prizes.

I loved the competition, particularly because a few blue ribbons gave me some extra spending money. The year I was thirteen was one I'll never forget. I managed to win both the fair's adult and youth divisions with a plate of chocolate chip cookies and a tall lemon chiffon cake made from my mother's recipe. I still make that chiffon cake, which is served plain or with an orange sauce. But try as I do, I can never make my modern cakes measure up to the height of the blue-ribbon cake of my memories. I have finally concluded that the ones I bake now seem smaller because I'm taller!

Barn raisings—when community members pitch in to help a young couple just starting out or to replace a barn destroyed by fire—have occurred whenever necessary. But most of those that are planned are finished by the time the brilliance of autumn has faded to winter grays and browns.

Going to a barn raising has always raised my spirits at least as high as the barn's main beams. There are the fellowship and the warm feelings that come from helping friends, to say nothing of the food that is unrivaled by any other social event. Wedding fare can't hold a candle to the groaning boards set out for barn raisings. After all, at a wedding there's usually just one meal and loads of people to eat it. At barn raisings, on the other hand, there's usually three or four times as much food and half as many people to eat it!

Barn raisings almost always begin at 6 A.M. and last until the roofing is nailed on a little after dusk. And food is served practically from the time the first hammer strikes the first nail. Hot and cold drinks and all kinds of cookies keep up the strength of the 150 (or more!) builders until break time when cold sliced meats and cheese platters are passed. But the main meal is the highlight of the day. There's a whole baked ham or fried ham slices, a rolled rib roast or brisket of beef, roast chicken, chicken pot pie or fried chicken, potatoes, three or four different vegetables, at least "two colors" of cake (white or yellow and chocolate or spice), any number of pies, two or three flavors of homemade ice cream, and at least three pud-

dings. It's a wonder the men are able to climb back up on the beams after a meal like that!

But autumn meant more than a round of social events and good eating. Although the tobacco crop was usually in by fair time, there was often one more cutting of hay and the corn harvest still to be done.

And there was a large culinary task that was as sure a sign of autumn as the sight of birds flying south and the smell of burning leaves in the air. That was the morning each October when my father and uncle built the outdoor fire and set up the copper kettles for the women to make the annual supply of applebutter. When I was young, my mother and aunt never gave me a chance at stirring the applebutter with the big wooden paddle because it could scorch too easily, but I put in many a shift at the apple peeler.

Although our day of making applebutter wasn't as grand an event as the Adams County Apple Harvest Festival (where city folk still can see how applebutter is made), I savored every minute of it. The smell of the apples cooking over the smoky open fire gave me a taste for the butter that lasted all year.

Our family experts always selected tart Staymen and Smokehouse apples for their recipe and combined them with dried apples (schnitz), sugar, and spices to provide the depth of flavor and rich brown color we all loved. The mixture was stirred and stirred from early morning until late afternoon when all the excess moisture had cooked away. We stored it in crocks and jars till we needed it.

A dish of applebutter was always on the table, ready to be spread over fresh homemade bread at a moment's notice. But we also put it in half-moon pies or filled cookies, glazed ham loaves with it, ate it with scrapple, matched it with wild game, and even dared to serve it, rather than cranberry sauce, with turkey.

When the cooler weather brought an end to garden chores and made us all feel more like firing up the kitchen range, we made the seasonal adjustments. Heavy, hearty bran and wheat breads went into the oven (though we lightened up again around the holidays by making festive yeast breads and cookies like the ever-popular sandtarts). Homemade ice cream and shortcakes with fresh fruit gave way to warm puddings and gingerbread topped with hot lemon rum sauce.

We experimented with flavored vinegars long before they became trendy. I particularly love the old-fashioned celery and onion vinegars which go a long way when it comes to adding extra flavor without adding calories or chemical additives.

There was time for making fun foods, too. Cinnamon heart candies were turned into the red coating for our own candy apples. Caramel corn was another treat that always had to be eaten quickly, before it became sticky and soggy. I've since discovered the candy shops' secret, that is, baking off the caramel corn for a little while in the oven to dry it out and keep it firm. Today, my caramel corn always cracks like the store-bought versions. Trouble is, I no longer have an excuse for eating so much of it so quickly.

Although I didn't enjoy fall cleaning nearly as much as autumn cooking, it was a necessary evil to prepare the house for the much more formal winter entertaining which replaced the casual summer gatherings that consisted of bowls of ice cream on the front porch. Table linens were starched and pressed. The silver was polished, and the china closet's entire contents were freshly washed.

The weeks before Thanksgiving were also the time for making our holiday supply of mincemeat. Ours always contained meat, but the beef was ground so finely that you wouldn't have realized it was in there unless someone told you. We added the dark red wine, apples, raisins, and currants to the meat and let the mixture simmer on the coal stove for hours and hours. But the finished mincemeat was worth all the trouble for it truly made festive pies. Even people who made a point of saying they didn't drink couldn't resist a slice or two of pie which was loaded with the taste of the alcohol; in addition to the wine the meat was cooked with, the mincemeat in each pie was topped off with another half cup of spirits just before baking.

Thanksgiving, of course, was autumn's most festive meal and required the most advance planning. My mother ordered our holiday turkeys from a nearby farm. Because there were always fourteen around the family table, nothing smaller than a twenty-two-pound bird would do.

The day before Thanksgiving, the turkey was picked up and my mother and aunt busily baked the cakes, cooked the sweet potatoes, peeled the white potatoes, and soaked the dried corn in milk overnight.

After Thanksgiving morning church services, the men in our family went hunting for rabbits and pheasants in nearby fields while the women went back to work in the kitchen. Before long, the wonderful aroma of celery and parsley being sautéed with butter and a bit of saffron began building our appetites. The basis of our moist bread stuffing, the sautéed vegetables were blended with the bread cubes, eggs, milk, pepper, and salt. Although Berks County residents served their turkey with potato filling (a mix of mashed potatoes with bread cubes, onion, celery, parsley, and butter) and still other Pennsylvania cooks dared to fill their turkeys with a mixture of chestnuts and oysters, we never wavered from our plain and simple stuffing. Once the breast and neck cavities of the turkey were stuffed full, the bird went into the oven to be slow-roasted, breast-side down.

The work for our 1 P.M. dinner was far from done, however. Pies and puddings were baked. The giblets and neck meat were cooked with onions and celery for the gravy. The dried corn went onto the stove, to be further flavored with sugar, butter, salt, and pepper. Cranberries, apples, and walnuts were ground together for a festive relish. Sweet potatoes were fried in butter and then sprinkled with granulated sugar. A traditional green salad or Waldorf salad was tossed. Lima beans came out of the freezer and were cooked in butter and cream and potatoes were mashed and whipped till they formed the perfect peaks over which to pour cascades of browned butter.

It didn't take long for the hungry hunters to devour a feast of these proportions. I still marvel that there was never anything left of that twenty-two-pound turkey. I didn't even know what turkey hash was until after Abe and I were married and had moved away from home. Thankfully, Thomas Jefferson faced the leftover problem before I had to. It is a modified version of his turkey hash, served at Jefferson's White House breakfasts, that we use in our home.

Fully fortified after Thanksgiving dinner, the hunters walked the same fields once more—supposedly to bag their limit of game on the season's last day but also, effectively, to miss the major clean-up operations in kitchen and dining room.

When we finished washing up, we talked about our plans for the Christmas season— everything from the gifts we were making to the cookies we would bake. As the hours passed, we kept an eye out for the men and hoped we'd see them come home empty-handed. In those days, women usually cleaned the game. (Today, most men clean their own game—at least at our house.)

Fall breakfasts on the farm were always hearty, for it seemed with every degree the temperature dropped, our appetites increased a few notches. Sometimes the early morning fare included fresh sticky buns studded with newly harvested walnuts, buckwheat cakes, and sausage or heavy cornmeal waffles with golden molasses. (Please note that I'm talking about light molasses here and in my recipes. The darker blackstrap molasses, which is heavily sulfured, on the farm was reserved for women with headaches and for bulls who didn't perform properly in the barn!)

Although maple trees are tapped and syrup was made in early spring, pouring it over pancakes brings it to my mind during the autumn. And while most people think of Vermont or Quebec when it comes to maple syrup, nearby Somerset County producers turn out enough for a good many Pennsylvanians.

Barb Adams, my friend and assistant, said her family managed to turn out 350 gallons of maple syrup from their own sugar camp on the family farm in Somerset. Saving it only for pancakes meant eating pancakes three times a day for the year, inviting Paul Bunyan for breakfast each morning, or finding additional uses for the syrup. It wasn't long before family members were candying sweet potatoes with maple syrup, baking apples with butter, cinnamon, and syrup, and brown sugar came to mean maple sugar. Although Barb notes that spotza, maple candy made by pouring the syrup onto a cold plate or pouring it over snow and eating it like a snowball, is popular (particularly at Pennsylvania's Maple Festival in April in Meyersdale), her family wasn't impressed with it. She said, "My grandmother said the family worked too hard cooking the sap down to syrup to waste it by pouring it on snow." I'm inclined to agree when I hear about the wonderful maple fudge and the taffy Barb's family made. They had the usual pull taffy but they also had pans of taffy that sat around the house, tempting anyone who dared go near them. Barb explained, "All you did was dip a dull table knife into the taffy and twirl it until it was covered with the sticky candy. Then you simply sat there and sucked on your knife until the candy dissolved!"

Autumn meals were often simple in Huntingdon County, where Barb spent most of her early years. Her grandmother was a great one for one-pot meals (another "new idea" that's not so new). A meal of ham, green beans, and potatoes was popular. So were homemade pot pie, corned beef with cabbage, and beef pot roasts. Her grandmother also liked to fry off a piece of meat in a pan and then brown slices of cabbage in the drippings.

Just a week or two after the fancy dishes from Thanksgiving were safely stowed in the cupboard, we knew my father and uncle would be anxious to begin butchering. After we'd had several good freezes in a row—several nights and early mornings when the breath billowed from our mouths like clouds of smoke—the weather meant the meat could be cooled down quickly without benefit of a modern refrigeration system.

Butchering meant extra work for everyone, but no one complained. Thanks to dad's vocation, we lived fairly high off the hog. The only time we ate pork variety meats was right after butchering, because dad didn't sell them in the shop. We didn't even make much of the stuffed pig's stomachs which were so popular in Lehigh and Northampton counties. Even when we had it, my mother fancied it up a bit by calling it "French Goose." We bought the pork we turned into sausage, bacon, and hams. The rows of hams, top rounds that would become dried beef, the beef tongues, and bacon laid out on planks in the old arched cellar (ten or twelve feet below ground and chilly all year) were sights I'll never forget. The meats were rubbed with a thick coating of salt and sugar that would seep into the meat for several days. Then, they were dipped in a salt brine and carried up narrow, winding stairs to the second-floor smokehouse that was above the butcher shop.

Already brimming with the rings of freshly made sausage and bologna, the smokehouse was a supernatural place. In summer, when you could see the rafters, they literally sparkled under layers of shiny black soot. In winter, the hickory and apple smoke swirled so thickly in the huge room that you couldn't see your hand when you held it six inches from your face. Unless you were very familiar with the room, a collision with an ugly beef tongue or two was entirely possible.

The fresh bologna was a real treat for me when it was new, lightly smoked, and still soft.

My grandfather, on the other hand, believed it was at its best when it was so smoky and dry that he could cut a quarter-inch slice and chew on it for an hour.

Paper-thin dried beef, the most expensive of all the smoked meats, was served in a milk gravy or went into sandwiches with cream cheese.

The flavor of the wonderful hams that came from the smokehouse is another taste I'll never forget. The hams were smoked and aged for nearly six months, the earliest ones in time for Easter. True fans, however, waited a year, rather than six months, for the special salty, smoky flavor that comes from a country ham.

Once the ham's rind is peeled and it has been soaked and baked in a small amount of water, it's shaved or served in very thin slices because a little of it goes a long way. Although the ham is half the weight it was the year before, it delivers at least twice the flavor.

Smokehouse delicacies like the smoked hams and dried beef were enjoyed on special occasions. But our daily diet also included plenty of fresh roasts, chops, and steaks as well as wonderful wild game, from pheasant and rabbit to venison.

Although farm families' diets often have been depicted as monotonous and bland, nothing could have been further from the truth in Pennsylvania, where each season heralded a new kind of feast.

Grains have always played an important role in history. Not only are we all dependent on them for our daily bread, but farmers count on the grain for income as well as straw for the cattle. It is difficult to imagine the physical work involved in harvesting this beautiful golden wheat crop since we live in a day of large automatic equipment.

While comparing our family's contributions to Pennsylvania Dutch cuisine, our friends Bob and Betty Shirk of Lancaster reminisced about Bob's distant relative, Michael Cromer, from Mercersburg, Pennsylvania, who on July 12, 1858, established a world's record—in one day, with only the aid of a grain cradle, he cut twelve-and-a-half acres of wheat. The illustration below, an imagined recreation of the event, is adapted from the original by Charles Stone.

WINTER
Moravian Christmas

Walk in Bethlehem's historic area on a December night when snow blankets streets, sidewalks, and trees like a freshly plumped down comforter.

Listen to the carolers who look for all the world like gilt figurines in the glow cast by an old-fashioned streetlamp. Linger on Church Street to absorb nearly 250 years of history and watch as women who simply can't make fewer than four Moravian sugar cakes at a time deliver the extras to friends and neighbors.

Breathe deeply to catch the aroma of paper-thin brown spice "cakes" baking in kitchens all over town. Longtime resident Alice Knouss declares it takes twelve of these cookies to make a single mouthful.

Have a thin Moravian mint and the crunch will recall the childhood sensation of biting into a wedge of crusted snow. It's moments like these that give visitors an insatiable appetite for Bethlehem and offer a taste of the reasons why eastern Pennsylvania cooks deserve recognition for their artistry. Although much of the activity in central Pennsylvania was devoted to agriculture and savoring the harvest, "Easterners" carefully nurtured bountiful gardens in their spare time and ate well from them, too.

Allentown, Bethlehem, and Easton cooks artfully prepare shad and its roe, thanks to the bounty in the nearby Delaware River. And they have become excellent bakers because area breweries have always kept them well-supplied with brewers' yeast.

From the earliest days, Bethlehem, in particular, gained a reputation for the hospitality extended to those who made the three-day horseback ride from Philadelphia to the frontier outpost.

Although the area's Moravians (Bethlehem's first settlers) were better known for their contributions in music and art, they also were teaching cookery in their seminary. Aided by the many cookbooks they had

brought with them from southeastern Germany, they practiced a high standard of cookery in their homes. No wonder Ben Franklin, George Washington, John and Samuel Adams, John Hancock, and even Benedict Arnold enjoyed tarrying in Bethlehem!

Today, no matter what the occasion for celebration, food is a part of it. When the men of the Central Moravian Church are finished decorating the sanctuary for Christmas, they have a "schmaus." As Alice Knouss explains, it's a party that always includes oyster stew, Moravian sugar cake, and other hearty fare like ham, potatoes, and beans.

During love feasts, simple Moravian worship services with plenty of singing and very little talk, women dressed in white pass baskets of sweetened rolls resembling buttersemmels and men follow with trays of coffee (or chocolate milk, if it's a special children's love feast). No one partakes until everyone is served and the minister gives the signal to begin.

Between stirring Christmas Eve vigil services (which are highlighted by the glow of hundreds of beeswax candles held aloft by the Moravian congregations in their darkened churches), choir members often dash home for lentil soup and sugar cake or have snacks in the church.

Between Christmas and New Year's Day, putzing parties go from house to house to see the putzes, which are elaborate nativity scenes set up beneath Christmas trees. The revelers particularly relish stopping at the homes where hosts frequently pass well-stocked trays of brown and white cakes (actually cookies), sandtarts, and pfeffernüsse.

Sugar pretzels—sweet rolls shaped like the familiar Pennsylvania Dutch snacks—glisten with melted butter and a sprinkling of granulated sugar. A New Year's Eve tradition, they add extra sparkle to the Watch Night church service that's climaxed by a burst of brass from the Central Church's trombone choir at the stroke of midnight.

Moravian sugar cake, though it is baked year round by Moravians living all over the Lehigh Valley, is particularly evident during holidays when hurried cooks still take the time to bake. Mrs. Lee Butterfield, who proclaims proudly that she was born and bred on Church Street within the shadow of the Central Church's belfry, commented, "There has been many a tooth-and-nail debate about whether sugar cake can be made with or without potato water." But Mrs. Pat Dimmick of Heller-town is convinced she knows the answer. She says, "Although my mother used mashed potatoes and potato water, I use instant mashed potatoes. I am convinced that if earlier Moravians had instant potatoes, they'd have used them, too!"

Cooks have definite opinions about the qualities of a good Moravian sugar cake. Explained Mrs. Butterfield, "It shouldn't be a quarter of an inch thick, but it shouldn't be two inches high either. The right height is about one-an-a-half inches and it has to have lots of butter and sugar holes. The cake shouldn't be overmoist but it shouldn't be dry, either. It shouldn't taste two days old when it isn't."

Eighty-eight-year-old Martha Luckenbach recalls how her mother's sugar cake was improved accidentally. "We mixed the dough as usual on Friday night, put it in cake pans and covered it with linen cloths so it would rise overnight. When we lifted the cloths in the morning, we discovered that the cat apparently had pranced across the tops of the cakes on the

way to his window perch for bird watching. My mother simply filled the paw holes with extra butter and sugar and baked the cakes. When my father asked why the sugar cake was so much better and heard the story, he gently stroked the cat and suggested that she make a habit of walking on the rising sugar cakes."

The molasses cookies called brown spice cakes are probably the most pervasive of holiday treats, according to Mrs. Knouss. "We also had sandtarts and chocolate cookies which were cut in rounds, but the brown spice cakes had to be cut into all kinds of fancy shapes."

The dough for the brown spice cakes ages for three or four days in a cool place (but not the refrigerator) so the spices can work their way through the dough. Miss Luckenbach, who recalls learning the art when she was eight or nine, first used a six-inch rolling pin and a cat cookie cutter to make her very own rolled cookies. "My mother and I always made the dough right after Thanksgiving and baked it at the start of December so the task was out of the way when it was time to begin work on the Christmas putz."

A well-seasoned expert on these cookies, Miss Luckenbach said the biggest challenge to these cookies was determining the proper baking time when all the gas ranges in Bethlehem were filled with baking goodies and the gas supply fluctuated wildly. Although it's not nearly as difficult to regulate temperatures today, she advises novices: "Grease your pans each time you're readying them for the oven. Rotate the top and bottom trays after five minutes. Don't take your eyes off them. And if the cookies blister, take a spatula and press them down lightly." She claims she manages to make about a thousand cookies from a single batch of dough so it's no wonder she says the cookies should be so thin that when you run the knife under them to pick them up, you should be able to see the knife clearly.

Mrs. Butterfield, whose family never opened their stash of brown spice cookies until Christmas Eve, noted it was something of a tradition to burn the last tray or two of cookies. It wasn't deliberate, however—just a matter of forgetting to watch them closely when there was so much cleaning up to do in the kitchen after a long day of baking.

Although the area's Christmas traditions are as varied as the many nationalities who eventually came to settle Bethlehem, there are a few culinary traditions that have been lost or are fading. Mrs. Knouss recalled a time when many a Bethlehem cook owned a "half-moon" cake pan specially made for baking half-moon cakes for holiday time. Made from a pound cake recipe, the cake was sliced thinly and each half round slice was iced with half chocolate icing and half lemon icing. But today, the taste is a fading memory and most of the pans are museum pieces.

There are those who worry that Moravian mints will become extinct, like the two-layered chocolate caramels with vanilla cream centers that were made by a local confectioner. Today, the thin red, white, and green mints are made almost exclusively by a group of elderly Moravians in the nearby town of Nazareth. These enterprising seniors worry about who will carry on their work in a time when traditions often are sacrificed to the demands of the modern world.

But food is only part of the celebration in Bethlehem. It's not hard to see why lifelong residents absolutely refuse to leave home over the holidays and why thousands of visitors make pilgrimages to this city first named on Christmas Eve of 1741. From that first Christmas Eve, when a small group of Moravian settlers gathered to worship in a log house that sheltered both man and beast, the residents of the town that would be Bethlehem were charged with the keeping of the holiday.

That night, Count Ludwig von Zinzendorf, of Hernnhut, Germany, and patron of the Moravians, had just arrived and was leading the service. He began the hymn, "Not Jerusalem, lowly Bethlehem, 'twas that gave us Christ to save us: Not Jerusalem." Then, still singing, he led the group to the stable within the log house and continued, "Favored Bethlehem, honored is that name; Thence came Jesus to release us, Favored Bethlehem." With that Zinzendorf suggested that the town had been named. Christmas had created Bethlehem.

The holiday traditions that can be traced to that Christmas Eve live on in Bethlehem, no matter what happens. In fact, keeping the holiday just may have prevented a massacre. Legend has it that Indians were ready to attack in 1755 when they were frightened off by the sounds of the Moravians' brass trombone choir heralding Christmas Day from the roof of the Brethren's House (now Moravian College).

During two winters of the Revolution, the Moravians nursed the Continental Army's wounded soldiers in the Brethren's House and noted that all the officers and doctors attended their Christmas Eve vigils.

In 1941, just one week before Pearl Harbor, fire raged through the Central Moravian Church and explosions blew out the windows. Though the church was blackened, the celebration of the two-hundredth anniversary of the founding of Bethlehem went on as scheduled on Christmas Eve.

Most years, Christmases in Bethlehem are marked less dramatically. In contrast to Lancaster County where the plain folk sew quilts, do tole painting, make clear toy candy, dip chocolates, and plan traditional plates of goodies for the children, Bethlehem is vibrant with the celebration. Elaborate putzes and putzing parties, multipointed Moravian stars, hundreds of Christmas trees sparkling with thousands of lights, carolers, pageants, lantern-light tours, candles in the windows of homes and historic buildings, church vigils, and love feasts, as well as distinct culinary traditions, overshadow department-store Santas, tinsel, and bows, and give this city a glow that shines as brightly as the Christmas star.

Chapter 1

Appetizers and Beverages

CHEESE STRAWS

This recipe is one of Barbara Hoerle's specialties. While researching old cookbooks, we found several cheese stix recipes, but I think this is the best one ever!

½ pound (2 sticks) butter
3 cups grated sharp cheese
3 cups all-purpose flour
1 teaspoon baking powder
1 teaspoon salt
¼ teaspoon paprika
⅓ teaspoon red (cayenne) pepper
Few drops of Worcestershire sauce
2 to 3 tablespoons water

A food processor works perfectly for this recipe, but you may use a heavy mixer or work it by hand.

Cream the butter and grated cheese together in a large mixing bowl till fluffy. Sift the dry ingredients together, then add to the butter-cheese mixture. Add the Worcestershire and water, starting with 2 tablespoons, mixing until thoroughly blended. If the dough is too dry, add the rest of the water—it must be pliable enough to press through a cookie press. Place the dough in a star cookie press. Press it onto greased cookie sheets in long strips. Cut into 3-inch lengths and bake in a preheated 350°F oven for 8 to 10 minutes or until golden brown. Cool and store in an airtight container.

YIELD: ABOUT 150 THREE-INCH-LONG STRAWS. THESE ARE SO GOOD, YOU HAD BETTER COUNT ON AT LEAST 4 PER PERSON.

DEVILED EGGS

Parties are not complete without deviled eggs. They are easy to pick up and perfect for picnics.

12 hardboiled eggs, cooled and peeled
¾ cup mayonnaise
1 tablespoon Dijon mustard
½ teaspoon salt
1 tablespoon mixed minced fresh herbs
    (parsley, chives, chervil, and oregano)
¼ cup sour cream
Paprika or minced fresh parsley for garnish

Cut the eggs in half, lengthwise. Remove the yolks and place in a mixing bowl. Add the rest of the ingredients and beat until smooth and creamy. Place in a pastry tube and pipe the yolk mixture into the whites. If you do not have a pastry tube or cake decorator tube, spoon the mixture into the whites. Garnish with paprika or minced parsley and chill until ready to serve.

YIELD: 24 HALVES

EASY SPICED PECANS

Pecans were much more plentiful in years gone by, but they are still grown in Pennsylvania.

10 tablespoons plus 2 teaspoons butter
2 large egg whites
½ teaspoon salt
½ teaspoon ground cinnamon
⅓ cup powdered sugar (superfine if
    possible)
1 teaspoon vanilla extract
1 pound pecan halves

Melt the butter in a small, heavy saucepan over low heat and place in a 9-by-13-inch baking pan. Beat the egg whites until nearly stiff and slowly add in the salt, cinnamon, sugar, and vanilla. Continue to beat until stiff peaks form and then fold in the nuts. Pour the mixture evenly into the pan and bake in a preheated slow oven, 300°F, for 40 minutes, stirring every few minutes to prevent the pecans from burning. Remove from the oven and place on a wire baking rack or slotted broiler pan top, then pour onto paper towels to remove excess butter. Store in an airtight container.

YIELD: ABOUT 1½ POUNDS

CANDIED WALNUTS

Nuts were candied for special holidays and important guests, but I suggest these year round.

1½ cups granulated sugar
½ cup water
½ teaspoon cider vinegar
½ teaspoon ground cinnamon (optional)
1 tablespoon butter
4 cups English walnut halves

Combine the sugar, water, vinegar, cinnamon, and butter in a deep, heavy saucepan over high heat. Stir until dissolved, then boil till a candy thermometer reaches 240° to 242°F, the hard ball stage, when you drop a bit of the mixture into ice water and it forms a hard ball. Stir in the nuts and then pour onto a large sheet of wax paper. Break into pieces when cool.

YIELD: ABOUT 2 POUNDS

Variation: Substitute any type of roasted nut.

GLAZED BACON

This is one of my favorite appetizers and one that will amaze every guest.

½ pound bacon, sliced
½ cup lightly packed light brown sugar
1 tablespoon Dijon mustard
2 tablespoons red wine

Place the bacon in a large baking pan and bake in a preheated 350°F oven for 10 minutes or until crisp. Drain the fat off. Mix the brown sugar, mustard, and wine together thoroughly, then pour over the bacon. Bake at 350°F until it bubbles, making sure the bacon glaze is covering both sides, approximately 10 minutes.

Remove the bacon from the pan and place on wax paper or aluminum foil. Cut the bacon slices in half, if desired. Do not refrigerate or cover, but let sit at room temperature until ready to serve. It should be dry to the touch, not sticky. If it is limp or sticky, bake a bit longer, about 2 minutes.

YIELD: 6 SERVINGS—PEOPLE REALLY LOVE TO EAT THIS, SO COUNT ON 5 POUNDS FOR 30 GUESTS.

TURKEY BITS

A great way to use up leftover turkey, this recipe may be made into turkey patties as a delicious substitute for hamburgers. Serve the turkey bits with a hot sauce or sweet and sour sauce or both.

4 cups minced turkey (roasted or cooked)
1 cup fresh bread crumbs
½ teaspoon salt
½ teaspoon ground white pepper
2 large eggs
½ cup cream cheese
2 scallions, with tops, chopped
½ cup salad olives
1 tablespoon vegetable oil or butter

Blend the first eight ingredients together thoroughly. Place a large, heavy skillet over medium heat and add the oil or butter. Drop the mixture by teaspoonsful into the heated skillet and fry until golden brown on each side, about 3 minutes per side. Add more oil as necessary while frying. Serve immediately or remove from skillet, place on a baking sheet, and keep warm in a 200°F oven until ready to serve. These freeze well before or after frying.

YIELD: 10 PATTIES OR 24 BITS

Variation: Substitute crushed crackers or potato chips for the bread crumbs and roll the bits in an egg wash of 1 large egg beaten with 1 tablespoon milk or water and then the fresh bread crumbs. This will make them crunchier.

OLD FASHIONED LEMONADE

Ice cold lemonade with sprigs of meadow tea (spearmint) brings back the best of every childhood memory. It was the highlight of all the threshing, haymaking, and summer work days. As a child, my family chose me to carry the bucket of lemonade to the fields, and I loved it. The funny thing was I didn't realize how special ours was and that not everyone had lemon slices floating on the top. The secret was pounding sugar into the lemon slices. This made the rind sweet and wonderful for keeping in the mouth long after the thirst was quenched. The nutmeg also gives it extra punch. Enjoy!

5 *large or 6 medium-size lemons*
1 *cup granulated sugar*
16 *cups cold water*
4 *cups ice cubes*
1/8 *teaspoon freshly grated nutmeg*
Several sprigs of fresh mint

Squeeze 4 of the lemons and reserve the juice. (If the lemons are cold, place in the microwave for 30 seconds or in a bowl of hot water for 5 minutes. The warmed oils in the rind will give extra flavor to the juice.) On a cutting board, cut the remaining lemons into 1/4-inch-thick slices, removing all the seeds. Press 1/2 cup of the sugar into the slices with a wooden mallet or potato masher. Place the sugared slices and any resultant juice into the container you plan to serve it in and let stand for at least 15 minutes. Add the reserved lemon juice and sugar, and cold water. Stir in the ice cubes, sprinkle with the nutmeg, and garnish with fresh mint.

YIELD: 20 CUPS

Variation: Add 2 cups of lime drink made from concentrate and 2 cups strong tea for a delightful summer cooler.

MULLED CIDER

This heartwarming beverage is always served warm to hot and is best when the weather is cold. Most important to remember when serving, always place a silver spoon in a glass punch bowl before pouring in the hot liquid. This will prevent the glass from cracking. If you prefer stirring the cider with teaspoons instead of cinnamon sticks, just sprinkle the top with ground spices.

1 cup lightly packed light brown sugar
6 cups apple cider, fresh or pasteurized
1 orange, seeded and sliced thin
1 lemon, seeded and sliced thin
2 cups dry white, rosé, or red table wine
   (cranberry juice may be used as a
   substitute)
Cinnamon sticks (optional)

Place the sugar and 2 cups of the cider in a large kettle. Stir until the sugar is dissolved. Place over medium heat and add the orange and lemon. Bring to a boil and simmer at that heat approximately 6 minutes until the rinds are clear. Add the remaining cider and the wine. Heat but do not let boil. Serve with cinnamon sticks for stirrers.

YIELD: 12 SERVINGS, ABOUT 10 CUPS

WINEBERRY SHRUB

Wineberries grow, and look, like red raspberries. They grow wild in meadows and fence rows mainly in the middle Atlantic states. They are very tart, so you will need to use more sugar or sugar substitute than you will with other berries. Shrubs are prepared juices that are canned or frozen as a syrup and diluted before drinking. The formula for making a punch is always one third shrub to two thirds ice and water, though many added soda for variety. The undiluted syrup is excellent over sponge cake, ice cream, or fresh fruit.

4 cups wineberries
2 cups cider vinegar
2 cups granulated sugar
1/2 teaspoon ground nutmeg
Dash of ground cinnamon
Lemon slices or 2 tablespoons fresh lemon
   juice (optional)

Combine the berries and vinegar and let stand overnight in a glass or stainless steel container, covered. The next day, press through a double thickness of cheesecloth or strain slowly. Add the sugar and spices to taste, remembering that the syrup will be considerably diluted before serving. Add lemon slices and let stand for at least 24 hours, then strain again and place in containers for freezing or can according to the cold pack method (see page 197).

YIELD: ABOUT 6 CUPS

Variations: Use any kind of berry, such as strawberries—with or without rhubarb—blueberries, cranberries, blackberries, gooseberries, or raspberries. A combination of cranberries and apples or raspberries and sour cherries makes a very interesting drink. Try your favorites or experiment. Adjust the amount of sugar according to the sweetness of the berries. To assure the best tasting shrub, start with 1 cup sugar, stir until it is dissolved, then taste and add more sugar until you reach the desired level of sweetness, again remembering that the shrub will be diluted before serving. Add a bit of orange or lime juice and rind for extra flavor.

DANDELION WINE

It takes forever to pick the blossoms, but the end result is well worth it. If made properly and you have enough patience to let it stand a year, dandelion wine will be so smooth you'll want to make it every year.

12 cups boiling water
12 cups dandelion flowers (without the
  stems)
3 oranges, sliced
3 lemons, sliced
1 pound seedless raisins
5 cups granulated sugar
6 cups water
1 teaspoon wine yeast (see note)

Pour the boiling water over the washed dandelion flowers. Let stand, covered, overnight. The next day, strain the mixture through a doubled thickness of cheesecloth, pressing out all the liquid. Discard the dandelions. Put the strained liquid in a plastic pail and add the oranges, lemons, and raisins. Combine 3 cups

of the sugar with 4 cups of the water in a large saucepan. Bring to a boil, stirring until the sugar has dissolved. Let syrup cool to lukewarm, then add to the dandelion liquid. Add the wine yeast and stir well. Cover and ferment for 15 days, stirring the mixture each day.

Combine the remaining sugar and water in a large saucepan and bring to a boil, stirring until the sugar is dissolved. Let cool to lukewarm. Meanwhile, strain the dandelion mixture again, then add the cooled syrup to the dandelion liquid. Pour into a gallon jug fit with a fermentation lock and leave in a warm place until all fermentation has ceased, approximately 6 to 8 weeks.

YIELD: 1 GALLON

NOTE: Wine yeast may be purchased from a home brewer's or winemaker's shop. If unavailable, substitute an equal amount of baker's yeast.

BLACKBERRY CORDIAL

This is a special after-dinner drink anytime, but when bottled in an old collector's bottle, it makes a valued and pretty gift.

4 cups blackberry juice
2 lemons, thinly sliced
2 cups granulated sugar
½ whole nutmeg, broken into small pieces
2 cinnamon sticks, broken into small pieces
1 teaspoon whole cloves
2 cups good brandy

Place the juice, lemon slices, and sugar in a large, stainless steel kettle. Stir until the sugar is dissolved. Place the spices in a muslin spice bag or tea infuser. Add to the juice and bring to a boil, simmering slowly for 15 minutes over low heat, occasionally skimming the top of foam. Turn the heat off, add the brandy, cover, and let set until completely cool. Strain through double cheesecloth and bottle, sealing tightly. This should be stored several weeks at least before serving. Store in a cool area away from direct sunlight.

YIELD: ABOUT 6 CUPS

Variation: The juice from mulberries, cherries, currants, or raspberries may be substituted.

Chapter 2

Soups and Salads

CREAMED CELERY SOUP

Celery is available all year. The Pennsylvania Dutch grow celery all summer long in their gardens. In the fall they put it in clay or cardboard tubes to bleach and tenderize for use as a relish. Celery hearts are usually served whole in beautiful cut glass "celery dishes." Celery is also a very important ingredient in soups and seasonings. Dry most of the leaves and use the stems for this soup.

2 bunches celery, cleaned, the leaves
   reserved for garnish
2 tablespoons (¼ stick) butter or vegetable
   oil
½ cup chopped onion
2 cups chicken stock
1 cup cooked rice
1 teaspoon salt

½ teaspoon ground white pepper
6 cups milk
½ cup crumbled Roquefort cheese (grated
   Cheddar may be substituted)
Paprika for garnish

Chop the celery and some of the leaves. In a 6-quart stock pot, melt the butter and sauté the celery and onion over medium heat until clear, about 10 minutes. Remove from heat and puree in a food processor, blender, or food mill. Add the chicken stock and simmer for 15 minutes over medium heat. Add the rice, salt, pepper, and milk. Reduce heat to low and heat thoroughly, about 15 minutes. Put about 1 tablespoon of the crumbled cheese in the bottom of each heated soup bowl, fill with soup, and garnish with paprika and celery leaves.

YIELD: 10 CUPS OR 6 TO 8 SERVINGS

27

POTATO-LEEK SOUP

Basic, but wonderful!

3 leeks
5 medium-size potatoes, peeled and diced
2 tablespoons (1/4 stick) butter
3 cups chicken broth
1/2 teaspoon dried chervil
1 teaspoon chopped fresh parsley
1/2 teaspoon dry mustard
1/2 teaspoon chopped fresh tarragon
1/2 teaspoon ground white pepper
1/2 teaspoon salt
3 cups milk
1/2 cup heavy cream or evaporated milk
Chopped fresh parsley or a few slices of leek
   for garnish

Clean the leeks, washing away all the sand, trim the coarse tops, saving as much of the top as is tender, and slice thin. Save several slices of leek for garnish. Sauté the potatoes and leeks in the butter over medium heat in a 6-quart stock pot for 5 minutes or until edges are golden. Add the chicken broth and bring to a boil. Simmer over medium heat for 20 minutes. Add all the seasonings and the milk and continue simmering for at least another 30 minutes, stirring occasionally to prevent sticking. Add the cream and check for salt, adding more if desired. Heat thoroughly. Garnish with parsley and or a few slices of leek on top of each bowl.

YIELD: 8 CUPS OR 4 SERVINGS

Variation: Vichyssoise: Puree the potatoes and leeks, reduce the milk to two cups and chill thoroughly. Serve ice cold.

LENTIL SOUP

See how many varieties of dried peas and beans you can combine in this colorful and nutritious soup.

2 cups dried lentils
14 cups water
1 large onion, chopped
2 stalks celery, chopped
2 pounds ham, veal hock, or beef short ribs
2 cups tomato or vegetable juice
1/2 teaspoon salt
1/2 teaspoon coarsely ground black pepper
1/2 teaspoon Tabasco sauce (optional)
Croutons for garnish

Wash the lentils and soak them in 8 cups water overnight in a 6-quart stock pot. Drain and add 6 cups water, the onion, celery, and meat. Cook until the meat is tender over medium heat, stirring every 10 minutes to prevent sticking. Depending on the thickness of the meat and bone, it will take about 1 1/2 hours. Remove the meat from the broth and remove the fat and bone. Dice the meat and put it back in the soup. Add the tomato juice, check for seasonings, and add the salt and pepper if desired. Add the Tabasco carefully, a few drops at a time, till you achieve the right level of hotness. (Some folks like to add the Tabasco at the table.) Simmer over low heat for 15 minutes. Serve hot with croutons. The longer the soup stands, the thicker it gets.

YIELD: 12 CUPS OR 6 SERVINGS

Variation: Dried Bean or Split Pea Soup: Use dried split peas or any combination of dried beans with the above recipe but substitute milk for the tomato juice.

SUNSHINE SQUASH SOUP

This will brighten up any meal and is a must for celebrating Halloween.

1/4 *pound bacon (about 4 slices)*
1 *medium-size onion, chopped*
1 *stalk celery with leaves, chopped*
1/4 *clove garlic, minced*
1/2 *teaspoon curry powder*
1/4 *teaspoon ground nutmeg*
8 *cups water*
2 *pounds butternut squash or neck pumpkin, peeled, seeded, and cut into 2-inch chunks*
3 *large carrots, peeled and sliced*
1 *medium-size potato, peeled and sliced*
1 *medium-size rutabaga, peeled and sliced (if unavailable, use another potato)*
1/2 *teaspoon salt*
1/4 *teaspoon ground white pepper*
1/4 *teaspoon ground thyme*
1/4 *cup rum*

2 *tablespoons fresh lemon juice*
1 *tablespoon granulated sugar*
Salt and freshly ground white pepper, if needed
Spiced Whipped Cream (page 170)
Fresh parsley sprigs for garnish

Fry the bacon in a heavy, 6-quart stock pot until crisp. Remove the bacon, drain, and crumble. Add the onion, celery, garlic, curry powder, and nutmeg to the bacon fat and sauté over medium heat for 5 minutes. Add the water, squash, carrots, potato, rutabaga, salt, pepper, and thyme. Cook over medium heat, covered, for 45 minutes. Cool slightly and pour by batches into a food processor, blender, or food mill. Puree thoroughly. Pour back into the pot and stir in the rum, lemon juice, and sugar. Check for seasonings and add the additional salt and pepper as desired. Simmer slowly over low heat until bubbles appear on top, about 10 minutes. Serve hot with a dollop of Spiced Whipped Cream. Garnish with parsley sprigs.

YIELD: 8 CUPS OR 4 SERVINGS

GERMAN TOMATO SOUP WITH DILL

I prefer most of my soups very hot, but this is excellent either cold or hot.

4 white onions, about 1 to 1½ cups
  chopped
1 carrot, scrubbed and chopped
1 stalk celery, scrubbed and chopped
½ green bell pepper, chopped (optional)
3 tablespoons butter
2 teaspoons salt, less if desired
1 teaspoon ground white pepper
2 cups water
5 cups tomato puree
¼ cup honey
1 tablespoon granulated sugar
2 tablespoons fresh lemon juice
2 cups tomato or vegetable juice
⅓ cup finely chopped fresh dill or 2
  tablespoons dried
1 cup sour cream
Fresh dill or parsley sprigs for garnish

In a 6-quart stock pot sauté the onions, carrot, celery, green pepper, and butter over medium-high heat until tender, about 3 minutes. Add the salt, pepper, and water; reduce heat to low and simmer for 5 more minutes. Remove from the heat and puree in a food processor, blender, or food mill. Pour puree back into the stock pot and add the tomato puree, honey, sugar, lemon juice, and tomato or vegetable juice. Blend and simmer over medium-low heat for at least 15 minutes, stirring frequently. Add the chopped dill and simmer another 5 minutes. Serve hot or cold with a dollop of sour cream and a sprig of fresh dill or parsley.

HINT: If the tomatoes are high in acid, add a pinch of baking soda.

YIELD: 12 CUPS OR 6 SERVINGS

Variation: Substitute watercress for dill and add 1 cup cooked rice.

CORN-SPÄTZLE SOUP

This soup is a special treat any time and is hearty enough for a meal.

2 cups water
1 tablespoon butter or vegetable oil
1 cup cooked Spätzle (page 44)
2 cups corn kernels, fresh or frozen
1 tablespoon chopped fresh parsley
½ teaspoon coarsely ground black pepper
½ teaspoon salt
⅛ teaspoon dried marjoram
⅛ teaspoon dried basil
2 cups milk
½ cup evaporated milk or half and half
Celery seed or chopped fresh parsley for
  garnish

In a 6-quart stock pot, bring the water to a boil and add the butter. If you are using fresh spätzle, boil them until tender in the boiling water. Once cooked, add the corn, parsley, pepper, salt, marjoram, and basil. If using cooked spätzle, add it now. Simmer over medium heat for 15 minutes. Add the whole milk and evaporated milk and heat thoroughly, about 5 minutes. Simmer until thickened, about 12 minutes, but be careful not to boil rapidly. Garnish with celery seeds or parsley.

YIELD: 6 SERVINGS

Variation: Add 6 slices crisply fried bacon, chopped, or 1 cup chopped celery when you add the corn.

CHICKEN-CORN SOUP

A meal in itself, this soup has helped many a volunteer fire company pay for a new engine or equipment in their sponsoring Chicken-Corn Soup Suppers.

*4 to 6 pound chicken (or 2 cups diced,
  cooked chicken and 6 cups chicken broth)*
8 cups water
¼ teaspoon salt
*¼ teaspoon coarsely ground black or white
  pepper*
2 tablespoons chopped fresh parsley
2 cups corn kernels, fresh or frozen
1 cup chopped celery
1 cup Egg Noodles (page 44)

If you are starting with a fresh chicken, remove the giblets and place the chicken in a 6-quart stock pot. Add the water, salt, pepper, and parsley. Cook over medium heat until tender, about 45 minutes. Remove and discard the skin, debone, and dice the chicken. Cool the broth, skim off the fat, and strain it through a double thickness of cheesecloth. Bring 6 cups

of the broth to a boil in a large saucepan over high heat and add the corn, celery, and noodles. Lower the heat to medium and simmer, covered, for at least 1 hour. Add the chicken and heat thoroughly. Serve in heated bowls.

YIELD: 12 CUPS OR 6 TO 8 SERVINGS

Variation: Substitute Spätzle (page 44) or sliced or cubed hardboiled eggs for the noodles.

OYSTER STEW OR SOUP

When I was a child I loved this stew, but I always gave the oysters to my parents. Now that I'm grown up I find many other children doing the same but it is a great way to learn to appreciate the flavor of oysters.

*1 pint stewing oysters with liquor,
  approximately 3 dozen*
2 tablespoons (¼ stick) butter
2 tablespoons all-purpose flour
½ teaspoon dried chopped chives
½ teaspoon chopped fresh or dried parsley
½ teaspoon dried chervil
¼ teaspoon paprika
½ teaspoon Old Bay (seafood) seasoning
½ teaspoon salt
¼ teaspoon ground white pepper
2 large eggs, well beaten
½ cup evaporated milk or heavy cream
4 cups milk
Fresh parsley sprigs or croutons for garnish

Check the oysters for shells. Melt the butter in a medium-size saucepan over medium heat. Add the flour and stir until smooth. Stir in the seasonings and oyster liquor. Heat thoroughly, but not to boiling. Blend the beaten eggs into the milk and heat in a heavy, 3-quart saucepan over medium heat until nearly boiling, stirring constantly with a wooden spoon. Blend the oyster liquor mixture into the milk mixture with a wire whisk. When slightly thickened, about 12 minutes, add the oysters and heat until the oysters begin to curl around the edges. Do not boil! If it does boil and curdle, add a pinch of baking soda. Serve immediately, garnished with parsley sprigs or croutons. Serve with lots of oyster crackers or crusty bread.

YIELD: 7 CUPS OR 4 TO 6 SERVINGS

Variation: Mock Oyster Stew: Substitute salsify (oyster plant) for the oysters. Scrub 1 pound of salsify and cook it in 2 cups of water, mild chicken broth, or veal stock over medium-low heat until tender, about 15 minutes. When cool, peel, cut into slices and use as oysters. Strain the broth and substitute for the oyster liquor.

OXTAIL SOUP

After the fat is removed, it's hard to believe this beef isn't filet mignon.

2 oxtails, about 4 pounds
1 large onion, chopped in 1-inch pieces
2 stalks celery, chopped in 1-inch pieces

1 teaspoon salt
1/2 teaspoon ground black pepper
1 tablespoon cider vinegar
6 cups water
2 medium-size potatoes, quartered or cut in 1-inch pieces
3 large carrots, cut into 1/3-inch slices
2 stalks celery, with leaves, coarsely chopped
1/2 pound tomatoes, cored and diced, or 1/2 cup tomato juice
2 scallions, with tops, cut in 1/2-inch pieces
1/2 large green bell pepper, coarsely chopped
1 tablespoon chopped fresh parsley for garnish

Cut the oxtails at each joint (half way through) and place in a heavy, 6-quart stock pot. Add the onion, celery, salt, pepper, vinegar, and water to the pot and bring to a boil. Skim the foam off as necessary and cook over medium heat, covered, until the meat is tender, approximately 2 1/2 hours. Remove the oxtails. When cool, remove all the fat and debone. Strain the broth and discard the celery and onion. Return broth to the stockpot. Chop, dice, or slice the remaining vegetables to their desired size and add to the broth. Cook over medium heat until tender, about 20 minutes, and add the meat. If the broth is too thick, add a little tomato juice or water. Reheat and garnish with parsley.

YIELD: 12 CUPS OR 6 SERVINGS

Variation: Oxtail Stew: Reduce the liquid to half before adding chopped vegetables.

PEACH BISQUE

So refreshing and tasty, this recipe may be adapted for many fruits.

1 pound fresh or frozen drained peaches, peeled
6 tablespoons light brown sugar
1 cup sour cream
1 quart half and half or milk
1 pint heavy cream
1 tablespoon ground cinnamon
1 teaspoon ground nutmeg
2 tablespoons brandy (optional)
Whipped Cream (page 170) or fresh peach slices for garnish

In a blender or food processor puree the peaches with the sugar. Add the sour cream, half and half, cream, and half of the spices. Refrigerate for several hours to draw the flavors. Stir in the brandy just before serving. Sprinkle the top of each serving with remaining spices, then top with a dollop of whipped cream or sliced peaches. If you chill the bowls before filling them, the soup will stay cold longer.

YIELD: 6 SERVINGS

BEET SALAD

You can't "beet" this salad for color and flavor, especially on a hot day.

3 cups shredded beets with liquid (add enough water to make 3¾ cups)
1 (6-ounce) package lemon gelatin
2 tablespoons prepared horseradish
½ teaspoon salt
1 tablespoon honey
Yogurt or sour cream for garnish

Heat the beet juice in a medium-size saucepan until nearly boiling over high heat. Dissolve the gelatin in the beet juice, then add the shredded beets, horseradish, salt, and honey. Pour into a 1½-quart mold or 8-inch square pan. Chill until set. Cut into servings and top with a dollop of yogurt or sour cream.

YIELD: 6 SERVINGS

BROCCOLI SALAD

This salad is not only beautiful but it is refreshing and nutritious.

Dressing:

2 to 3 tablespoons cider vinegar
3 ounces cream cheese
⅛ teaspoon garlic or onion salt
2 to 3 tablespoons granulated sugar
Dash of ground black pepper
1 tablespoon prepared mustard
2 large eggs, well beaten
2 to 3 tablespoons vegetable oil

Salad:

12 slices of bacon, crumbled
6 to 7 cups chopped broccoli
⅓ cup raisins
3 tablespoons chopped red onion

Place all the ingredients for the dressing in a blender, food processor, or mixer. Blend thoroughly and set aside. Fry the bacon in a saucepan and dry on paper towels; then crumble into small pieces. Place the broccoli, chopped or broken into buds, raisins, onion, and bacon in large salad bowl. Pour the dressing over the salad and let it stand for at least 1 hour, covered with plastic wrap. Toss before serving.

YIELD: 6 SERVINGS

Variation: Cauliflower may be substituted for the broccoli.

CUCUMBERS AND ONIONS IN DILL SOUR CREAM

Weiner Schnitzel would not be the same without this side dish.

1 large cucumber
1 medium-size onion
1 tablespoon salt
1 tablespoon cider or white wine vinegar
1½ teaspoons granulated sugar
½ cup sour cream
¼ teaspoon dried dill weed
Paprika

Clean and peel the cucumber. Slice the cucumber and onion as thin as possible. Place slices in a bowl and sprinkle with the salt. Let stand at least 1 hour. Rinse slices in cold water and drain thoroughly. Add the vinegar and sugar to the cucumbers and onions and press with hands until sugar is dissolved. Add the sour cream and dill, mixing well. Sprinkle with paprika before serving.

YIELD: 4 TO 6 SERVINGS

SAUERKRAUT SALAD

Delicious with pork or ham dinners, it is also a wonderful salad for summer picnics (especially if you have hot dogs or cold cuts). This salad is the perfect way to use up extra sauerkraut. It can be substituted for cabbage or pepper slaw (see page 36).

4 cups chopped sauerkraut, fresh or canned, drained
½ cup chopped onion
1 cup chopped celery
1 tablespoon chopped pimiento
¼ cup chopped green bell pepper
½ cup cider vinegar
¼ cup vegetable oil
1½ cups granulated sugar (less if desired)
Lettuce leaves, washed and patted dry

Mix all the ingredients but the lettuce and let stand in the refrigerator for at least one hour. Serve on lettuce leaves.

YIELD: ABOUT 6 CUPS OR 6 SERVINGS

MUSHROOM SALAD

This is a great winter salad, especially when you realize that Pennsylvania is the largest producer of mushrooms in the United States.

Dressing:

1/3 cup olive or walnut oil
1 tablespoon fresh lemon juice
3 tablespoons Herb Vinegar, 1 each of
  thyme, rosemary, and chive (page 206)
1/4 cup chopped fresh parsley
2 teaspoons granulated sugar
1/2 teaspoon chopped fresh basil
1/8 teaspoon crushed garlic
1/4 teaspoon salt
1/2 teaspoon coarsely ground black pepper
1/4 cup red table wine

Salad:

10 to 12 ounces fresh mushrooms, cleaned
  and sliced
Fresh cutting lettuce or Boston lettuce
  (about 3 cups)

Combine all the ingredients for the dressing until thoroughly blended. If you are preparing the salad ahead of time, slice the mushrooms into the dressing to prevent discoloration. Wash and tear the lettuce. Drain and pat dry with a clean cloth. Arrange the lettuce on individual plates or in large bowl. Add mushrooms and dressing and serve chilled.

YIELD: 4 SERVINGS

Variation: Add wedges of tomatoes or hard-boiled eggs to the salad.

PERFECTION SALAD

We all love molded salads, and this recipe is no exception!

3 tablespoons gelatin (I use Knox)
1/2 cup cold water
1/2 cup white wine vinegar
2 cups boiling water
1 teaspoon salt
1 cup finely shredded cabbage
2 tablespoons fresh lemon juice
1 teaspoon grated lemon rind
1/2 cup granulated sugar
2 cups finely diced celery
1/2 cup finely diced red or green bell
  peppers
1 teaspoon celery seed
1 tablespoon sesame seeds
Lettuce
Chopped pecans for garnish

In a large mixing bowl soak the gelatin in the cold water for 5 minutes. Add the vinegar, boiling water, salt, cabbage, lemon juice and rind, sugar, celery, peppers, celery seed, and sesame seeds. Stir until the sugar dissolves. Pour the mixture into a 1 1/2-quart mold or 9-by-13-inch baking pan and chill until set. Place on crisp, cleaned lettuce and garnish with chopped nuts. Serve mayonnaise on the side.

YIELD: 6 TO 8 SERVINGS

DANDELION SALAD WITH HOT BACON DRESSING

Even though we specify dandelions, any greens are great with this hot dressing. Since we have microwave ovens, we can make a full recipe of the dressing and refrigerate or can it until we need it.

6 cups loosely packed dandelion greens, washed and cleaned
4 hardboiled eggs, peeled and sliced

Dressing:

1/2 pound bacon
2 tablespoons cornstarch
1 1/2 teaspoons salt
3 tablespoons granulated sugar
2 large or medium-size eggs, lightly beaten
1/3 cup cider vinegar
2 cups milk

Tear the dandelion greens into pieces as you would for any salad. Fry the bacon in a saucepan or deep skillet until crisp. Remove and drain on paper towels, then crumble into small pieces. Combine the cornstarch, salt, and sugar. Blend in the beaten eggs, then the vinegar. Heat the milk in the pan with the leftover bacon fat over medium heat and add the egg mixture slowly, stirring with a whisk until thickened. Remove from the stove and add the crumbled bacon, cool slightly, and pour over the greens. Top with the hardboiled eggs and serve any extra dressing on the side.

YIELD: 6 SERVINGS

CABBAGE SLAW

When I was a child, one of my jobs was squeezing the slaw, sugar, and vinegar until I could see the liquid in the bottom of the bowl. Only after I made slaw for myself did I realize the difference it makes to squeeze it. The raw cabbage taste disappears because the flavors are so thoroughly blended. Try it; I know it works!

1 1/2 pound head of cabbage
1 cup granulated sugar
1/2 cup cider vinegar
1/2 teaspoon ground white pepper
1/2 teaspoon salt
1/2 teaspoon celery seed
1 tablespoon chopped fresh parsley
1 carrot, grated (optional)

Core the cabbage and shred or grate into slaw. Place in a large bowl and add the sugar, vinegar, pepper, salt, and celery seed. Press together with your hands until completely blended and liquid starts to form in the bottom of the bowl. Fold in the parsley and carrot (for added color and flavor). Cover and chill in the refrigerator for at least one hour.

YIELD: ABOUT 5 CUPS

Variation: Creamed Cole Slaw: Add 1 cup mayonnaise or 1/2 cup mayonnaise and 1/2 cup sour cream when mixing in the parsley.
Pepper Slaw: Add 1 medium-size green bell pepper, chopped, and 1 medium-size red bell pepper, chopped.

CHARLIE'S POTATO SALAD

Ever since our son, Charles, developed this recipe, everyone asks for it. Our guests from Germany say it tastes the way they remember it from "Grandma," while others remember it tasting the same but with the addition of chopped sweet pickles. Try it this way and then add sweet or dill pickles or maybe a bit of chopped fresh tarragon, whichever way you prefer.

3 pounds firm, all-purpose potatoes
1 tablespoon salt
3 cups water
1½ cups mayonnaise
¾ cup sour cream
2½ tablespoons cider vinegar
⅓ cup granulated sugar
1 teaspoon ground white pepper
2 teaspoons dry mustard
1 tablespoon celery seed
2 teaspoons Worcestershire sauce
2 teaspoons fresh lemon juice
2½ tablespoons chopped fresh parsley
2 teaspoons chopped fresh chives
⅓ cup minced onion
⅓ cup minced celery

Peel and cook the potatoes in the salt and 3 cups of water over medium heat in a large saucepan until medium soft. Drain, slice, and let cool. Mix the mayonnaise and sour cream together in a large mixing bowl, then add all the rest of the ingredients. Stir in the sliced potatoes. If possible, let the salad stand for at least 3 hours or overnight before serving. It will keep, refrigerated, for nearly a week if stored in an airtight container.

YIELD: ABOUT 7 TO 8 CUPS OR 4 TO 6 SERVINGS

Variation: Sunchoke Salad: Substitute 3 pounds of Jerusalem artichokes (sunchokes) for potatoes in potato salad, cooking as you would potatoes. It will have extra crunch and holds its shape well.

GERMAN HOT POTATO SALAD

This is a meal by itself if you add sliced smoked sausage.

6 slices bacon
2 tablespoons cornstarch
¼ cup water
1 cup chopped onion
¾ cup diced celery
2 teaspoons salt
1 teaspoon granulated sugar
⅛ teaspoon freshly ground black pepper
½ cup cider vinegar
6 cups firm potatoes (red skins are great),
   cooked, peeled, diced, and still hot
6 large pimiento-stuffed green olives or 12
   small green olives, sliced

Fry the bacon in a large, heavy skillet until crisp. Remove the bacon, drain on paper towels, then crumble; reserve the bacon fat. Dissolve the cornstarch in the water. Sauté the onion and celery in the bacon fat over medium heat about 5 minutes until the onions are translucent. Add the salt, sugar, pepper, and dissolved cornstarch to the skillet. Next, add the vinegar and bring to a boil over medium heat for 3 minutes. Add the hot potatoes and crumbled bacon, stirring gently. Serve hot, garnished with sliced stuffed olives.

YIELD: 6 TO 8 SERVINGS

NOTE: It takes 8 medium-size potatoes cooked in salted water for about 30 minutes to make 6 cups of diced potatoes. They may be cooked in the skins and peeled while still hot.

Variation: For added flavor, cook the potatoes in chicken stock instead of water.

WALDORF SALAD

All the ingredients for this salad are available during the fall, winter, and spring. The old-fashioned way of making this salad always topped it with Cooked Dressing (see page 129). It seems a bit too sweet for those not accustomed to it, so I prefer to use regular mayonnaise.

2 cups cored and diced apples
1 cup chopped celery
1 cup raisins
½ cup broken nuts
½ cup mayonnaise
Fresh lettuce or watercress
Nut halves or maraschino cherries for
   garnish

Combine the apples, celery, raisins, nuts, and mayonnaise gently in a large bowl. Chill in the refrigerator until ready to serve. Serve on crisp greens. Garnish with nut halves or cherries.

YIELD: 6 SERVINGS

CHICKEN SALAD

In the summer, the chicken is cut in chunks, nuts and sometimes grapes or white raisins are added, and the resulting salad is scooped onto fresh cutting lettuce. For sandwiches, the chicken is ground and spread between slices of buttered homemade bread.

2 cups diced, cooked chicken
1 cup chopped celery
4 hardboiled eggs, peeled and chopped
$\frac{1}{4}$ cup chopped pecans (optional)
$\frac{1}{4}$ cup red or white seedless grapes, halved
  or quartered (optional)
$\frac{1}{4}$ cup white raisins (optional)
1 cup Cooked Dressing (page 129)

Combine all the ingredients; stir until thoroughly blended. Chill and serve on lettuce. If making a sandwich spread, omit grapes.

YIELD: 4 CUPS

Chapter 3

Cheeses, Doughs, and Batters

MACARONI AND CHEESE

I have made this ever since I was in 4-H club. My family never gets tired of it but my grandchildren like it with Velveeta instead of the sharp cheese. Try it either way.

8 cups water
2 cups (8 ounces) macaroni
Pinch of saffron threads
½ teaspoon salt
1 tablespoon butter or vegetable oil
½ cup grated sharp cheese
1½ cups grated white American cheese
⅓ teaspoon salt or salt substitute
½ teaspoon coarsely ground white pepper
2 cups milk
Several dashes of paprika for garnish
Sliced olives for garnish (optional)

Bring the water to a boil in a 6-quart pot. Add the macaroni, saffron, salt, and butter, and boil uncovered until tender, approximately 12 minutes. Drain and place in a large mixing bowl. Stir in the cheeses, salt, pepper, and milk. When thoroughly blended, pour into buttered 2-quart baking dish and bake in a preheated 375°F oven for approximately 35 minutes or until golden brown. Remove from the oven and top with the paprika and sliced olives.

YIELD: 6 SERVINGS

WELSH RAREBIT

This is one of the first dishes I mastered in home economics class and my favorite light supper dish. It must be smooth and creamy, so use a wire whisk as well as a wooden spoon when stirring it. The toppings or accompaniments vary according to season.

1 tablespoon butter or margarine
1 tablespoon Worcestershire sauce
1/4 teaspoon ground white pepper
1/8 teaspoon red (cayenne) pepper
1/4 teaspoon curry powder
1/2 teaspoon dry mustard
1/2 teaspoon paprika
1 tablespoon cornstarch
1/2 cup ale or beer (water may be substituted)
2 cups (about 8 ounces) shredded Cheddar cheese
6 to 8 slices toast
Accompaniments (see below; optional)

Melt the butter in a heavy, 2- to 3-quart saucepan over medium-low heat (a double boiler may be used to insure it won't stick). Blend in the Worcestershire. Gradually stir in all the dry seasonings but the cornstarch until blended. Dissolve the cornstarch in the ale and slowly add to the mixture. Stir until mixture is warm, but not hot. Add the cheese by the handful, making sure it is fully melted before adding more. Continue until all the cheese is stirred in and melted until hot but not boiling. Serve over toast with desired accompaniments.

ACCOMPANIMENTS: Chopped or thinly sliced roast beef, ground or thinly sliced baked ham or turkey, crisp bacon, or thinly sliced tomatoes, onions, or peppers.

YIELD: 4 TO 6 SERVINGS

CHEESE SOUFFLÉ

For those who prefer a meatless meal, this is as attractive and impressive as its flavor.

3 tablespoons butter or margarine
3 tablespoons flour
1/2 teaspoon salt
1/2 teaspoon ground white pepper
2 tablespoons dried chopped chives
1 teaspoon prepared mustard
1 teaspoon Worcestershire sauce
Dash of Tabasco sauce
1 cup milk
1 cup grated Cheddar cheese
6 large eggs, separated
1/4 teaspoon cream of tartar
1 tablespoon butter
1 tablespoon grated Parmesan cheese or flour

In a large saucepan over medium heat, melt the 3 tablespoons of butter, slowly stirring in the flour until smooth. Add salt, pepper, chives, mustard, Worcestershire, and Tabasco. Heat the milk in a microwave or small saucepan. Slowly add the warm milk to the butter and flour mixture, stirring until thickened. Remove from heat and stir in the Cheddar cheese. Beat the egg yolks until fluffy and lemon colored. Stir slowly into the cheese sauce. Beat the egg whites with cream of tartar in a large mixing bowl until stiff but not dry. Coat the bottom and sides of a soufflé dish with 1 tablespoon of butter and dust with cheese or flour. Gently fold cheese mixture into egg whites and pour into prepared soufflé dish. Bake in preheated 350°F oven for approximately 40 minutes or until lightly browned. It should pull away from the sides a bit but will shake slightly in center. Serve immediately.

YIELD: 4 TO 6 SERVINGS

EGG CHEESE

All kinds of cheese are very important to the Pennsylvania Dutch. It is probably due to the frugality of the dairy farmers. If the milk price is low, they make more cheese. This cheese is made with fresh ingredients and often served

as a snack, appetizer, or as a dessert with fresh fruit. The molds that were used for generations to make this cheese are very valuable and sought after, though reproductions of the old molds are now being made. The old heart molds are the most valued (they have little feet on the bottom and the design is pierced from the inside out so the whey can drain, still leaving the design intact when unmolded) but a natural basket—handles removed—works the same way and looks great when unmolded.

I consider it a special treat when I can have a loaf of hearty bread, golden table molasses, and an egg cheese. It will always be one of my favorites.

2 quarts milk
6 large eggs
2 cups buttermilk
1 teaspoon salt
2 teaspoons granulated sugar

Warm the milk in a large, heavy 3-quart saucepan or kettle. Beat the eggs until fluffy and add the buttermilk, salt, and sugar. Slowly add to the warm milk, stirring constantly. Reduce heat to low and cover. Simmer for several minutes, stirring occasionally. Remove lid and gently stir with a slotted spoon. Watch for the curds and whey to separate (the liquid will start to clear). Place the molds in a pan large enough to hold all the liquid. Immediately spoon the curds into the molds with the slotted spoon. Allow to drain—if using baskets, place a ring under the basket to allow the liquid to drain properly. The more gently you treat the curds, the lighter the cheese will be. A heavy cheese either has been cooked too long or was bounced carelessly when removed from the liquid. When cooled, unmold and serve as desired.

YIELD: 3 MOLDS (1¼ POUNDS)

Variation: Add 3 tablespoons chopped fresh chives, chopped green onions, or parsley as the curds begin to form. Grate nutmeg on top and serve with fresh fruit on the side.

SPÄTZLE

Often served instead of potatoes, spätzle is great as a garnish when sautéed in butter and bread crumbs or pan-fried in butter until golden brown. My friend Sue Hoffman, owner of the Kitchen Shoppe, in Carlisle, Pennsylvania, uses this recipe in her cooking school classes and it is light, airy, and delicious.

1½ cups all-purpose flour
¾ teaspoon salt
⅛ teaspoon ground nutmeg
2 large eggs, lightly beaten
½ cup milk
8 cups water

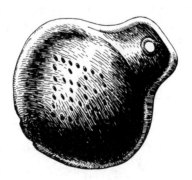

Combine the flour, salt, and nutmeg in a mixing bowl. Stir in the beaten eggs and add the milk gradually. Beat until smooth. Force the dough through the holes of a colander or use a spätzle maker. Bring the water to a rapid boil in a large pot (add 1 tablespoon oil or shortening to prevent the spätzle from sticking together), and drop in the dough. Boil until they rise to surface, about 2 to 3 minutes. Continue to cook over low heat for 12 minutes. Remove with a slotted spoon and drain. Serve as desired.

YIELD: 3 CUPS

EGG NOODLES

The Pennsylvania Dutch often serve noodles as well as potatoes, especially if sweet potatoes are on the menu. Variations on the basic egg noodle have been added in the past few years, giving color and variety to one of our best loved starches.

2½ cups all-purpose flour
½ teaspoon salt
3 large eggs
¼ cup cold water

Put 2 cups of the flour and the salt in a deep bowl or on a pastry board. Make a well in the middle of the flour and add the eggs and water. Mix with your hands or in a food processor until well blended and smooth. Form into a ball and wrap with wax paper or cover until the dough feels tender, at least 30 minutes. If using a food processor, mix until the dough forms a ball, adding extra flour if necessary. When ready to roll out, cut the dough into three parts if rolling by hand, six parts if using a pasta machine. Dust a little flour over and under the dough to prevent sticking. (It will take more flour if using a pasta machine.) Roll paper thin and flour both sides again. Starting at one end of the dough, roll up into a neat, tight roll, jelly-roll fashion. With a very sharp chef's knife, cut the roll into thin slices, about ¼ inch wide. As the slices fall onto the board, toss them lightly with your hand so they do not stick together. Unroll the noodles and let them dry on paper towels. If using a pasta machine, roll and cut dough to the desired thickness. Be sure to add plenty of flour as they fall from the machine to prevent them from sticking together. Uncooked noodles may be stored in an airtight container and refrigerated up to 3 days. To cook, drop noodles into 8 cups of water (add a tablespoon of vegetable oil or butter to prevent them from sticking together) brought to a rolling boil in a large pot and continue to boil another 5 minutes or until they reach the desired level of doneness. Pour into a colander to drain. Serve in a heated bowl with Browned Butter (see page 123) or your favorite sauce. To cool and store, or use for cold salads, run cold water over the noodles in the colander, making sure they are not sticking together. When completely drained and cool, store in an airtight container and refrigerate until ready to use. These will keep for 3 to 4 days.

YIELD: 1 POUND OF NOODLES (ENOUGH FOR 6 TO 8 SERVINGS)

Variations: Use ¼ cup chopped, drained, cooked spinach or tomato paste instead of the water.

POT PIE SQUARES

This is similar to a noodle dough, but the Pennsylvania Dutch roll it out very thin, about ⅛ inch thick, and cut it into 2- to 3-inch squares. It dries nicely if placed on a clean sheet or linen towels. When properly dried, it will keep in an airtight container for at least 4 weeks, unrefrigerated. To freeze, place layers between sheets of wax paper and wrap in double plastic bags. Squares will keep in the freezer for at least 2 months.

2½ cups all-purpose flour
2 large eggs
⅓ cup water
1 tablespoon butter or vegetable shortening, melted
½ teaspoon salt

Mound the flour on a pastry board or marble slab and make a well in the center. Break the eggs into this well. Add the water, butter, and salt. Gradually work the flour into the other ingredients with your hand or fork until well blended. Gather into a ball and knead the dough until very tender, smooth, and elastic. Generously flour the board and roll the dough out very thin, no more than ⅛ inch thick. The thinner it is rolled, the more delicate it will be when cooked. If using a pasta machine, roll out strips of the dough. Cut the rolled-out dough into 2- to 3-inch squares. Follow instructions for cooking Pot Pie on page 109.

YIELD: 1½ POUNDS OR 6 SERVINGS

DUMPLINGS

The secret of having beautiful light dumplings is to never lift the lid while they are cooking. Dumplings are often served with sauerkraut as well as poultry or meat.

1½ cups all-purpose flour
1 tablespoon baking powder
1 teaspoon salt
2 tablespoons (¼ stick) butter
1 large egg
½ cup milk
Chopped fresh parsley (optional)

Sift the flour, baking powder, and salt together. Cream the butter and egg together in a large mixing bowl, then add the flour mixture and milk to it alternately, blending thoroughly after each addition. Drop by tablespoons into a pot of boiling water or the liquid in which the sauerkraut or meat is cooking. When all are dropped into the pot, cover with a lid and boil over medium heat for 12 minutes. DO NOT LIFT THE LID during cooking. Remove with a slotted spoon and serve hot. Garnish with chopped parsley.

YIELD: 12 TO 15 DUMPLINGS OR 6 SERVINGS

KNEPP

Schnitz und Knepp (recipe on page 107) is one of the best known and publicized dishes of the region, yet few people make it frequently. I suppose it is the combination of salty ham and sweet apples that make it unique. If the ham broth is mild, this dish can be extremely pleasant, but knepp can be used in many other recipes.

2 cups all-purpose flour
1 tablespoon baking powder
¼ teaspoon salt
2 tablespoons (¼ stick) butter or vegetable
  shortening, at room temperature
1½ cups milk

Sift the flour, baking powder, and salt together in a large mixing bowl. Cut in the butter with a pastry blender or your fingers. Add the milk and stir until the dough is smooth. Drop by tablespoons into a large pot of boiling water or the liquid in which the ham is cooking. Cover the pot with a lid and simmer over medium heat for 12 minutes. DO NOT LIFT THE LID during cooking. Remove with a slotted spoon, drain, cover, and keep hot until serving.

YIELD: 6 SERVINGS OR 10 DUMPLINGS

RIVELS

Chowders and soups may be considered the main course when rivels are added.

1 large egg, lightly beaten
½ cup milk
½ teaspoon salt
¾ cup all-purpose flour

Pour the beaten egg into a 1-cup measure and add enough milk to make it ¾ of a cup. Pour into a mixing bowl and add the salt and enough flour to make a dough you can crumble. Rub the dough between your fingers to form small drops about the size of large grains of cooked rice. Drop into rapidly boiling soup or chowder, and cook for 3 minutes. Serve immediately.

YIELD: 6 SERVINGS WHEN ADDED TO CHOWDER OR SOUP

WAFFLES

The earliest waffle irons were brought along with the first settlers. They had beautiful designs, many with tulips, long handles and many different shapes. It is hard to believe the strength needed to hold the iron over the hot coals, but a few had stands to hold the iron.

2 large eggs, separated if desired
2 cups all-purpose flour
1/2 teaspoon salt
3 1/2 teaspoons baking powder
4 tablespoons (1/2 stick) butter or vegetable
    shortening, melted (bacon fat may be
    partially substituted)
2 cups milk

Heat the waffle iron while you are preparing the batter. (The iron is ready when a drop of water dances around on it and quickly evaporates.) If you want fluffy, light waffles, separate the eggs and beat the whites until stiff in a small bowl. In a large bowl, beat the egg yolks or whole eggs until light in color. Sift the flour, salt, and baking powder together. Add the melted shortening and mix till just blended.

Alternately add the flour mixture and milk to the beaten eggs, stirring until blended, about 30 seconds. Do not overbeat. If the eggs were separated, now fold in the stiffly beaten egg whites. Pour about 3/4 cup batter onto the heated waffle iron and bake until golden brown, about 5 minutes.

YIELD: 6 TO 8 WAFFLES

Variation: Nut Waffles: Add 1 cup chopped, toasted nuts to the batter.
Wholewheat or Buckwheat: Use 1/2 cup all-purpose flour and 1/2 cup whole wheat or buckwheat flour.

CORNMEAL WAFFLES

These have a beautiful color and a flavor you can't forget.

2 large eggs
1 cup buttermilk
1 cup sour cream
1 teaspoon baking soda
1 cup all-purpose flour
1 cup cornmeal, sifted
2 teaspoons baking powder
1/2 teaspoon salt
1 teaspoon granulated sugar (optional)
1/3 cup vegetable shortening, softened or
    melted

Heat the waffle iron while mixing the batter. In a large mixing bowl, beat eggs until light in color. Gradually add the remaining ingredients and blend thoroughly. Pour about 3/4 cup batter onto hot iron and bake until golden, about 8 minutes. Serve with butter and maple syrup.

YIELD: ABOUT 8 WAFFLES

Variation: Cheese Waffles: Fold ⅓ cup grated Cheddar or white American cheese into the batter.

BUTTERMILK PANCAKES

We often served Creamed Frizzled Dried Beef (page 104) and buttermilk pancakes for an easy supper.

2 cups all-purpose flour
¼ cup cornmeal
1 teaspoon baking powder
1 teaspoon salt
2 teaspoons granulated sugar (optional)
1 large egg, lightly beaten
½ cup milk
1 teaspoon baking soda
1 cup buttermilk
2 tablespoons (¼ stick) butter, melted

Sift the flour, cornmeal, baking powder, salt, and sugar into a large bowl. Stir in the beaten egg and milk. Dissolve the baking soda in the buttermilk and add to flour mixture. Add the melted butter and stir until blended. Pour about ¼ cup of batter for each pancake onto a hot, seasoned griddle. When golden on bottom and the top starts to bubble, turn. If the griddle becomes dry, add ½ teaspoon corn oil

to the hot surface. Serve pancakes immediately.

YIELD: 12 TO 14 PANCAKES

FLANNEL CAKES

The stiffly beaten egg whites make these flannel cakes light and fluffy.

2 cups all-purpose flour
1 tablespoon baking powder
¾ teaspoon salt
2 large eggs, separated
2 cups milk
2 tablespoons (¼ stick) butter, melted

Sift the flour, baking powder, and salt together into large bowl. Lightly beat the egg yolks into the milk and add to the flour mixture. Stir in the melted butter. Beat the egg whites until stiff and fold into the batter. Pour about ¼ cup per cake onto a hot, oiled griddle and cook until golden brown on both sides.

YIELD: 14 OR MORE CAKES

BUCKWHEAT CAKES

There was always a yeast starter stored in a crock on the arched cellar steps. It was made with potatoes and was used for breads and griddle cakes. Today it is easier to use packaged yeast. These cakes are lighter than the usual baking powder griddle cakes.

1 package dry granular yeast or 1 yeast cake
1 cup warm water
Pinch of granulated sugar
1 cup milk, scalded
1 teaspoon salt
1 cup all-purpose flour
1 cup buckwheat flour
½ teaspoon baking soda
2 tablespoons table molasses (golden, barrel, or King Syrup), do not use baking molasses
1 tablespoon butter, melted
1 large egg, lightly beaten

Proof the yeast by combining it with the water and sugar in a small bowl. If it foams, it's active and ready. Cool the milk to lukewarm, then mix with the salt and both flours in a large mixing bowl. When thoroughly blended, gradually stir in the yeast mixture. Cover and let stand in a warm, draft-free place overnight. When ready to use, preheat the griddle and

spray with nonstick vegetable spray or brush lightly with vegetable oil. Then, dissolve the baking soda in 1 tablespoon of water. Stir it, the molasses, butter, and egg into the flour mixture. This should create a thin batter. If it is too thick, add extra milk. Pour about ¼ cup of batter for each cake onto the hot griddle (it's hot enough when a drop of water dances around on it until it disappears). Turn when golden or when bubbles break and the top begins to look dry, about 5 minutes.

YIELD: 4 SERVINGS OR ABOUT 12 MEDIUM TO LARGE CAKES

CREPES OR THIN PANCAKES

The country folks serve thin pancakes in many ways. They fill them with thinly sliced meats, roll, and stack them on a heated platter, topping them with beef or chicken gravy. For dessert (see Variation), they're often filled with ice cream, folded tightly and fried in butter, brown sugar, and orange juice. When served hot with meat, they are known as Pfatzlings in Pennsylvania Dutch. When used as desserts, they're called Fancy Pancakes.

1 cup all-purpose flour
3 large eggs
½ teaspoon salt
½ cup beer or water
¾ cup milk
¼ cup water
2 tablespoons (¼ stick) butter, melted
1 tablespoon vegetable oil

Combine all the ingredients but the oil in a large mixing bowl and stir until well blended. Cover and refrigerate overnight or at least several hours (this will make the crepes more tender). Season your crepe pan by adding the oil to it and heating it until it smokes. Remove the pan from the heat and sprinkle it with salt. Wipe the pan with paper towels and it's ready. If you always use this pan for making crepes, you only need to clean it with a clean towel and spray the pan with nonstick vegetable spray or brush it with a few drops of oil whenever you use it.

Return the pan to the stove and heat it over a medium-high flame. When hot, pour ¼ cup of batter into the pan and cook until a light, golden brown on the bottom. Flip over and remove when golden. Store between sheets of wax paper until ready to fill.

YIELD: 12 TO 14 CREPES

Variation: Fancy Pancakes: Add 2 tablespoons granulated sugar and ½ teaspoon fresh lemon juice or extract to the batter. These are delicious with Fried Ice Cream (page 195).

Chapter 4

Vegetables and Side Dishes

APPLESAUCE

A staple in Pennsylvania Dutch cookery, homemade applesauce is so tasty and satisfying, it is a shame to buy store-bought unless you add some extra flavor to make it your own. For this recipe, I like to use one of the following types of apples: Stayman, Smokehouse, Winesap, Baldwin, York Imperial, Rome, or Jonathan.

8 apples (about 3 pounds), peeled, cored,
 and quartered
1½ cups water
2 teaspoons fresh lemon juice
½ teaspoon grated orange rind
¼ teaspoon salt
⅛ teaspoon ground nutmeg
¼ cup lightly packed light brown sugar
¼ cup red cinnamon candies (optional)
Ground cinnamon or nutmeg for garnish

Place the apples in a large, heavy 6-quart saucepan or kettle. Add the water and cook over low heat, covered, until soft, about 15 minutes. Stir to prevent them from sticking to the bottom of the pan. If there is any extra liquid, drain off before pureeing. Put the apples through a food mill or processor until they are smooth (or chunky, if you wish). Pour them back into the saucepan and add all the ingredients but the cinnamon. If you want your applesauce to have a cinnamon flavor and pinkish color, add the candies. Bring the apples to a boil over low heat and let boil for at least 2 minutes. Serve warm, garnished with a sprinkle of cinnamon or nutmeg. If making a large amount, can the applesauce in hot, sterilized jars with new lids after boiling for 5 minutes (see the section on canning, pages 197–98).

YIELD: ABOUT 4 CUPS

APPLE DUMPLINGS

Apple dumplings are sold individually at most of our markets and bakeries. When there were twelve around our table, we made deep-dish dumplings, cutting them into large slices. I much prefer baking them separately, basting them with the syrup. They're almost as good cold as hot.

6 baking apples, such as Stayman,
    Smokehouse, or Granny Smith, peeled
    and cored
1/2 cup cinnamon hearts (hard candies)
2 cups all-purpose flour
2 1/2 teaspoons baking powder
1/2 teaspoon salt
1/2 pound (2 sticks) butter or margarine
1/2 cup milk
2 cups lightly packed light brown sugar
2 cups water
1/8 teaspoon ground cinnamon
1/8 teaspoon ground nutmeg

Fill the cored center of each apple with cinnamon candies. Sift the flour, baking powder, and salt together. Cut 2/3 cup of the butter into the flour mixture until fine and crumbly. Sprinkle the milk over the mixture until moist, pressing it into a ball. Roll out the dough about 1/4 inch thick on a floured board and cut into 6-inch squares. Place an apple on each square and bring the dough up around to cover it completely. Moisten the top edges with water and fasten securely on top of the apple—whole cloves may be used to secure it. Place the dumplings 1 inch apart in a greased 9-by-13-inch baking dish or pan. Combine the brown sugar, water, cinnamon, and nutmeg in a large saucepan and bring to a boil. Simmer over low heat for 3 minutes, remove from the heat and stir in the remaining butter. Pour the syrup over the dumplings and bake in a preheated 375°F oven for 35 to 40 minutes, basting every 15 minutes. Serve hot with chilled rich milk, cream, or whipped cream.

YIELD: 6 SERVINGS

APPLE FRITTERS

Fritters are eaten as a snack, vegetable, or dessert. They're so good, you'll have to decide how many ways you can serve them. I suggest using either Smokehouse, Winesap, Jonathan or Stayman, Rome, or York Imperial.

4 or 5 large apples
1 1/2 cups all-purpose flour
2 large eggs, separated
1/2 cup water or milk

1 tablespoon butter, melted
1 tablespoon fresh lemon juice or white
  wine
1 teaspoon baking powder
¼ teaspoon salt
¼ cup granulated sugar
2 cups vegetable oil (or 2 inches deep in the
  skillet)
Confectioners or cinnamon sugar for
  topping

Peel, core, and slice the apples into rings about ¼ to ⅓ inch thick. Dredge in ½ cup of the flour. Whip the egg yolks in a large mixing bowl until light in color, then whip in the water, butter, and lemon juice. Sift the baking powder, salt, sugar, and remaining flour together. Slowly add to the egg yolk mixture until thoroughly blended. Beat the egg whites until stiff and fold into the batter. Dip the apple slices in the batter, covering them completely. Heat the oil in a large, heavy skillet or fryer to 375°F and fry until golden brown, about 2 minutes on each side. Drain on paper towels, sprinkle with sugar, and serve hot.

YIELD: 20 TO 25 FRITTERS, 4 TO 6 SERVINGS

JERUSALEM ARTICHOKES

These artichokes grow wild along fencerows and meadows. Even though they were growing here before the first settlers arrived, they were nearly forgotten over the past 40 years. Now they are making a comeback, but are called sunchokes (because they are a member of the sunflower family). Use them as a substitute for water chestnuts or serve raw with a dip.

1½ pound Jerusalem artichokes (or
  sunchokes)
1 cup water
½ teaspoon salt
3 slices bacon or 3 tablespoons butter
½ teaspoon celery salt
½ clove garlic, minced, or 1 tablespoon
  minced onion
½ teaspoon ground black pepper

Scrub the chokes and cook them in the water and salt, covered, in a large, deep saucepan until nearly tender over medium heat, about 15 to 20 minutes. Drain, cool a bit, and peel. Cut into ⅓-inch slices or wedges. Fry bacon in a large, heavy skillet until limp, then drain off the fat, add the chokes, celery salt, minced garlic, and pepper, and continue to fry over medium heat until chokes are golden. The extra fat from the bacon will be enough to fry the chokes and the bacon should be crisp by the time the dish is ready to be served, about 4 minutes. If you prefer not to have the bacon, follow the same instructions, only frying the chokes in the 3 tablespoons butter.

YIELD: 4 SERVINGS

ESCALLOPED ASPARAGUS

This is a very delicate dish. Make sure you serve it immediately from the oven (almost like a soufflé).

3 cups asparagus, cleaned and cut in pieces
2 large eggs, lightly beaten
1/2 teaspoon ground white pepper
1 1/2 teaspoons salt
1 1/2 cups milk
2 cups fresh bread crumbs
1/4 cup grated Cheddar cheese
Several slices of Cheddar cheese for topping

Blanch, steam, or microwave asparagus for two minutes until bright green but not fully cooked. Blend eggs, pepper, salt, and milk thoroughly. Butter or oil a 1 1/2-quart casserole dish and alternate layers of bread crumbs, asparagus, cheese, and the milk mixture until all are used. Top with slices of cheese and bake in a preheated 350°F oven for 40 minutes. If the cheese starts to darken, lightly cover with foil for last 15 minutes. Serve immediately.

YIELD: 6 SERVINGS

Variation: Add 2 cups diced, cooked chicken, alternately between the asparagus and cheese layers.

ASPARAGUS IN CREAM

This is the old standby. Everyone served it with toast tips or poured it into patty shells (pie dough baked in muffin cups) for a special occasion.

1 1/2 pounds asparagus
1/2 cup water
1/2 teaspoon salt
Pinch of granulated sugar
1 cup Medium White Sauce (page 124) or heavy cream
2 tablespoons Browned Butter (page 123)
Toast Cups (page 86) or Patty Shells (page 149)

Make sure all the tough ends are removed, then cut the asparagus into 1-inch pieces and place in a saucepan. Add water, salt, and sugar, and bring to a boil. Cover and blanch for only a few minutes. Drain the water off, then add the white sauce or cream to the asparagus and simmer over low heat until thoroughly heated. Pour into a heated serving dish, warm toast cups, or warm patty shells and top with browned butter.

YIELD: 6 SERVINGS

BAKED BEANS

Everyone loves baked beans but this recipe is exceptionally versatile.

8 slices bacon
1/2 cup chopped onion
1 teaspoon dry mustard

½ teaspoon ground white pepper
1 teaspoon chopped fresh chives
1 teaspoon dried parsley flakes
½ teaspoon salt
½ cup pure maple syrup
½ cup catsup or barbecue sauce
½ cup red or white wine
4 (15-ounce) cans butter beans, drained, or
    1 pound dried lima beans soaked in
    water overnight
3 slices bacon or ½ cup fresh bread crumbs
    for topping

Fry the bacon in a large, heavy skillet until crisp. Remove the bacon, drain on paper towels, and crumble when cool. Sauté the onion in the bacon fat over medium heat until golden brown, about 3 minutes. Add the crumbled bacon, the mustard, pepper, chives, parsley, salt, syrup, catsup, wine, and beans. Blend thoroughly. Pour into a greased 9-by-12 inch casserole or baking dish and top with the bacon or bread crumbs. Bake in a preheated 350°F oven for 1 hour, uncovered.

YIELD: 6 TO 8 SERVINGS

Variation: Add 2 cups chopped beef or pork and substitute an equal amount of beef broth for the wine and maple syrup.

BEAN LOAF

A great substitute for meat loaf, this is perfect for stretching the budget as well as pleasing to the vegetarian.

3 cups dried beans, cooked, or 5 cups
    canned and drained (use navy, great
    northern, butter or kidney beans, or chick
    peas)
2 tablespoons vegetable shortening
½ cup chopped celery
1 medium-size onion, chopped
1 tablespoon chopped fresh parsley
1 tablespoon chopped green or red bell
    pepper
½ teaspoon chopped fresh marjoram
½ cup chopped tomatoes or catsup
1 teaspoon salt
½ teaspoon ground black pepper
2 large eggs, lightly beaten
1½ cups fresh bread crumbs

Chop beans in a food processor if you prefer a smoother loaf. If the shells of the beans are not a problem for your family, leave the beans whole. Heat the shortening in a skillet and sauté the celery, onion, parsley, bell pepper, and marjoram for 5 minutes over medium heat or until celery and onion are clear. In a large mixing bowl combine the beans, tomatoes, celery mixture, salt, pepper, eggs, and bread crumbs. Mix thoroughly, form into a loaf. If the loaf seems dry, add a little tomato or vegetable juice. Place in a greased 9-by-5-inch loaf pan or a 9-by-13-inch cake pan and bake in a preheated 350°F oven for 45 minutes.

YIELD: 6 SERVINGS

HINT: For extra flavor, add strips of bacon to the top of the loaf before baking.

GREEN BEANS

Plain green beans, lightly steamed and crunchy, are still the most colorful vegetable to complement any dish.

1 pound green beans, washed and trimmed
¼ (if steaming beans) to ½ cup (if boiling
   beans) water
½ teaspoon salt
1 tablespoon Browned Butter (page
   123—optional)
1 tablespoon Mushroom-Herb Sauce (page
   126—optional)

Leave beans whole or cut into desired lengths. Place the beans and water into a covered saucepan or deep skillet. Bring to a boil and cook or steam over high heat until the beans are bright green and give a bit when squeezed. Drain and sprinkle with salt if desired. Top with browned butter or sauce of choice.

YIELD: 4 SERVINGS

Variation: Cook the green beans with 4 white potatoes, whole or quartered, and a ham hock in a large saucepan until everything is tender. Remove the meat from the bone, cut off the fat and cut the meat into chunks. Serve with the beans and potatoes in deep serving dish. Top with Hollandaise Sauce (page 124).

HAPPY BEETS

One day while making Harvard Beets, our cook mistook the homemade wine for vinegar and this recipe became a favorite of everyone in the restaurant. Some folks who wouldn't think of eating beets just ask for the "sauce."

4 cups beet juice from pickled beets
2 tablespoons arrowroot or cornstarch
¼ cup water
½ cup dry red wine or dry fruit wine
¼ cup granulated sugar
4 cups Pickled Beets (page 57)

Place the beet juice in a large saucepan and bring to a boil over high heat. (If you do not get 4 cups beet juice from the pickled beets, add equal parts water and part wine to make the proper amount.) Dissolve the arrowroot in the water and add to the wine along with the sugar. Stir into the beet juice and cook until thickened over medium heat, about 5 minutes. Add the beets and continue to simmer for several minutes until thoroughly heated and the flavor goes through the beets. Check for seasonings and add salt or sugar as desired.

YIELD: 4 TO 6 SERVINGS

Variation: Sunshine Beets: Add juice and grated rind of 1 orange, ¼ cup maple syrup, ½ teaspoon ground ginger, and 2 tablespoons (¼ stick) butter to above recipe. Omit wine if desired and substitute ¼ cup white vinegar. *Harvard Beets:* Substitute an equal amount of red wine vinegar for the wine.

STUFFED BEETS

The extra work of stuffing the beets will be rewarded when you try this old recipe.

6 large beets, with tops
2 cups water
½ teaspoon salt
2 green onions
2 tablespoons (¼ stick) butter
¾ cup fresh bread crumbs
¼ teaspoon dried dillweed
½ teaspoon salt
⅛ teaspoon ground white pepper
⅓ cup sour cream
1 hardboiled egg, chopped

Scrub the beets and cut the tops one inch from the beets to prevent bleeding. Place in a large saucepan with the water and salt. Cook over medium heat, covered, until tender, about 1 hour. While beets are cooking, wash the tops thoroughly, save a few choice tops for garnish, and chop the rest coarsely. Chop or slice the onions, tops and all. Melt the butter in a large, heavy skillet and sauté the tops, onions, bread crumbs, dillweed, salt, and pepper over medium heat approximately 6 minutes. When the beets are ready, let cool a bit, then slip off the skins. Scoop or cut the center out of each beet. Chop the centers and add to the crumb mixture. Trim the bottom of each beet so it will stand upright in a 9-inch baking dish and on the plate. Add those trimmings to the crumb mixture. Fill each beet with the mixture and place the filled beets in a 9-inch buttered baking dish or pan. If you have extra filling, arrange it around the beets and bake in a preheated 350°F oven for 25 minutes. Top with a dollop of sour cream and some chopped egg

and continue baking for 5 more minutes. Serve on a heated plate garnished with beet tops.

YIELD: 6 SERVINGS

HINT: Any of the homemade vinegars will complement this dish nicely. Serve the vinegar in a cruet, letting each person sprinkle a few drops on the beet after cutting it.

PICKLED BEETS

These are usually made with small beets and used as a relish or for making Harvard Beets (page 56). If using large beets, cut them into quarters after they are cooked.

2½ pounds fresh beets
½ cup granulated sugar
½ cup cider vinegar
½ cup water
1 teaspoon salt
1 teaspoon coarsely ground black pepper
1½ teaspoons minced mixed herbs (dried salad herbs are fine)

Wash but do not peel the beets. Cut the tops 1 inch above the beets to keep them from bleeding. Place them in a large pot and cover with water. Bring to a boil and cook over medium heat until tender, approximately 30 minutes. Drain, reserving the beet liquid. Peel the beets and cut up if necessary. Place all the ingredients (except the beets) and 1 cup of the beet juice back into the pot, stir together, and bring to a boil. Add the beets and boil an additional 2 minutes over medium-high heat. Pack and seal in hot sterilized jars or store in a covered container in the refrigerator until ready to use.

YIELD: 3 PINTS

NOTE: Save any remaining beet juice to pickle hardboiled eggs.

BROCCOLI

Many folks prefer eating broccoli raw, but if steamed for a very short time, it takes on a beautiful bright green color.

1 pound broccoli
½ cup water
½ teaspoon salt
1 tablespoon butter
½ teaspoon dried salad herbs (optional)
2 tablespoons Browned Butter (page 123), your favorite sauce, or Herb Vinegar (page 206)

Wash and trim the broccoli. Break into flowerets and peel the stem. Cut the stem into ⅓-inch-thick slices or into strips to cook with the flowerets. Put the broccoli, stems, water, salt, butter, and herbs in a large saucepan, cover, and bring to a boil over high heat. Reduce heat to medium, cover, and simmer 3 to 5 minutes, depending on how crunchy you like them. Drain and top with browned butter, your favorite sauce (walnut-mustard sauce or hollandaise is very nice), or a few splashes of herb vinegar.

YIELD: 4 SERVINGS

BRUSSELS SPROUTS WITH CHESTNUTS

I cannot understand why folks shy away from this wonderful vegetable. Maybe it's because it's a member of the cabbage family. After you try this combination I think you will be pleasantly surprised.

2 pounds small Brussels sprouts
2 cups water
½ teaspoon salt
6 tablespoons (¾ stick) butter or margarine
1 tablespoon granulated sugar
1 cup boiled or canned chestnuts (do not use water chestnuts; pecans may be substituted)
⅓ cup seasoned beef broth
Freshly ground black pepper

Clean and trim the sprouts. (If freshly picked, some people like to soak them in cold salted water for 15 minutes to remove any garden insects that may be inside.) Place the sprouts, water, and salt in a large saucepan, cover, and cook until tender, about 8 minutes. They should not fall apart, but give a bit when squeezed. Drain. Melt 3 tablespoons of the butter in a large, heavy skillet and sauté the sprouts over medium heat until lightly golden, about 5 minutes. Pour into a heated serving dish; keep warm. Melt the remaining butter in the same skillet, add the sugar and stir over medium heat until lightly caramelized, about 3 minutes. Add the chestnuts and stir until golden brown, about 4 minutes. Add the beef broth, simmer a bit, still over medium heat, check for seasonings, then pour over the sprouts. Top with pepper and serve immediately.

YIELD: 4 TO 6 SERVINGS

BAKED CABBAGE

I have to include this recipe because everyone asks me why they like this cabbage when they do not eat cabbage—could it be the cheese?

1 medium-size head cabbage
1/2 cup water
2 tablespoons all-purpose flour
1/2 teaspoon salt
1/2 teaspoon ground white pepper
1 tablespoon granulated sugar
3 tablespoons butter
1 cup milk
1/2 cup grated Cheddar or white American cheese

Cut the cabbage into wedges and parboil in the water in a covered saucepan for about 4 minutes. Drain and place the cabbage in a buttered or greased 2-quart casserole. Sprinkle with the flour, salt, pepper, and sugar. Dot with the butter or melt and pour over evenly. Pour the milk over the cabbage and top with the grated cheese. Bake in a preheated 350°F oven for about 35 minutes or until golden brown on top and bubbling around the sides. The time will be affected by the depth of the baking dish.

YIELD: 4 SERVINGS

SAUERKRAUT

Every good "Dutchman" eats pork and sauerkraut on New Year's Day to bring the family good luck for the coming year.

2 pounds sauerkraut (4 cups), fresh or canned
2 cups beer or water
1 tablespoon light brown sugar
1 tablespoon caraway seeds (optional)

Wash and drain the sauerkraut and place it in a large, heavy kettle. Cover with the beer or water. If you use the water, add several cored and sliced apples to mellow the kraut. Add the brown sugar and caraway. Bring to a boil and simmer over low heat for at least 1 hour. The longer it simmers, the better it tastes. If you want to add meat, put this in during the last 15 minutes before serving. The brownings from a pork or beef roast give an excellent flavor.

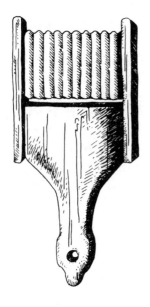

To make your own sauerkraut, finely shred fresh cabbage with a coarse grater or the thin slicer of a food processor. A firm medium head of cabbage will fill 3 pint jars of kraut. Pack into sterilized jars. Sprinkle the top of each quart with one teaspoon of salt (if using pints, ½ teaspoon salt per pint) and fill to the neck of the jar with boiling water. Seal with new lids and rings and store in a cool place. To prevent the liquid from staining the shelves mold foil in a baking pan to form a tray. Place the jars of kraut on the foil—it will ferment in the jars and seep from the lids—to age. Let the kraut age for at least 1 month—the longer the better—but 3 months is good. The old-fashioned way was to place it in a crock and let it ferment, partially covered with a plate weighted down with a washed stone, until it was tender, about 35 days. This method keeps the kraut much lighter and is so easy—without near the odor!

YIELD: 6 SERVINGS

Variation: Sauerkraut and Knepp: Add extra liquid to the sauerkraut and drop the knepp in tablespoonsful into the boiling broth, following the recipe on page 46.

RED CABBAGE

Our ancestors raised red cabbage and considered it an ordinary part of a meal. I think it is exciting and delicious, especially when served with a fine red wine.

½ cup granulated sugar
1 tablespoon salt
½ cup water
½ cup cider vinegar
8 cups shredded red cabbage
1 tablespoon butter
*½ cup red wine (grape jelly may be
    substituted)*

Combine the sugar, salt, water, and vinegar in a large 6 quart saucepan or kettle. Bring to a boil and add the cabbage and butter. Lower the heat to a simmer and cook, covered, until tender, at least 30 minutes. Add the red wine and check for seasoning, adding extra salt and pepper if desired. Simmer 10 minutes more or until ready to serve.

YIELD: 6 SERVINGS

HINT: Several apples, peeled, cored, and sliced thin may be added to the cabbage while it is boiling.

CARROTS

Nutritious and colorful, carrots are loved by children. Here are some of my favorite recipes for tempting them.

1 pound carrots, peeled and cut into 1-inch pieces
1 cup water
½ teaspoon salt
2 tablespoons Browned Butter (page 123)

Place the carrots into a large saucepan, add the water and salt, cover, and cook over medium heat until tender but not mushy, about 12 minutes. Drain and serve in a heated serving dish. Top with browned butter.

YIELD: 4 TO 6 SERVINGS

Variations: Substitute beef broth for the water.
Minted Carrots: add 1 tablespoon chopped fresh mint while cooking and garnish with a few sprigs of mint.
Fried Carrots: After draining the cooked carrots, roll them in ½ cup flour, coating thoroughly. Melt 2 tablespoons butter or vegetable oil in a large, heavy skillet over medium heat. Add the carrots and 1 teaspoon granulated sugar and fry until golden brown around the edges, approximately 6 minutes. Serve immediately. This recipe is especially good with whole baby carrots.

CARROT SOUFFLÉ

Many folks think soufflés are new, but my research proves they've been made for many, many years.

1 pound carrots, peeled and coarsely chopped
5 tablespoons butter
1 tablespoon minced onion
2 teaspoons dried chervil
½ teaspoon dried tarragon
½ teaspoon chopped fresh mint
1 teaspoon Worcestershire sauce
¼ teaspoon paprika
½ teaspoon salt
¼ teaspoon ground black pepper
3 tablespoons all-purpose flour
1½ cups milk
3 large eggs, separated

Place the carrots in a large saucepan and cover with water. Bring to a boil, then simmer over medium heat until the carrots are tender, about 10 minutes; drain. Melt 2 tablespoons of the butter in a large heavy skillet or saucepan over medium heat. Add the carrots, onion, chervil, tarragon, mint, Worcestershire, paprika, salt, and pepper, and sauté for 4 minutes or until thoroughly heated. Remove from the heat and let cool slightly. In a 1½-quart saucepan, melt the remaining butter and gradually stir in the flour with a whisk over medium heat, stirring until smooth and bubbly, about 2 minutes. Slowly add the milk and cook about 3 minutes or until thickened. Beat the egg yolks. Remove the milk mixture from the heat and whip in the yolks. Fold it into the carrot mixture. Beat the egg whites until stiff and fold into the warm mixture. Pour into a buttered 1½-quart ring mold, bundt pan, or baking dish. Place it in a pan with 1 inch of water and bake in a pre-heated 350°F oven for approximately 45 minutes or until a knife inserted in the deepest part of the soufflé comes out clean. Work the point of a knife around the outer edge to loosen the soufflé and invert it onto a heated serving dish. Do not remove the mold immediately—let the soufflé come out gradually.

YIELD: 4 TO 6 SERVINGS

Variation: Before serving, fill the center of the baked soufflé with cooked snow peas, garden peas, green beans, or buttered spinach.
Corn Soufflé: Substitute 4 cups corn kernels for the carrots and omit the mint. For a fine, light soufflé, puree the corn in a food processor or blender.
Broccoli Soufflé: Substitute 1½ pounds broccoli buds for the carrots and omit the mint. If baking in a ring mold or bundt pan, fill the baked soufflé with any sautéed or steamed vegetables.

CAULIFLOWER

You can also make this recipe using the whole head of the cauliflower; it's more showy looking for company.

1 head cauliflower, about 10 inches across the top
1 cup water
½ teaspoon salt
1 teaspoon chopped fresh chervil (optional)
½ teaspoon ground white pepper

1½ cups Medium White Sauce (page 124)
½ cup grated Cheddar or white American cheese
Paprika or chopped fresh chervil for garnish

Trim and wash the cauliflower, breaking it into flowerets if you prefer. Place in a large saucepan with the water, salt, chervil, and pepper. Cook over medium heat until tender, about 10 minutes if separated into flowerets, 20 minutes if whole. Drain the cauliflower and top with butter pats if you like it plain and serve immediately. If you plan to sauce it, heat the white sauce while the cauliflower is cooking, adding the grated cheese and stirring until completely blended. Pour the sauce over the drained cauliflower and sprinkle with paprika or chervil. Serve immediately or place under a preheated broiler until top is golden brown.

YIELD: 4 SERVINGS

NUTTY SWEET AND SOUR CAULIFLOWER

With the abundance of walnuts in Pennsylvania Dutch country, is it any wonder they are used in sauces and as garnishes?

1 large head cauliflower
1 cup water
1 teaspoon salt
2 tablespoons (¼ stick) butter
1 large egg, lightly beaten
2 tablespoons granulated sugar
¼ teaspoon ground white pepper

3 tablespoons light brown sugar
2 tablespoons Dijon mustard
1 tablespoon cornstarch
⅓ cup cider vinegar (herb or wine vinegar may be substituted)
½ cup milk or evaporated milk
½ cup broken or coarsely chopped walnuts, toasted
Walnut halves for garnish

Trim and wash the cauliflower. Place it in a large saucepan with the water and ½ teaspoon of the salt. Cover and cook over medium heat until tender but crisp, approximately 20 minutes. Meanwhile, melt the butter in a small skillet or saucepan and whisk in the egg, sugar, pepper, salt, brown sugar, mustard, and the remaining salt. Cook over low heat until slightly thickened, about 3 minutes. Dissolve the cornstarch in the vinegar and add to egg mixture, stirring till well blended. Add the milk and stir until thickened and smooth, about 6 minutes. Add the walnuts. Drain the cauliflower and place in heated serving dish. Spoon the sauce over the cauliflower and garnish with walnut halves.

YIELD: 4 SERVINGS

CELERY BAKED WITH ALMONDS

Bleached celery hearts are always presented chilled and usually in an antique glass celery dish. The green stems around the outside of the stalk were used to their best advantage in this recipe.

8 to 10 stems of green celery or 2 whole stalks of celery with leaves, washed, trimmed, and cut into 1-inch pieces
1 cup chicken broth
1 teaspoon chopped fresh parsley
½ cup grated carrots (optional)
½ teaspoon salt
½ teaspoon ground black pepper
3 tablespoons butter
3 tablespoons all-purpose flour
1 cup milk
⅓ cup toasted slivered or sliced almonds
⅓ cup fresh bread crumbs
⅓ teaspoon celery seed and ⅓ cup toasted, slivered almonds for garnish

Place the celery in a large saucepan with the broth, parsley, carrots, salt, and pepper. Bring to a boil and simmer over medium heat until tender but still crisp, about 10 minutes. Strain, reserving the liquid for the sauce. Melt the butter in a deep skillet or saucepan and stir in the flour over medium-low heat until smooth and bubbly. Gradually add the celery liquid and the milk. Cook over medium heat, stirring constantly until the sauce is thick and creamy, about 6 minutes. Add the almonds and sauce to the celery and pour into a buttered 2-quart baking dish. Top with the bread crumbs, celery seed, and almonds and bake in a preheated 400°F oven for 10 minutes or until golden brown, or place under a preheated broiler until lightly browned.

YIELD: 6 SERVINGS

Variation: Use ½ cup grated Cheddar cheese instead of the almonds.

CELERY WITH SESAME-HONEY PEANUT BUTTER

This takes very little time to make and lasts forever in the refrigerator (if you can keep from eating it!).

1/4 cup sesame seeds
3 tablespoons honey
1 cup creamy peanut butter (crunchy if desired)
Celery stems, cleaned and cut in 3-inch lengths

Toast the sesame seeds in a small skillet over medium heat or toaster oven at 350°F for 5 minutes, stirring constantly until golden brown. Blend the honey into the peanut butter and add 3 tablespoons of the sesame seeds. Mix well and spread on celery stems. Top with remaining sesame seeds.

YIELD: 1 1/2 CUPS

Variation: Place the spread in a small bowl and serve with fresh carrot sticks, cauliflower or broccoli florets, or sliced turnips. Fill leaves of fresh cabbage with the peanut butter mixture, roll them, and serve as a finger food.

CORN SOUFFLÉ

For extra corn flavor in a meal, try this.

1 cup milk
4 large eggs, separated
2 tablespoons (1/4 stick) butter or margarine
1 teaspoon salt
1/2 teaspoon ground black pepper
1/2 cup cornmeal
1/4 cup all-purpose flour
1 cup corn kernels, fresh or frozen
1 cup grated Cheddar cheese
1 tablespoon chopped pimiento
1 1/2 teaspoons chopped fresh chives

Heat the milk in a large, heavy saucepan over medium-high heat until very hot but not boiling. While heating the milk, beat egg yolks and butter together in a large mixing bowl until fluffy. Combine the salt, pepper, cornmeal, and flour together in another bowl and gradually whisk into the hot milk, stirring constantly until thickened. Remove from the heat and beat into the egg yolk mixture. Whip the egg whites until they form soft peaks. Fold corn, cheese, pimiento, and chives into the yolk mixture. Gently fold into the egg whites. Pour into a greased baking dish and bake in a preheated 375°F oven for 30 minutes or until golden brown and will not jiggle in the middle when shaken.

YIELD: 4 SERVINGS

CORN, TOMATOES, AND OKRA

Our neighbors, when I was growing up, raised okra. I prefer it fried or pickled, so I love to include it in mixed vegetable stir fries. It's beautiful to serve as a main dish.

1 pound okra
5 or 6 ears sweet corn or 5 cups corn kernels
¼ cup vegetable shortening or oil
1 teaspoon salt
1 teaspoon ground black pepper
1 teaspoon granulated sugar
½ teaspoon Krazy or steak salt (coarse salt with herbs added)
5 medium-size tomatoes, cored and cut into slices or wedges
¼ teaspoon coarsely ground black pepper
½ teaspoon chopped fresh parsley

Clean and cut the okra into ⅓-inch slices. Cut the corn off the cob. Melt the shortening or oil in a large, deep skillet. Fry the okra and corn seasoned with the salt, pepper, sugar, and seasoned salt over medium heat until both are light brown around the edges, stirring frequently to prevent sticking, approximately 25 minutes or until the vegetable liquid is absorbed. Add the tomatoes, reduce the heat to low, and simmer 5 minutes more or until tomatoes are thoroughly heated. Sprinkle with ground pepper and parsley before serving. It's nice to serve this in the skillet in which it was prepared.

YIELD: 6 SERVINGS

CORN, LIMAS, AND RED PEPPER STIR FRY

When everyone is enjoying the outdoors, make this recipe in your wok or electric skillet or use your heavy iron skillet on the grill and prepare it outdoors—that way you can keep the heat out of the kitchen and be part of the family fun.

6 slices bacon
6 ears corn or 4 cups corn kernels
2 medium-size red bell peppers, sliced or diced
2 cups fordhook or baby lima beans
¾ teaspoon salt
½ teaspoon coarsely ground black pepper

Fry bacon until crisp in a large skillet. Remove and drain on paper towels. Cut the corn kernels from the cob and add to the hot bacon fat along with the peppers, lima beans, salt, and pepper; stir fry over medium-high heat until vegetables are tender but crunchy, about 8 minutes. Top with the crumbled bacon and serve immediately.

YIELD: 6 TO 8 SERVINGS

Variation: Substitute green or yellow beans of your choice for the limas and add other vegetables as desired.

CORN FRITTERS

Excellent as a vegetable dish, fritters are a perfect finger food to serve from an electric skillet during a buffet (or at poolside).

3 cups corn kernels, fresh or frozen
1 teaspoon salt
½ teaspoon granulated sugar (optional)
¼ teaspoon coarsely ground black pepper
½ teaspoon crushed dried basil (optional)
2 large eggs, lightly beaten
2 tablespoons butter or vegetable oil

Blend all the ingredients together, coarsely, in a food processor or blender, unless you are using frozen corn; in that case, add all the other ingredients first or the frozen corn will harden and burn out the blender's motor. Heat the butter or oil to medium-high in a large, heavy skillet and drop the batter in by table-spoonful. Turn over when golden brown. Remove from skillet when other side has browned. Serve with maple syrup, molasses, or powdered sugar. (I like my corn fritters plain.)

YIELD: 25 TO 30 FRITTERS

DRIED CORN

When fresh sweet corn is dried it retains all its natural sugar. When reconstituted, it almost tastes as though there was a bit of caramel syrup added. You can purchase dried corn by mail: Write John F. Cope Co., Inc., Rheems, Lancaster County, PA. 17570

8 ounces dried sweet corn, almost 2 cups
3½ cups milk
2 tablespoons (¼ stick) butter or
   margarine
¼ teaspoon salt (optional)

Grind the corn in a food processor or mill until fine. Soak the corn in a 2-quart buttered casserole overnight, refrigerated, in the milk. Pour into a 2-quart saucepan, add the butter and salt, and simmer over low heat for at least 40 minutes, stirring frequently to prevent sticking. Take off the heat, stir once, and let stand for 15 minutes. Return to low heat and cook 15 minutes more. Serve immediately.

YIELD: 6 SERVINGS

Variation: Baked Corn: Add 4 eggs, lightly beaten, and 1 teaspoon salt to the corn and bake in a preheated 350°F oven for 45 minutes.

BATTER DIPPED CUCUMBERS

When cucumbers are plentiful, this will be one of your favorite ways to enjoy them.

4 to 6 medium-size cucumbers
1 recipe of Beer Batter (page 131)
Vegetable oil for frying

Do not peel the cucumbers unless they are waxed. Cut into ¼-inch slices and dip in the batter. Heat 3 inches of oil in the fryer to 380°F; fry the batter-dipped slices until golden brown. Drain on paper towels. Serve hot with catsup on the side.

YIELD: 4 SERVINGS

DANDELION, LIMAS, AND POTATOES

An excellent way to enjoy the first fresh dandelions.

6 slices bacon
1 cup baby limas, fresh or frozen
2 cups diced potatoes
1/2 cup water
4 cups fresh baby dandelion leaves
1/2 teaspoon salt
1/2 teaspoon ground black pepper

Fry bacon until crisp. Remove from pan and drain on paper towels. Reserve 2 tablespoons of the bacon fat. Cook limas and potatoes over medium-high heat with water in a saucepan, covered, until tender, approximately 12 minutes. Drain. While vegetables are cooking, wash dandelion leaves thoroughly and trim stems and roots. Heat the bacon fat over medium heat and sauté the leaves until wilted; then add the potatoes, lima beans, salt, and pepper. Stir and cover, simmering over medium heat for about 3 minutes. Do not overcook or the dandelion leaves will become bitter. Top with crumbled bacon or stir in before serving. Serve from the skillet or a heated serving dish.

YIELD: 4 SERVINGS

EGGPLANT CASSEROLE

This recipe is so simple and delicious I had to include it for you to enjoy.

2 eggplants, peeled
1 medium-size green bell pepper
1 medium-size onion
1/2 cup water
1 1/2 teaspoons salt
1 1/2 cups grated Cheddar cheese
1 cup broken saltine crackers
1/2 teaspoon coarsely ground black pepper
4 tablespoons (1/2 stick) butter, melted

Slice, dice, or chop the eggplants, pepper, and onion, and place them in a 3-quart saucepan with the water and salt. Cover and cook over medium heat until the eggplant is clear, about 5 minutes. Drain well. Generously butter a 2-quart baking dish or pan and layer vegetables, cheese, and crackers. Sprinkle with the pepper and dribble the melted butter over the top. Bake in a preheated 350°F oven for 30 minutes until golden brown.

YIELD: 6 TO 8 SERVINGS

FRIED EGGPLANT

The secret to good eggplant is the weighting-down process. It has a lot of liquid which is best removed before preparation by slicing the eggplant, sprinkling it lightly with salt, covering the slices with a dish, and weighting it down with a heavy can, stone, or jar. This presses out all the liquid in less than 1 hour. Many folks used eggplant as a substitute for oysters.

2 eggplants, about 1 pound, peeled
Salt
2 cups fresh bread crumbs or half cracker
  and half bread crumbs
½ teaspoon dry mustard
½ teaspoon ground white pepper
3 large eggs, lightly beaten
1 cup vegetable oil

Slice the peeled eggplants ¼ to ⅓ inch thick. Place in a large bowl or casserole, sprinkling each layer lightly with salt. Cover the slices with a dish and weight it down with a heavy object. Let stand for at least 1 hour. Drain the liquid. Mix the crumbs, mustard, and pepper together on a plate or a sheet of wax paper. Dip the eggplant slices into the beaten egg, then dredge completely in the crumbs. Fry in the oil, heated to 375°F, in a large, heavy skillet or deep fat fryer until golden brown, about 4 minutes.

YIELD: 4 TO 6 SERVINGS

NOTE: You may broil the eggplant instead of frying it, placing the slices in a preheated broiler until golden brown, about 3 minutes per side.

Variation: Slice 3 firm tomatoes ½ inch thick and fry or broil the same way. When serving, alternate the tomato and eggplant slices around the serving dish. Two large zucchini may be substituted for the eggplant.

HOMINY CAKES

These can be baked in the oven, but most people find it easier to fry them. Hominy is a great substitute for potatoes or rice and may be served for breakfast, lunch, or dinner.

1¼ cups cooked hominy, drained
½ cup milk
1 large egg
1 tablespoon butter, melted
½ teaspoon salt
1 teaspoon granulated sugar
Flour for dredging
2 tablespoons (¼ stick) butter or vegetable
  oil

Place the hominy, milk, egg, melted butter, salt and sugar in a food processor or mixer and puree. Form into cakes about 3 inches round and dredge in flour. Melt butter in skillet and fry until golden brown on each side. Cover the pan with a lid to keep from splattering during frying. If baking in an oven, generously grease a baking dish, put a dab of butter on top of each cake, and bake them in a preheated 375°F oven for 20 minutes.

YIELD: 6 CAKES APPROXIMATELY 3 INCHES IN DIAMETER

HOMINY CROQUETTES

Hominy, the center of a grain of corn, was an important part of the early settlers' diets. Today we have the advantage of the availability of flaked hominy, known as grits, or canned hominy. Hominy picks up the flavor of anything it is cooked with, much like noodles, potatoes, or rice. Usually served with pork or ham dishes, these croquettes, when sweetened, are served with poached fruit as a dessert.

1¼ cups instant grits
1½ cups water
1¾ cups canned hominy (small or
  chopped), drained
3 large eggs, separated
1 tablespoon butter, melted
1 teaspoon granulated sugar
¼ teaspoon salt
2 cups milk

Cook the instant grits in the water over medium heat in a covered saucepan for about 4 minutes. If using whole canned hominy, chop in a food processor. Lightly beat the egg yolks with a fork. Whip the whites until they form peaks. Mix the grits, hominy, butter, sugar, salt, and beaten egg yolks together until well blended. Gradually add the milk and mix until smooth. Fold in the beaten egg whites. Pour into a buttered 2- to 2½-quart casserole dish. Bake in a preheated 350°F oven for 1 hour or until golden brown.

YIELD: 6 SERVINGS

Variation: Add 1 cup of grated Cheddar cheese to the mixture before baking.
For Dessert: Add 2 to 3 tablespoons granulated sugar and 1 teaspoon vanilla extract to the mixture before folding in the egg whites.

KOHLRABI

Kohlrabi, like turnips, are delicious peeled, sliced, and eaten raw with a sprinkle of salt. It is such an interesting vegetable, reasonably priced and nutritious.

1½ pounds kohlrabi, peeled and cut into
  ½-inch slices
1 cup chicken broth or water
½ teaspoon salt (less if broth is salty)
½ teaspoon ground black pepper
2 tablespoons Browned Butter (page 123)

Place kohlrabi, broth, salt, and pepper in large saucepan. Cook, covered, over medium heat until tender, about 25 minutes. Drain and top with browned butter.

YIELD: 4 SERVINGS

Variation: ½ pound turnips and ½ pound rutabaga, peeled and sliced, may be added to the above recipe, for 6 to 8 servings. For *Creamy Mashed Kohlrabi,* add ½ cup evaporated milk to vegetable and whip thoroughly. Serve with or without browned butter on top. *Baked Kohlrabi, Turnips, and Rutabaga with Pork or Beef Roast:* Place the vegetables, peeled, around the roast for the last 2 hours of cooking, turning once so flavor of the roast seasons the vegetables.

LANCASTER COUNTY LIMA BEANS

My Dad's family always served their vegetables in cream. Limas do need more cooking than some of the green vegetables, and when they are simmered in cream, they are unbelievable. We still make them with cream for special occasions.

4 cups (about 2 pounds) fresh or frozen
   lima beans (I prefer the pole limas or
   Fordhook limas)
1/2 cup water
1/2 teaspoon salt
1/2 teaspoon granulated sugar
1 tablespoon butter
Pinch of ground white pepper
1 cup half and half
1 tablespoon Browned Butter (page 123)

Put the beans in a large saucepan with the water, salt, sugar, butter, and pepper. Cover and bring to a boil. Simmer over medium heat for 10 minutes. Add the cream and heat to nearly boiling. Turn off the heat and let stand covered until ready to serve (the cream thickens as it stands). Pour into a heated serving dish and top with browned butter.

YIELD: 4 TO 6 SERVINGS

Variation: Baby Limas with Herbs: Omit the cream and add 1/2 teaspoon each of ground thyme, dried chervil, and dried parsley to the lima beans while cooking. A pinch of baking soda added while cooking will make them more tender. Top with Browned Butter if desired.

Limas with Roquefort: Use 1 cup Thin White Sauce (page 124) instead of the cream and add 1/3 cup crumbled Roquefort just before serving or top with the cheese instead of the browned butter.

LIMAS IN TOMATO SAUCE

A great winter dish. Everyone dried their own beans and canned their own tomatoes. Today it is much easier to buy the canned ones.

6 slices bacon
2 1/2 cups prepared tomato sauce
2 or 3 tablespoons light brown sugar
   (depending on your taste)
1/2 teaspoon salt
1/2 teaspoon celery salt
1/2 teaspoon ground black pepper
2 1/2 cups canned butter beans, drained
Seasoned croutons

Fry the bacon in a large, heavy skillet until crisp. Remove bacon and drain on paper towels. Discard all but 2 tablespoons of the bacon fat. Put the fat in a large saucepan, over medium heat, stir in the tomato sauce, brown sugar, salt, celery salt, and pepper. When thoroughly heated, add the beans and simmer over medium heat for 30 minutes or until they absorb some of the liquid. Crumble the bacon and stir about 3/4 of it into the beans. Serve beans in saucers topped with the croutons and the remaining bacon.

YIELD: 4 TO 6 SERVINGS

ONION RINGS

Fried (pan fried with butter) onions were the normal way to serve onions as a side dish. I like to fry them in deep fat in single rings, but many people prefer to partially fill the basket and fry them altogether. Either way, they're great with this light batter.

*6 large onions, cut into 1/4-inch slices
(Bermuda or red onions are best because
they are mild and sweet)
Vegetable oil for frying
1 recipe Beer Batter (page 131)*

Separate the onion slices into rings. Preheat 3 inches of oil to 375°F in a deep fryer. Dip the rings in the beer batter and drop them into the oil. Fry until golden brown, about 4 minutes. Drain on paper towels. Place on a heated platter and serve immediately.

YIELD: 4 TO 6 SERVINGS

BAKED ONIONS

Grandma always said, "When you feel a cold coming on, eat lots of onions." Most of the time we ate them raw, but I love baked onions because they are so sweet after baking.

*6 to 8 medium-size onions, peeled and cut
in half
Salt and ground black pepper or herbed salt
3 tablespoons butter, margarine, or
vegetable oil*

Place the onion halves in buttered muffin cups. Sprinkle with the seasonings and add a pat of butter (or brush with oil) to each half. Bake in a preheated 350°F oven for 45 minutes or until golden on top. Serve hot.

YIELD: 4 TO 6 SERVINGS

Variation: Baked Stuffed Onions: Follow the above recipe but remove the centers of each half and chop them up. Fry 3 slices bacon in a skillet until golden and crisp. Remove the bacon and drain on paper towels. Sauté the chopped onion in the bacon fat over medium heat until golden brown. Remove from the heat and add 1/2 cup fresh bread crumbs, 1 egg, lightly beaten, 1/2 teaspoon salt, 1/3 teaspoon coarsely ground black pepper, 1/2 teaspoon chopped fresh chives, 1/4 teaspoon celery salt, and the crumbled bacon. Mix thoroughly and spoon into the onion halves. Dot with butter or oil. Bake in a greased 9-inch square or 9-by-13-inch baking dish as directed above.

GLAZED ONIONS

Glazed onions were always served for special occasions. I can't understand why we didn't use them all the time—maybe because it takes time to peel them. I think any onions are wonderful and exciting when prepared this way, even if you quarter the large ones.

1 pint pearl onions (about ½ pound), cleaned
½ cup water
½ teaspoon salt
2 tablespoons (¼ stick) butter
1 tablespoon granulated sugar
Dash of ground white pepper

Parboil the cleaned onions in the water and salt in a covered saucepan over high heat for 3 minutes. Remove from the heat and let stand for another 2 minutes. Drain and pat dry the onions between paper towels. Melt the butter in a heavy skillet and add the sugar and onions. Cook slowly over medium heat, stirring constantly with a wooden spoon until all sides are golden and shiny, about 5 minutes. Serve as a vegetable side dish or as a garnish around the entree. Sprinkle with pepper before serving.

YIELD: 4 SERVINGS

Variation: Creamed Onions: Follow the above recipe. When the onions are gold and shiny, add 1 cup of Thick White Sauce (page 124). Heat through and serve.

PARSNIPS

Parsnips have a rather sweet flavor and are usually fried or added to beef stew. This recipe will give you several choices. Try them all.

1 pound parsnips
1 cup beef broth or water
¼ cup wine
2 tablespoons vegetable shortening or oil
Salt and ground black pepper to taste (depending on strength of broth)
½ cup heavy cream or Medium White Sauce (page 124)

Scrub the parsnips, prick them several times with a fork, and place them in a large saucepan with the broth and wine. Bring to a boil over medium heat and boil until tender, about 40 minutes. Remove from the heat and cool until able to hold in hands. Peel and either slice, cut in half, or leave whole. Heat the shortening in a large, heavy skillet and sauté the parsnips over medium heat until golden brown, about 5 minutes. Check for seasonings and add salt and pepper if desired. Add the cream and heat through.

YIELD: 4 SERVINGS

Variation: Glazed: Cook as the recipe above but omit the cream. Mix together 2 tablespoons white wine and ¼ cup light brown sugar or maple syrup and pour over the parsnips. For extra flavor, add 1 tablespoon Dijon mustard to the glaze.

GARDEN PEAS
WITH MINT

Peas are always colorful, and the mint makes them taste extra fresh.

4 lettuce leaves
2 cups peas, fresh or frozen
½ teaspoon salt
½ teaspoon granulated sugar
1 tablespoon butter
2 or 3 sprigs fresh mint or 1 teaspoon dried
⅓ cup water
2 tablespoons Browned Butter (optional; page 123)

Line a 1½-quart saucepan or vegetable steamer with the lettuce leaves. Add peas, salt, sugar, butter, and mint. Pour the water underneath the lettuce, cover the pan, and bring to a boil, then turn down to medium heat. Steam the peas for 3 minutes or until tender. Drain the peas, discard the lettuce, and serve the peas in a heated serving dish. Top with Browned Butter.

YIELD: 4 SERVINGS

Variations: Sauté or steam 2 cups small pearl onions or chopped green onions in 1 tablespoon butter until tender. Add to the peas before serving.

Scrub 6 tiny new potatoes and leave their skins on and cook in 1 cup lightly salted water over medium heat until tender, approximately 20 minutes. As it will take longer to cook the potatoes, start them before you steam the peas. Add the peas before serving.

In Patty Shells: Use the Basic Pie Dough recipe (page 149) to make shells or use Toast Cups (page 86). Fill with peas. If you prefer, add ½ cup heavy cream to peas and heat thoroughly before topping with Browned Butter.

SUGAR PEAS

The original sugar peas grown in the Pennsylvania Dutch country were of two varieties. One was the flat, thin ones, much like the snow peas available everywhere but sweeter and smaller. The other was the sickle pod sugar peas which were rounder and plumper, since developed into the sugar snap peas. The pods of both are a delicate surprise; newcomers to the area often thought the peas were to be shelled and threw the best part away.

4 cups sugar peas
½ teaspoon salt
1 tablespoon butter
½ cup water
2 tablespoons Browned Butter (page 123)

Wash the peas, then remove the stem end and pull the string back to the blossom end. Trim any browned or dry tips. Place the peas, salt, butter, and water in a 2-quart saucepan. Cover and bring to a boil. Reduce heat to medium and cook for about 2 minutes. Do not overcook. Serve in heated serving dish and top with Browned Butter.

YIELD: 4 SERVINGS

UNBELIEVABLE PEAS
IN SOUR CREAM

The name says it all!

1 large cucumber or zucchini, peeled
Pinch of chopped fresh chervil
Pinch of chopped fresh tarragon
Pinch of chopped fresh dill
Pinch of chopped fresh mint
1 pound fresh or frozen garden peas
1 tablespoon butter
1/2 teaspoon salt
1/4 cup water
1/2 cup sour cream
1/2 cup Cooked Dressing (page 129),
   mayonnaise, or salad dressing
1 tablespoon fresh lemon juice

Slice cucumber into 1/4-inch slices. Place them in a large saucepan and add the herbs, peas, butter, salt, and water. Cover and bring to a boil. Reduce heat to low and simmer for 6 minutes, less if frozen peas are used. Blend the sour cream, mayonnaise, and lemon juice, and pour over the peas. Heat thoroughly, stirring to prevent sticking. Serve immediately.

YIELD: 6 SERVINGS

BAKED POTATOES

So many young cooks find it hard to believe that few cookbooks tell how to bake a potato. Since I am a potato freak, I'll give you several ways to enjoy them.

It saves time and insures uniform baking if you choose fresh baking potatoes, not wrinkled ones or ones with sprouts, and preferably the same size.

1 potato per person
Butter, salt, pepper, sour cream, chopped
   chives, and all your favorite extras

Scrub the potatoes thoroughly and prick with a fork several times to prevent the skin from exploding during baking. If you like the skin soft, rub with vegetable oil or salad dressing. Place on the oven rack or in a shallow baking pan and bake in a preheated 400°F oven for 1 hour or until the potato feels soft when squeezed gently with a pot holder. Cut a slit on the top of each potato and squeeze each end, popping it enough to let in the butter or sour cream, etc. Serve immediately.

For microwave baking, place potatoes on a paper towel in a circle, leaving at least 1 inch between each. Prick each potato with a fork. Each medium-size potato takes about 4 minutes on high (meaning, if you are baking 2 potatoes they should be in the microwave for 8 minutes). Halfway through, turn the potatoes over. When cooked, cover with a clean towel and let stand at least 10 minutes or until ready to serve.

Variation: Baked Sweet Potatoes or Yams: - Follow the same recipe as baked potatoes, but reduce the baking time to 45 minutes.
Baked Potatoes Stuffed with Sausage: When the potatoes are nearly baked, cut them in half and scoop out the middles. Crumble 1/2 pound fresh or smoked sausage in a large, heavy skillet and fry over medium heat for 6 minutes. Drain off most of the fat. Mash the scooped-out potatoes with a fork and add them to the

sausage in the pan. Add chopped chives and ground black pepper if desired and simmer over medium heat until thoroughly cooked, about 10 minutes. Spoon the filling back into the potato skins and continue baking at 400°F until golden brown, approximately 15 minutes.

SCRAPED NEW POTATOES

Don't bother trying to scrape new potatoes for a large dinner party if you haven't tried it before. It takes about one hour to scrape enough for 6 people. Of course, it is well worth the effort, but I would suggest preparing them the day before and storing them in cold water until needed. When you buy new potatoes, scrape one with your nail. If the skin does not come off easily, they are not freshly dug and will be hard to scrape.

8 small new potatoes, scrubbed clean
2 cups water
1/2 teaspoon salt
2 tablespoons Browned Butter (page 123)
  or browned bread crumbs

Place the potatoes in a large bowl of water (dipping the potato in water as you scrape off the skin speeds up the scraping time). Scrape toward you with a paring knife, holding the potato firmly in one hand and guiding the knife with the other. Do not pare, but scrape gently, with the blade at a 90° angle to the potato, until all the skin is removed. Place the scraped potatoes in another bowl filled with cold water to prevent them from turning

brown. When ready to cook, put the potatoes in a large saucepan with the 2 cups water and salt and cook over medium heat with the lid cracked until tender, about 20 minutes. The edges should crack a bit; if they don't, just prick the potato with a fork several times. Drain and place in a heated serving dish. Top with the browned butter.

YIELD: 4 SERVINGS

PAPRIKA BROWNED POTATOES

These are so easy to make and so good to eat.

6 medium-size potatoes, peeled
1/2 cup all-purpose flour
1 tablespoon paprika
1 teaspoon salt
1/2 teaspoon ground white pepper
2 to 3 tablespoons corn oil

Cut potatoes into wedges or thick slices. Combine flour, paprika, salt, and pepper in a paper bag. Shake the cut potatoes in the flour mixture until thoroughly covered. Heat oil in a skillet and fry over medium heat until potatoes brown and are soft in middle, approximately 20 minutes.

YIELD: 4 TO 6 SERVINGS

POTATO CAKES

These are often served with chipped beef or Creamed Frizzled Dried Beef as a light lunch or supper dish. I like them with everything.

3 cups seasoned, cooked mashed potatoes
2 large eggs, lightly beaten
¼ teaspoon coarsely ground black pepper
⅓ cup all-purpose flour, 2 tablespoons if the potatoes are stiff
2 teaspoons chopped fresh chives
2 tablespoons (¼ stick) butter or vegetable oil

Mix everything but the butter together until blended thoroughly. Form into 3-inch-diameter cakes about 1 inch thick. Heat the butter or oil over medium-high heat until bubbly hot, then add the potato cakes. Reduce heat to medium and fry until golden brown on each side. Serve immediately or place in low oven until ready to serve.

YIELD: 6 TO 8 CAKES

RAW FRIED POTATOES

It took me years to realize why some raw fries were so much better than others. The secret is to add water while frying. The best ones I ever ate were made by George Yoder of Shoemakersville. He prepares them on his huge outdoor grill. First he fries the onions, slides them to the side, then fries the potatoes, covered with a lid. Every time he turns them he adds a little water. Unbelievable!

1½ pounds white potatoes
6 slices bacon or 3 tablespoons vegetable shortening
½ teaspoon salt (optional)
½ teaspoon coarsely ground black pepper
1 medium-size onion, thinly sliced (optional)
1 tablespoon chopped fresh chives
⅓ cup water

Scrub the potatoes, peel if desired, and slice very thin in a food processor. Fry the bacon in a large heavy skillet until crisp. Remove and drain on paper towels. If you do not use bacon, melt 3 tablespoons shortening or oil in a skillet; otherwise, reserve 3 tablespoons of the bacon fat and heat in the skillet over a medium flame. Add the sliced potatoes, salt, pepper, onion, and chives, cover and fry, turning the potatoes often to prevent burning. Each time you turn the potatoes, sprinkle a little of the water in the pan before you cover it with lid. Fry until potatoes brown on each side and are soft in the middle, approximately 25 minutes. Crumble the bacon on top before serving.

YIELD: 4 TO 6 SERVINGS

POTATO FILLING

The Dutch of Berks County make this dish more beautifully than anyone else I've met. It is soupy when mixed and bakes high and golden brown, but they make swirls in the batter with a spoon before baking that gives it that "extra touch."

3 tablespoons butter or vegetable oil
¾ cup chopped celery with leaves
½ cup chopped onion
Pinch of saffron threads
¼ cup chopped fresh parsley
½ teaspoon salt
½ teaspoon ground black pepper
2 cups cooked mashed potatoes
2 cups white bread cubes
1 cup milk

Heat butter or oil in a skillet and sautée the celery, onion, saffron, parsley, salt, and pepper over medium heat until celery is tender, approximately 6 minutes. Mix with mashed potatoes, bread cubes, and milk until well blended. Pour into a buttered 2-quart soufflé dish and bake in a preheated 350°F oven for 40 to 45 minutes or until golden brown.

YIELD: 6 SERVINGS

POTATO CHIPS

With all the wonderful equipment and food processors we have today, making chips is not as hard as it used to be, but the secret is in the temperature of the potato and how it is stored. They must never get below 52 degrees or they will not stay crisp and will have a dark ring around the outside edge. One little secret we found recently helps to keep the potatoes from turning pink after cutting. Add 1 tablespoon vinegar to the sliced potatoes while they are soaking in water. And believe it or not, they really do taste better when you make them yourself.

2 pounds Irish Cobbler or good baking
  potatoes
1 tablespoon cider vinegar
2 cups peanut oil
Salt (optional)

Wash and peel the potatoes. Slice as thin as possible, the thickness of a penny, place them in a deep bowl, add vinegar, and cover with cold water. Heat the oil to 360°F in a deep skillet or deep-fat fryer. Dry the chips on clean towels a handful at a time to prevent them from discoloring, and drop them into the hot fat one at a time. As they turn golden, remove them with a slotted spoon and drain on paper towels. Sprinkle lightly with salt if desired. After the chips cool, store them in an airtight container. Chips fried in peanut oil will keep longer than those fried in lard or shortening.

YIELD: 1½ POUNDS

Variation: Sweet Potato Chips: Substitute an equal amount of sweet potatoes.

ESCALLOPED SALSIFY

The best substitute for oysters, salsify was brought in from the garden before the first frost. Stored in the root cellar or the coolest part of the cellar in a tub and layered with dirt, they stayed firm and fresh for most of the winter. It still works today, but for many folks without cellars it is easier to buy salsify at the local grocery or farmers' market. Most folks know this vegetable as "oyster plant" and use it in casseroles, stews, or fritters. Mother Groff often fries the slices like oysters, but this is her favorite way to use salsify.

1 pound salsify
1 cup water
½ teaspoon salt
1 cup fresh bread crumbs
1 cup small oyster crackers (broken Saltines may be substituted)
½ teaspoon salt
½ teaspoon coarsely ground white pepper
4 tablespoons (½ stick) butter or part margarine, melted, less if desired
1 cup light cream or milk

Scrub the salsify and cook in the water and salt in a large saucepan until tender over medium-high heat, about 15 minutes. Drain and peel. Cut in ½-inch-thick slices. Use a bit of the butter to grease a 1½-quart baking dish. Layer the crumbs, salsify, crackers, butter, and cream. Sprinkle with half the salt and pepper and layer the rest, ending with butter poured over the remaining crumbs. Bake in a preheated 375°F oven for 35 minutes.

YIELD: 4 SERVINGS

Variation: Scalloped Salmon: Substitute 2 cups flaked, cooked salmon for the salsify, add ½ teaspoon dried dill weed, ½ teaspoon celery salt, and substitute lemon pepper for the white pepper.

CREAMED SPINACH

If people would eat spinach that is lightly steamed, they would never say they hate it again. I hate to wash sandy spinach, so I put it in a net bag and agitate it in the washing machine (no soap, of course) in cold water and in a minute it is as clean as a whistle.

1 pound spinach, with stems if they are young leaves
1 teaspoon salt
½ cup heavy cream or Medium White Sauce (page 124)
2 tablespoons Browned Butter (page 123)

Wash the spinach thoroughly, trim the stems (I like to chop them into pieces) and shake. The water that is left on the leaves will be just enough to steam it perfectly. Place the leaves in a saucepan, add salt, and cover. When it starts to steam and the leaves turn bright green, turn off the heat. Add the cream and heat thoroughly over medium heat until slightly thickened. Serve hot with the browned butter dribbled over it. Many folks prefer omitting the cream and use just the browned butter—the choice is yours.

YIELD: 4 SERVINGS

HINT: Grated cheese or a chopped hardboiled egg makes an excellent garnish.

FRIED SPINACH

Many people of Pennsylvania Dutch country served vinegar—often an herb vinegar—with their spinach. It gives a special added flavor.

2 pounds spinach, including stems if leaves
   are young
6 slices bacon or 3 tablespoons butter or
   vegetable shortening
1/2 clove garlic, minced (optional)
1/2 teaspoon salt
1 teaspoon coarsely ground black pepper

Wash spinach thoroughly and dry thoroughly. Chop the stems into 1-inch pieces and tear the leaves as you would for a salad. Fry the bacon until crisp in large skillet; remove the bacon and drain on paper towels. If you don't use the bacon, heat the butter or oil in a skillet; otherwise add the garlic to the fat and sauté over medium heat until golden. Then add the spinach, salt, and pepper and fry over medium-high heat for about 2 minutes. Do not overcook. Remove the spinach from pan with a slotted spoon, place in heated serving dish, and crumble the bacon on top.

YIELD: 4 TO 6 SERVINGS

Variation: Use 1 teaspoon lemon pepper instead of the garlic and ground black pepper.

BAKED SQUASH
AND CRANBERRIES

This casserole will brighten any winter day. Fill two small baking dishes, bake, and serve one, freeze the other.

2 pounds butternut squash, peeled, seeded,
   and cubed
1/2 teaspoon salt
2 cups water
2 large eggs, lightly beaten
5 1/3 tablespoons (2/3 stick) butter, melted
1/3 cup lightly packed light brown sugar
1 teaspoon salt, less if desired
1/2 teaspoon coarsely ground black pepper
1 1/2 cups raw cranberries, washed and
   picked over for stems
Freshly grated nutmeg

Cook the squash, covered, in the salt and water in a large saucepan over high heat until soft, about 15 minutes. Drain well; let stand in a colander for at least 30 minutes or press down with your hand to force out most of the liquid. Puree the pulp in a food processor or put through a food mill; it should yield about 4 cups. Add the eggs, butter, sugar, salt, and pepper. Blend thoroughly. Fold the cranberries into the mixture. Pour into a buttered 2-quart baking dish or two smaller ones. Top with grated nutmeg and bake in a preheated 350°F oven until golden and does not shake in the middle when jiggled, about 45 minutes for one casserole, 30 minutes for two.

YIELD: 8 SERVINGS

STUFFED ACORN SQUASH

Acorn squash are so attractive and, when stuffed, they become individual one-dish meals. Our early settlers roasted them over an open fire and we can enjoy the same flavors by using our outdoor grills.

3 pounds acorn squash (2 or 3, depending on the size), washed, halved crosswise, and seeded
1 cup water
1/2 teaspoon salt

Stuffing:

1 1/2 cups long-grain rice
3 cups water
1/2 teaspoon salt
3 tablespoons butter
1 small onion, chopped (about 1/2 cup)
2 stems celery, chopped
2 cups chopped, cooked ham
1/2 cup chopped fresh parsley or 3 tablespoons dried
1/2 teaspoon dried marjoram
1/2 teaspoon dried mint, crushed
1/4 teaspoon dried rosemary, crushed
1/2 teaspoon Krazy or seasoned salt
1/2 teaspoon lemon pepper
2 tablespoons (1/4 stick) butter or vegetable shortening, melted
1/2 recipe Tomato Sauce (page 125) but add 1/2 teaspoon each chopped fresh basil and chopped fresh oregano to the recipe
1 tablespoon chopped fresh basil for garnish

Boil the squash in a large, heavy saucepan in the water and salt, covered, over high heat for about 10 minutes. Drain upside down until ready to fill.

To make the stuffing, cook the rice in the water and salt over high heat until almost tender, about 20 minutes. Drain. Melt the butter in large skillet and sauté the onion and celery over medium heat until clear, about 6 minutes, then add the ham, herbs, salt, and pepper. Stir in the rice and mix thoroughly.

Brush each squash half with melted butter and fill by placing a tablespoon of tomato sauce in the bottom of each half and then filling with the stuffing, topping with at least 2 tablespoons of sauce. Bake in a preheated 350°F oven for 20 minutes, turn off the heat and let stand in the oven until ready to serve. Garnish with chopped basil. If you have extra stuffing and sauce, mix it together and bake it in a buttered baking dish to serve on the side or freeze for later use.

YIELD: 4 SERVINGS

Variation: Maple Baked Squash: Prepare the squash as above, omitting the stuffing. Brush with melted butter and 1/2 cup pure maple syrup. Sprinkle with a dash each of grated nutmeg and ground cinnamon. Bake in a preheated 350°F oven for 30 minutes or until tender and golden brown.

FRIED SWEET POTATOES

There's a big difference between Jersey White sweet potatoes and yams. Jersey Whites are small, dry, and firm compared to the big orange sweet potatoes and yams. Yams and sweets have more liquid and are sweeter than the whites.

1½ pounds sweet potatoes
½ teaspoon salt
2 cups water
3 tablespoons butter or vegetable oil
Salt and ground black pepper (optional)

Scrub the potatoes and put them in a large saucepan with the salt and water. Cook over medium heat, covered, until tender, about 30 minutes. Drain, cool, and peel. Cut in half, lengthwise, or into thick slices to fry. Heat the butter or oil in a large, heavy skillet and fry over medium heat until golden brown on all sides, about 10 minutes. Sprinkle with salt and pepper if desired. (My family always sprinkled a bit of sugar on the Whites during frying.) The potatoes may be frozen for future use before they are fried.

YIELD: 4 TO 6 SERVINGS

Variations: Maple Glazed Sweet Potatoes: Add ⅓ cup pure maple syrup to the butter while frying.
Sweet Potatoes and Apples: Fry 4 apples, cored, peeled if desired, and sliced into rings or wedges with the potatoes.

TOMATOES STUFFED WITH SPINACH

A perfect color combination for the holidays, this dish can be prepared ahead of time and slipped in the oven as the guests arrive. Serve it as a vegetable or use cherry tomatoes and serve them as an appetizer.

1½ pounds tomatoes
1 pound fresh spinach or 10 ounces frozen
¼ cup water
4 ounces cream cheese, at room temperature
1 large egg
¾ cup fresh bread crumbs
½ cup shredded Cheddar cheese
¼ cup grated Parmesan cheese
¼ cup milk
½ teaspoon salt
½ teaspoon ground nutmeg
Dash of ground white pepper

Wash the tomatoes, cut off the top of each, and carefully scoop out the center and seeds. Chop about ½ cup of the pulp. If using fresh spinach, remove the stems and wash the leaves thoroughly. Place them in a large saucepan, add water, and steam over high heat until limp, about ½ minute. Drain and chop fine. If using frozen spinach, allow to defrost and then chop. In a large mixing bowl, beat the cream cheese and egg together until fluffy. Gradually add the crumbs, cheeses, milk, salt, nutmeg, pepper, chopped tomato pulp, and chopped spinach, blending thoroughly. Fill each tomato shell with the mixture and place in a greased baking dish. Bake in a preheated 350°F oven for 35 to 40 minutes or until a toothpick comes out clean when inserted in the middle of a tomato. If baking cherry tomatoes, reduce the baking time to 15 minutes. If you want to freeze these, do so before baking; they will keep for at least 6 weeks, if tightly covered. Defrost them for 10 minutes before baking.

YIELD: 6 SERVINGS OR 25 TO 30 STUFFED CHERRY TOMATOES

PLAIN BAKED TOMATOES

These are a great addition to any meal.

1½ pounds tomatoes
¾ cup all-purpose flour
5⅓ tablespoons (⅔ stick) butter or
　margarine, melted
1 tablespoon light brown sugar
½ teaspoon dry mustard
½ teaspoon salt
½ teaspoon ground black pepper

Peel the tomatoes by dipping them in boiling water for ½ minute or until the skins slip off easily. Core and cut in half crosswise. Dredge each half completely in flour then dip in the melted butter; place in a buttered baking dish. Mix the brown sugar, mustard, salt, and pepper together and sprinkle over the tomato halves. Bake in preheated 375°F oven for 25 to 30 minutes or until golden brown. If broiling, place the halves on the rack of a broiler pan and broil for 5 to 7 minutes until golden brown.

YIELD: 4 TO 6 SERVINGS

Variation: Baked with Wine: Bake with 1 cup white wine added to the baking dish.

HINT: For extra flavor, sprinkle the tomato halves with chopped fresh herbs and herb blossoms, such as chives, chervil, oregano, parsley, or mint before baking.

SCALLOPED TOMATOES WITH CORN

Perfect for picnics and dramatic when served in a beautiful casserole dish or basket.

1½ pound tomatoes
6 slices bacon or 3 tablespoons butter or
　margarine
2 cups corn kernels, fresh or frozen
½ cup chopped onion
½ teaspoon salt
½ teaspoon ground black pepper
1 tablespoon chopped fresh parsley

1 teaspoon chopped fresh sweet basil
1 teaspoon chopped fresh chervil
1 teaspoon granulated sugar (optional)
1 cup fresh bread or cracker crumbs

Core and slice the tomatoes about ⅓ inch thick. Fry the bacon or melt the butter in a large skillet. When the bacon is crisp, remove and drain on paper towels. Add the corn, onion, salt, pepper, parsley, basil, chervil, and sugar (if desired) to the skillet and sauté for several minutes. Butter a 2-quart baking dish or casserole and alternate layers of the tomatoes, corn mixture, and bread crumbs, ending with about ⅓ cup crumbs for topping. Bake in a preheated 350°F oven for 45 minutes, covered. Top with the crumbled bacon and bake until bubbly and golden brown, about 10 minutes more.

YIELD: 6 SERVINGS

Variations: Core and scoop out the whole tomatoes. Sauté the bread crumbs with the corn mixture. Stuff the tomatoes with the corn mixture and place them in a buttered baking dish or in buttered muffin cups and any extra corn mixture in a casserole. Bake in a preheated 350°F oven for 35 to 40 minutes.
With Cheese: Add 1 cup grated cheese of your choice when layering the casserole.

FRIED TOMATOES

The tomatoes must be firm to fry. Some fry green tomatoes with onions—super good!

2 pounds firm tomatoes
1 cup all-purpose flour
2 tablespoons light brown sugar
½ teaspoon ground white pepper
½ teaspoon salt
1 teaspoon chopped fresh chervil
¼ cup vegetable oil
Chopped fresh chervil or parsley for garnish

Core tomatoes and trim ends. Cut into ⅓-inch-thick slices. Combine the flour, brown sugar, pepper, salt, and chervil on a plate or sheet of wax paper. Dredge the slices completely and fry one layer at a time in the heated oil over medium heat in a large, heavy skillet until golden brown and crispy, about 3 minutes on each side. Place the slices in a buttered baking dish and keep warm until all are fried and ready to serve. Garnish with chopped fresh chervil or parsley.

YIELD: 4 TO 6 SERVINGS

Variation: Use green tomatoes and 1 medium-size onion, sliced. Sauté the onions without dredging in flour, adding them along side the tomatoes while frying.

STUFFED ZUCCHINI

What do you do with all your large zucchini? For one, you can stuff them with any of your favorite meats or stuffings. They make a one-dish meal that's attractive and filling.

1 large zucchini or several smaller ones,
  totaling 1 pound
1 teaspoon vegetable oil
½ pound lean ground beef
½ cup chopped onion
1 cup Tomato Sauce (page 125) or 1½
  cups chopped tomatoes, canned or fresh
1 tablespoon chopped fresh parsley
½ teaspoon salt
½ teaspoon ground black pepper
½ teaspoon celery seed
½ teaspoon chopped fresh basil
Dash of Tabasco sauce
1 teaspoon fresh lemon juice or Herb
  Vinegar (page 206)

Clean and cut the zucchini in half lengthwise. Scoop out the center of each half, leaving at least a ½-inch thick shell, then discard the seeds and chop up the good pulp. Heat the oil in a large, heavy skillet over medium-high heat, crumble the beef, and brown it with the onion; then add the chopped zucchini, tomato sauce, parsley, salt, pepper, celery seed, and basil. Reduce the heat to medium and stir until thoroughly heated. Spoon into the zucchini shells. Whisk the Tabasco and lemon juice together and sprinkle over the top. Place in a 9-by-13-inch baking pan and bake in a pre-heated 350°F oven for 30 minutes. Cut the baked zucchini into 3- to 4-inch pieces for serving.

YIELD: 4 SERVINGS

FILLED ZUCCHINI BLOSSOMS

The best way to keep from getting too many zucchini is to break off the blossoms. They're good batter dipped and fried, but this recipe is so dramatic it will be remembered forever.

1 dozen zucchini blossoms (must be fresh,
  picked the morning they fully open)
½ recipe Cheese Soufflé (page 42)

Rinse the blossoms and remove any green stems. Spray or butter muffin cups. Pour the soufflé batter ½ inch deep in each cup. Place a blossom in each cup and fill to a little below the top with batter, leaving a bit of room for the soufflé to expand while baking without running over. If the blossoms are very long, fold the blossom tips into the middle, over the top of the soufflé batter. Bake in a preheated 350°F degree oven for 18 minutes, or until lightly browned. Serve immediately.

YIELD: 12 (MUFFIN-CUP SIZE) FILLED BLOS-SOMS, 6 SERVINGS

Chapter 5

Poultry and Wild Game

CHICKEN AND ASPARAGUS

This is perfect for spring entertaining. Wild asparagus grows on lots of country roadbanks and fence rows. The tender tiny tips make this an elegant dish that tastes as good as it looks.

2 cups chunked cooked chicken
2 cups fresh asparagus, cut in 1½-inch
  pieces
¼ cup water
4 tablespoons (½ stick) butter or
  margarine
¼ cup all-purpose flour
½ teaspoon salt
¼ teaspoon ground white pepper
½ teaspoon paprika
1 cup light cream or milk
1 cup chicken broth or milk

Toast Cups (recipe follows)
Paprika or fresh parsley sprigs for garnish

If you are starting with a fresh chicken, cook, covered, over medium heat, until tender, about 45 minutes, in 6 cups water seasoned with ½ teaspoon each salt and ground black pepper. When cool, remove the skin and debone. Cut into chunks and set aside. Place the asparagus and ¼ cup water in a saucepan, cover and cook until just tender—no more than *5 minutes*. Do not overcook! Drain. Make a roux in a heavy saucepan by melting the butter over medium heat, slowly adding the flour, salt, pepper, and paprika. Stir until smooth and golden-colored. Gradually whisk in the cream and broth, stirring until smooth and thickened. Reduce the heat to low and add the chicken. When it is warmed through, add the asparagus and heat thoroughly. Serve in warm Toast Cups or over toast points. Garnish each cup with a dash of paprika or a sprig of parsley.

To make Toast Cups, remove the crusts from slices of bread. Butter each slice on one side. Generously butter or oil muffin cups and mold the bread, buttered side down, to form cups. Bake in a preheated 400°F oven for 10 to 12 minutes or until lightly browned. (These may be made ahead of time and stored in an airtight container.)

YIELD: FILLS 6 TO 8 TOAST CUPS

OLD-FASHIONED CHICKEN PIE

A country favorite, we can't have a complete cookbook without one chicken pie!

1 roaster chicken, 4 to 5 pounds
2 cups water
1/8 teaspoon paprika
2 stems celery, with leaves
1/4 cup chopped onion
1/4 teaspoon ground black pepper
1/2 teaspoon chopped fresh parsley
1/2 teaspoon salt

Place the chicken in a large pot with the above ingredients and cook, covered, over medium heat for about 45 minutes, or until tender. Strain the broth, skim off the fat, reserve, and debone the chicken.

4 medium-size potatoes, peeled and sliced
2 large carrots, peeled and sliced
1 large onion, chopped
4 stems celery with leaves, diced
3 cups reserved chicken broth
3 tablespoon cornstarch
1 teaspoon salt
1/2 teaspoon ground black pepper
1 tablespoon chopped fresh parsley
1 recipe Baking Powder Crust (page 150)

Cook the potatoes, carrots, onion, and celery in 2/3 cup chicken stock, covered, over medium-high heat until nearly tender approximately 15 minutes. Drain and use the broth from the vegetables and add enough stock to make 3 cups. Stir the cornstarch into the broth until it dissolves. Bring to a boil over medium heat, check for seasonings, and add the salt and pepper if desired. Add the parsley and cook until thickened. Combine the diced chicken, vegetables, and gravy, and pour into a buttered 9-by-13-inch baking dish. Top with a baking powder crust, making sure to slit the crust to allow steam to escape. Bake in a preheated 350°F oven for 45 minutes or until golden brown.

YIELD: 6 SERVINGS

Variation: Use any type of meat or wild game instead of chicken.

CHICKEN CROQUETTES

The white sauce is the secret to this moist, delicious croquette.

2 cups diced cooked chicken
1/3 cup finely chopped celery
1 teaspoon dried celery leaves
1/4 teaspoon celery salt
1 teaspoon fresh lemon juice
1 teaspoon chopped fresh parsley
3/4 cup Thick White Sauce (page 124)
1/2 teaspoon salt
1 1/4 cups fresh bread crumbs
1 1/4 cups fresh cracker crumbs
2 large eggs, lightly beaten
Vegetable oil for frying
2-3 cups Chicken Gravy (page 88, using
    the gravy recipe for Chicken Fricassee)
Fresh parsley sprigs for garnish

Combine the chicken, celery, celery leaves, celery salt, lemon juice, parsley, white sauce, and salt thoroughly in a large mixing bowl. Refrigerate until easy to form croquettes, about 30 minutes. Use about 1/2 cup each of the mixture to form into cones or rectangular croquettes. Mix the crumbs together, then roll the croquettes in the crumbs, dip them in the beaten eggs, and roll them in the crumbs again. Chill for at least 30 minutes until firm. Deep fry in 3 inches of vegetable oil in a large, heavy skillet or fryer at 375°F until golden brown, about 5 minutes. Keep on a plate in a preheated 300°F oven until ready to serve. Serve with gravy on the side and garnish with fresh parsley.

YIELD: 8 TO 10 CROQUETTES

HINT: These make a great appetizer when made small and served with a dipping sauce, such as sour cream, dill, or mustard sauce.

Variation: Any type of meat may be substituted for the chicken. Turkey is excellent, too.

CRISPY FRIED CHICKEN

Everyone loves fried chicken and this recipe is perfect for picnics.

1 cup fresh cracker crumbs
1/2 cup all-purpose flour
1 teaspoon Krazy salt (a coarse salt with
    herbs added)
1/2 teaspoon dried chervil
1/2 teaspoon dried parsley
1/2 teaspoon ground white pepper
1/2 teaspoon celery seed
2 pounds chicken parts
1 large egg, lightly beaten
1 tablespoon milk or heavy cream
1/3 cup vegetable oil

Combine all the dry ingredients, including the herbs. Roll or shake the chicken parts in the crumb mixture. Let it stand 15 minutes. Combine the beaten egg and milk. Dip the chicken parts in the egg mixture and roll in crumbs again. Heat oil in a deep skillet and fry over medium heat, turning occasionally, until golden brown, approximately 15 minutes.

YIELD: 4 TO 6 SERVINGS

CHICKEN STOLTZFUS

I couldn't write a book without including my trademark dish. You may make the pastry the day before if time is limited.

1 roaster chicken, 4 to 5 pounds, giblets removed
6 cups water
2 teaspoons salt
1/2 teaspoon ground black pepper
Pinch of saffron threads
12 tablespoons (1 1/2 sticks) butter or margarine
3/4 cup all-purpose flour
1 cup heavy cream, or half milk and half evaporated milk or all milk
1/4 cup finely chopped fresh parsley
1/2 recipe Pastry Squares (page 149)
Fresh parsley sprigs for garnish

Put the chicken, water, salt, pepper, and saffron in a 6-quart kettle and bring to a boil. Reduce the heat to medium, partially cover with a lid and simmer for 1 hour. Remove the chicken, cool, debone, and remove the skin. Cut chicken into bite-size pieces. Strain the stock through a double thickness of cheesecloth and reduce it over high heat until it makes 4 cups. Melt the butter in a heavy saucepan, whisk in the flour, and stir over medium heat until golden and bubbling. Slowly whisk in the stock and cream, stirring constantly until smooth, creamy, and thickened, about 10 minutes. Add the chicken and parsley and heat thoroughly. Arrange the pastry squares on a heated platter and pour the chicken on top. (Make sure to leave the edges of the pastry squares showing.) Garnish with parsley sprigs. Serve immediately or the pastry will become soggy.

YIELD: 6 TO 8 SERVINGS

Variation: Chicken Fricassee: Follow the above recipe, but while reducing the broth, add 1/2 cup each of chopped celery and onion. Use an equal amount of chicken broth instead of the cream. Most chicken fricassee is prepared with a stewing hen but I prefer to use a roaster; it is more tender, takes half the time to cook, and has better flavor. Serve over biscuits instead of pastry squares.

PAPRIKA CHICKEN

Paprika and saffron are spices that have been used and valued highly by Pennsylvania Dutch cooks. Their antique spice boxes are family treasures that give us an insight into their early cooking techniques.

4 pounds chicken parts
1 teaspoon salt
1 teaspoon ground black pepper
6 tablespoons (¾ stick) butter or margarine
1 cup chopped onion
1½ teaspoons paprika
1 tablespoon all-purpose flour
2 cups chicken broth
1 cup sour cream
1½ tablespoons chopped fresh dill
Fresh dill sprigs for garnish

Sprinkle the chicken parts evenly with the salt and pepper and let stand, covered, for a few minutes. Melt the butter in large, heavy saucepan and sauté the onion over medium heat until clear, about 3 minutes. Stir in the paprika. Add the seasoned chicken parts, sprinkle with flour and simmer over medium-low heat for 30 minutes, turning the pieces as they get golden brown on all sides. Stir in the broth, cover, and simmer for 15 minutes more. Remove the chicken to a heated serving dish and keep covered. Stir the sour cream and dill into the chicken broth and heat thoroughly over medium heat. Pour over the chicken and garnish with dill sprigs (or parsley).

YIELD: 6 SERVINGS

ROAST TURKEY

One of the most versatile meats, turkey is so easy to prepare. Turkey is a great substitute in veal recipes, too.

one 15-pound turkey
Salt and ground black pepper to taste
½ teaspoon salt
½ teaspoon ground black pepper
2 cups water
8 cups stuffing (A moist bread stuffing is the
*   most popular but if you want to save one*
*   hour of baking time, omit the stuffing or*
*   cook it in its own dish)*

Remove the giblets and neck from the inside cavity. Rinse the bird thoroughly, pat dry, and lightly salt and pepper the inside. Put the giblets and neck in a small saucepan with water to cover, add the salt and pepper. Bring to a boil and simmer, covered, over low heat until soft, about 45 minutes. Remove, trim the fat and gristle, and debone the neck meat; set aside in a small bowl. Spoon the stuffing lightly into the cavity, taking care not to press it together. This prevents heavy stuffing and seepage while baking. Truss the bird with skewers and baking cord, folding the wings under its back. Generously salt and pepper the outside of the turkey, rubbing the skin with vegetable oil to brown the skin evenly if desired. Add the water to a roasting pan, place the turkey breast down, tent with aluminum foil and bake a in preheated 375°F oven for 4 hours. Remove the foil, drain the broth into a bowl, turn the turkey breast side up, and continue to bake until golden brown and legs are easily moved, about 45 minutes. After removing the turkey, deglaze the pan with ½ cup water to get all the pan juices and brownings. Skim the fat from the reserved broth and add to the brownings. Add 2 tablespoons cornstarch dissolved in ¼ cup water for every 2 cups broth. Cook over medium heat until thickened, about 3 minutes. Add the chopped giblets to the gravy and serve on the side with the turkey.

YIELD: 15 SERVINGS

TURKEY HASH

What do you do with leftover turkey?—that old, familiar refrain. For one thing, never re-heat more than once or it will lose all the flavor. Use what you need for serving, then freeze or refrigerate the rest. This is an excellent brunch or breakfast dish.

4 tablespoons (½ stick) butter or
*   margarine*
½ cup chopped onion
½ cup chopped bell peppers, preferably ½
*   red and ½ green*
1 cup sliced mushrooms
3 tablespoons all-purpose flour
1½ cups turkey or chicken broth
4 cups coarsely chopped turkey
2 tablespoons chopped fresh parsley
1 teaspoon Worcestershire sauce
⅛ teaspoon red (cayenne) pepper
⅛ teaspoon curry powder
½ teaspoon salt
¼ teaspoon ground white pepper
½ cup heavy cream or evaporated milk
Fresh parsley sprigs or pimiento slices for
*   garnish*

Melt the butter in a large, heavy skillet over medium heat and sauté the onion, peppers, and mushrooms for 5 minutes. Sprinkle with the flour and stir, then gradually pour in the broth, stirring until thickened, about 5 minutes. Add the turkey and seasonings. Blend thoroughly, then add the cream. Heat well but do not bring to a boil. Garnish with the parsley. Serve in the skillet.

YIELD: 6 SERVINGS

MAPLE-GINGER DUCK
WITH WILD RICE

The use of maple syrup and ginger is interesting and traditional.

1 large duck, about 6 pounds
Salt and ground black pepper, to taste
1 cup pure maple syrup
1 tablespoon ground ginger
3 cups chicken broth
1½ cups wild rice
1 tablespoon butter or margarine
½ cup chopped onion
½ cup chopped celery with leaves

Sprinkle inside and outside of duck with salt and pepper. Place duck, breast side down, on a wire rack in a roaster pan and pour in ½ inch of water—this is to prevent the duck from drying out. Roast in a preheated 400°F oven for 30 minutes, then turn on its back and roast 30 minutes more. Reduce heat to 350°F. Mix the syrup and ginger together and spread over the duck. Continue to roast until duck is tender and leg joints are easy to move, approximately 45 to 60 minutes more. After you glaze the duck, bring the chicken broth to a boil in a large kettle. Add the rice, butter, onion, and celery. Lower heat to a simmer and cook until rice is tender. Place the rice on a heated platter with the carved duck or place the duck whole and carve tableside.

YIELD: 6 SERVINGS

ROAST DUCK WITH APPLE GLAZE AND APPLE STUFFING

The worst thing about duck is getting the feathers off. When we were children, cousin Dick and I raised ducks and chickens for extra spending (or saving) money. We had to dress them ourselves (that made us real money), which wasn't too pleasant but taught us the economics of business. To get the pin feathers off the ducks, we dipped them in scalding water with paraffin melted into it. This caused all the feathers to stick together, making it much easier to pull them out, and the birds always looked terrific when they went to our customers.

1 large duck, about 6 pounds
Salt and ground black pepper
Apple Stuffing (page 131)
1 cup orange juice
1/4 cup grated orange rind
1 cup applesauce
1 tablespoon cornstarch
Pinch of ground thyme
Pinch of dried or fresh hyssop (optional)

1/2 cup sherry or sweet red or white wine
1/2 cup lightly packed light brown sugar
1 teaspoon grated lemon rind
1 tablespoon fresh lemon juice
1/2 cup water
1/3 cup brandy (optional)

Remove the giblets from the duck and sprinkle it inside and out with salt and pepper. Stuff loosely with the apple stuffing, baking the rest of the stuffing in a buttered baking dish for the last 30 minutes of the duck's cooking, and place it, breast side down, on a rack in a roasting pan. Prick the skin several times on each side to allow the fat to drain. Add 1/2 inch of water. Roast the duck in a preheated 400°F oven for 45 minutes. Then turn it breast side up, reduce the heat to 375°F and roast another 45 minutes. Combine the orange juice and rind, applesauce, cornstarch, thyme, hyssop, sherry, brown sugar, and lemon rind and juice in a large saucepan and cook over high heat until thickened, about 5 minutes. Pour one cup of the sauce over the duck and continue to roast until tender, about 45 minutes to 1 hour more. The duck is ready to serve when the legs move easily. After removing the duck to a heated serving platter, skim off all the fat in the roasting pan. Add the 1/2 cup water and loosen all the brownings from the bottom over low heat, stirring constantly with a wooden spoon until all the brown particles are dissolved. Add this to the remaining sauce along with the brandy and ignite at table for that extra touch.

YIELD: 6 SERVINGS

Halve the duck and score skin with a sharp knife several times on each side. Brush the skin with the honey (if you heat it, it will spread more easily). Mix all the herbs, substituting mild herbs if you cannot get the ones mentioned above, with half of the orange liqueur in a small bowl and brush it over the duck. Sprinkle with the pepper and salt. Let stand for 1 hour or more to absorb all the herb flavors. Place on a wire rack in a roasting pan and roast in a preheated 400°F oven for 1 hour, basting with the remaining orange liqueur mixture until tender. It should be browned and crispy on the outside and tender on the inside. Serve with your favorite rice or stuffing.

YIELD: 4 TO 6 SERVINGS

HONEY-HERBED DUCK

Duck was not considered a delicacy years ago, but with the addition of fresh herbs it took on a different and interesting flavor. This was especially true of wild duck. If using wild ducks for this recipe, use two. I prefer fresh herbs, but if you use dried herbs, cut the amounts listed in half.

1 duck, 5 to 6 pounds
1/3 cup honey
1 teaspoon chopped fresh rosemary
1 1/2 teaspoons chopped fresh hyssop
1 teaspoon chopped mint
1 teaspoon chopped fresh chervil
1 teaspoon chopped fresh dill
1/2 teaspoon chopped fresh thyme
1/2 teaspoon ground fresh marjoram
1/4 cup orange liqueur or orange juice
1/2 teaspoon coarsely ground black pepper
1/2 teaspoon salt

ROAST GOOSE

Goose is considered very fatty and hard to prepare. That's just not true—it's as easy to prepare as turkey. For those who love the dark meat of fowl, goose is hard to beat. I like to count on 1 pound per person when serving whole roasted fowl because of the bones.

1 large goose, 6 to 8 pounds
1/4 cup Herb Vinegar (page 206)
1 teaspoon salt
1 teaspoon ground black pepper
Stuffing of your choice; I recommend Apple
*   or Dried Fruit Stuffing (see Index)*
3 1/4 cups water
2 tablespoons cornstarch
1/4 cup water

Remove the giblets and neck from the dressed goose and rinse them thoroughly. Pat dry with paper towels. Sprinkle the goose with the vinegar, salt, and pepper inside and outside. Pat it with your hands to insure the seasonings stick to the skin. Stuff the cavity loosely, secure it with skewers, tie the legs together with cord, and fold the wings under the back. Pour 2 cups of the water in the bottom of a roasting pan fitted with a wire baking rack. Place the bird, breast side down, on the rack. Place the giblets, not including the liver, alongside the goose. Tent it with foil and roast in a preheated 350°F oven for 4 hours for a 6-pound goose to 5 hours for an 8-pound goose. When the legs move easily, remove the foil, turn the breast side up, and brown it, about 20 minutes. This cooking method will keep the meat moist. Transfer the goose to a heated platter. Deglaze the pan with the 1 cup of water and simmer over low heat until the brownings are easily scraped from the pan. Pour into a bowl and cool until the fat comes to the top, about 15 minutes. Remove the fat. To make a gravy, pour the broth into a 1-quart saucepan, dissolve the cornstarch in the ¼ cup water, and add to the broth. Bring to a boil over medium heat and cook until thickened, approximately 5 minutes. Check for seasonings, adding salt and pepper if desired.

YIELD: 6 TO 8 SERVINGS

ROAST SQUAB OR QUAIL

Count on at least one bird per person. They are so delicate in flavor and look so nice when served whole, it is a pity to debone them in the kitchen.

4 to 6 birds, about 3 to 4 pounds, total
Salt and ground black pepper
1½ cups stuffing of your choice—I
  recommend Salsify or Chestnut Stuffing
  (pages 132, 134), or filling the cavity
  with fried oysters (see page 118)
1 cup water

Remove the giblets and neck from the dressed birds and rinse thoroughly. Sprinkle lightly with salt and pepper inside and out. Stuff the birds lightly, baking any extra stuffing in the oven for the last 15 minutes. Truss the birds with cord or skewers, folding the wings under the backs. Add the water to a roasting pan, place the birds breast side down, and tent with aluminum foil. Bake in a preheated 400°F

oven for 40 minutes. Meanwhile, cook the giblets and necks in the remaining water with the salt over medium heat until tender, about 30 minutes. When soft, trim the fat, debone the meat, and cut into small pieces to add to the gravy.

Remove the foil from the roasting pan, drain the broth into a bowl and turn the birds breast side up to brown. Add the extra stuffing to the pan and continue roasting for another 15 minutes. Remove the birds and stuffing from the pan onto a heated serving platter. Deglaze the pan with ½ cup water to make gravy. Thicken with the cornstarch dissolved in ¼ cup water over medium heat and add the giblets. Taste for seasoning, adding salt and pepper if needed. Serve in gravy boat.

YIELD: 4 TO 6 SERVINGS

Variations: Braised Squab: Split birds in half, sprinkle lightly with seasoned salt and ground black pepper. Melt 3 tablespoons butter or vegetable oil in a heavy skillet and sauté them breast side down over medium-high heat until golden brown, about 12 minutes. Turn, add ½ cup dry white wine and ¼ cup pure maple syrup. Cover and simmer over medium heat until birds are tender, about 20 minutes. Baste sauce over birds while cooking. Place on heated platter and spoon over sauce or serve it on the side.

Grilled Squab, Quail or Partridge: Marinate in ½ cup white wine vinegar and ½ cup walnut or vegetable oil with your favorite herbs for one hour before placing on grill. Do not overcook; if grill is very hot, needs approximately 7 minutes on each side.

ROAST GUINEA HEN

Considered the best "watch dog" because they make so much noise when strangers arrive, guineas are delicious, tender, and unique in flavor. They have a rather spicy taste, much like that of pheasant. The meat is very dark, especially the legs, and moist if roasted properly. Many farmers raise the fowl for the feathers, which they sell to fishermen for fly-tying. The eggs are sought after for pickling because they are so small and the beautiful brown speckles make them attractive for egg decorators.

2 guineas, 2½ to 3 pounds each
Salt and ground black pepper
1 tablespoon vegetable oil
Stuffing of your choice (I recommend
  Raisin-Pecan on page 134)
3 cups water
½ teaspoon salt
½ cup currant or grape jelly
½ cup dry white wine or water
2 teaspoons cornstarch (optional)

Remove the giblets and neck from the dressed birds and rinse the birds thoroughly. Pat dry inside and out with paper towels. Sprinkle lightly inside with the salt and pepper. Rub the outside with the oil and sprinkle lightly with salt and pepper. Stuff lightly, baking the extra stuffing in a buttered baking dish for the last 15 minutes of the birds' cooking. Truss the birds with skewers or cord. Add 2 cups of the water to the bottom of a roasting pan. Place the birds, breast down, in the pan and tent with aluminum foil. Bake in a preheated 350°F oven for 2 hours. Meanwhile, cook the giblets and necks in the salt and remaining water over medium heat until tender, about 45 minutes, if you want to add them to the gravy. When soft, trim the fat and gristle from the good meat and chop into ½-inch pieces. After 2 hours of baking, remove the aluminum foil and brush the birds with the jelly. Bake another 15 to 20 minutes or until the jelly bubbles. Remove the birds from the pan when the legs or wings move easily, and deglaze the pan with ½ cup white wine or water. Continue to stir with a wooden spoon until all the brownings are loosened from the pan. If you prefer gravy, dissolve 2 teaspoons cornstarch in ⅓ cup water and add to the brownings. Heat over medium heat until thickened, approximately 4 minutes or until smooth.

YIELD: 4 TO 6 SERVINGS

Variation: Roast Pheasant with Bourbon: Follow recipe above, substituting 2 pheasants of equal weight, and stuff with any of your favorite stuffings. Baste with ½ cup bourbon instead of the jelly.

RABBIT

Rabbit tastes very much like chicken, so I recommend substituting it in any of the chicken recipes. Our family always loved rabbit pot pie and fried (really crispy) rabbit. If the hare is fully grown, wild and large, it is best to marinate the meat in wine and herbs overnight before roasting or frying.

SQUIRREL

Squirrels are small, but the meat is so mild and delicious, you will need several for a meal for four. Much like rabbit, they are wonderful in stews or pot pie. Follow the same recipes as for chicken, pork, or veal.

VENISON

Venison is very popular in this area for hunters' families. Deer feed on many things, but most of the time they graze on corn or acorns. The taste is very similar to that of beef, but if the season has been dry, or the deer is old, the meat has a tendency to have a "wild" taste. Here's a recipe that will overcome that gamey flavor; the secret is in the marinade and the removal of the fat before preparation.

2 tablespoons cider vinegar
2 tablespoons soy sauce
1 pound venison, fat removed

Mix the vinegar and soy sauce together in a shallow baking dish. Dip both sides of the meat in it and let it marinate overnight in the refrigerator, covered. Then follow any beef recipe. If pan frying, steaks will need a bit more time than three minutes to cook. If the steaks are 1 inch thick, fry over high heat for 3 minutes on each side.

VENISON CHOPS

Count on at least 2 chops per person.

*1 recipe Venison Marinade (see preceding
    recipe)*
*4 venison chops (about 1 pound), cut ¾
    inch thick and trimmed of fat*
⅓ cup all-purpose flour
Salt and ground black pepper
3 tablespoons vegetable oil or butter
1 small onion, chopped
⅓ cup chopped green or red bell pepper
*½ cup sliced water chestnuts or sliced
    broccoli stems*
*1 large tomato, diced, seeded, and juice
    drained*
1 stem celery, chopped
½ cup grated Cheddar cheese
½ cup sour cream
¼ cup brandy
1 tablespoon chopped fresh parsley

Marinate the chops in the marinade overnight. Pat dry, dredge in the flour and sprinkle with the salt and pepper. Set aside. Melt the oil or butter in a large skillet and sauté the onion, pepper, chestnuts, tomato, and celery for several minutes over medium-high heat until clear and thoroughly heated. Remove everything from the pan and add the chops, sautéing them to a golden brown on each side over medium-high heat, no more then 4 minutes per side. When browned, add the vegetables and reheat completely, covered. Remove and place on a heated platter. Melt the cheese in a small saucepan over low heat, add the sour cream, brandy, and parsley and heat through but do not boil. Pour over the chops before serving or serve on the side.

YIELD: 4 SERVINGS

Chapter 6

Meats

BRISKET OF BEEF WITH BEANS

This dish has terrific flavor but little eye appeal. Serve it with a bright salad or colorful relishes on the side.

2 to 2½ pounds beef brisket
2 slices bacon or 1 tablespoon vegetable oil
¾ teaspoon salt
½ teaspoon ground black pepper
2 cups water
4 cups dried navy, butter, or lima beans, cooked and drained, or 1 pound of dried beans soaked overnight in 8 cups of water and drained
¼ cup pure maple syrup or table molasses (golden, barrel, or King Syrup), do not use baking molasses
⅓ cup lightly packed brown sugar
½ teaspoon dry mustard

Fresh parsley or watercress sprigs for garnish

Brown the fat side of the beef in a Dutch oven or heavy pot over medium-high heat. Add the bacon or oil and brown the other side. Add the salt, pepper, water, and beans. Reduce the heat to medium and cook, covered, for 2 hours or until the beef and beans are tender, stirring occasionally to prevent sticking. Remove the beef and keep warm. Add the maple syrup, brown sugar, and mustard to the beans. Mix thoroughly and simmer over medium heat another 10 minutes. Slice the brisket thin and serve with the beans garnished with fresh parsley or watercress.

YIELD: 6 SERVINGS

CORNED BEEF

There is a certain pride in saying "I made this" when everyone enjoys a meal. Corned beef takes a while to cure, but after it is made, it can be frozen. It will keep in the freezer for months if properly sealed, so make a good amount at one time or you can cut this recipe in half.

5 cups salt
1/4 cup saltpetre (this is available in drug stores, but should be ordered in advance)
10 pounds beef, brisket, round, or rump
20 cups water
1 teaspoon ground white pepper
1/2 cup pickling spices
1 teaspoon paprika
1/2 teaspoon ground nutmeg
3 bay leaves
3 cloves garlic
1 teaspoon whole black peppercorns, cracked
1 1/2 cups lightly packed light brown sugar

Combine 1 cup of the salt and 1 tablespoon of the saltpetre and rub it into the beef, covering it generously on all sides. It should take about half the mixture; reserve what's left over. Let stand in a cold place or the refrigerator, covered, for one day. The next day cover the beef with the rest of the salt mixture and let stand overnight again. Wipe the salt mixture from the meat the next day. Make a brine of the water, 4 cups salt, 3 tablespoons saltpetre, and remaining ingredients in a large pot. Bring to a boil and simmer over medium heat for 5 minutes. Let cool. Place the meat in a crock or container big enough to hold it along with the brine. Use stainless steel or plastic; the brine will react with aluminum. Pour the brine over the meat, weight down the meat with a plate to keep it submerged. Refrigerate and leave in the brine for 3 to 4 weeks, turning every other day. If the brine seems to lose its strength, add more salt or make a new brine. Wash several times in cold water to remove the extra salt before cooking or freezing. Cut the meat, remembering that it is strongly flavored, into the size desired. Three pounds of meat will serve at least six people. Freeze the remainder by double wrapping it in heavy aluminum foil or plastic freezer bags.

YIELD: ABOUT 9 POUNDS BEEF

Variation: Pickled Beef Tongue or Heart: Use the recipe above, but with the same amount of either fresh tongue or heart, leaving it in the brine for two weeks. Wash off the salt, peel the skin from the heart, and cook the same as for tongue on page 111. They freeze well and keep for months.

GLAZED CORNED BEEF

Although boiled corned beef is most common, glazing it looks better, tastes better, and is worth the extra baking time.

3 pounds corned beef (see preceding recipe)
Whole cloves
1/2 cup pure maple syrup
1/4 cup dry white wine

Place the beef in a large, heavy saucepan or Dutch oven, cover it with water, bring to a boil, and simmer it over medium-low heat for about 3 hours, covered, or until it's tender. Remove, stud with whole cloves and place in a greased baking dish. Combine the maple syrup and wine and pour it over the meat. Bake in a preheated 350°F oven for 20 minutes or until the glaze is lightly browned. Baste the meat with the syrup several times during baking. Serve thinly sliced.

YIELD: 6 SERVINGS

Variation: Boiled Corned Beef: Cook as above, omitting the glaze.

BEEF PIE
WITH POTATO CRUST

Old-fashioned, tasty, and great for those busy days, this pie also freezes well.

3 tablespoons butter or vegetable shortening
½ head cabbage, sliced
1 medium-size onion, sliced
1 pound thinly sliced roast beef or corned beef
2 cups seasoned mashed potatoes
½ cup beef broth

For crust:

1 cup mashed potatoes
1 large egg, lightly beaten
2 tablespoons (¼ stick) butter, melted
1 cup all-purpose flour
About ¼ cup milk
1 large egg
1 tablespoon water

Melt the butter in a large, heavy skillet over medium heat and sauté the cabbage and onion until clear, about 6 minutes. Butter a 1½-quart baking dish or pan and layer half of the beef, mashed potatoes, and cabbage mixture. Pour the broth over everything. Repeat again and top with the potato crust. To make the crust, place the mashed potatoes, 1 egg, the butter, and flour in a food processor or blender, and mix until it forms a large ball. Gradually add the milk until the right consistency to roll out. It should not be too dry. Place the dough between 2 sheets of wax paper and roll about ⅓ inch thick. Place on top of the beef pie, and slit a design in the center. Mix the beaten egg and water together and brush over the crust. Bake in a preheated 350°F oven for 35 minutes or until golden brown on top.

YIELD: 6 SERVINGS

HINT: This potato crust is super for any meat or vegetable pie.

RIB ROAST

Many folks ask why our prime rib is so moist, rare in the middle, and consistently excellent. We buy top quality standing ribs, we roast in a slow oven with a small amount of water in the bottom of the roasting pan, and we season the meat under the fat. It is hard to get all of these advantages if you are roasting anything less than a 6-pound roast. The roast should be thick enough to insure getting it rare in the middle.

6 pounds standing prime rib roast of beef
1 teaspoon salt (less if desired)
1/2 teaspoon coarsely ground black pepper
2 1/2 cups water
2 tablespoons cornstarch (optional)
1/4 cup water (optional)

With a very sharp knife trim the fat close to the meat—making smooth, clean cuts, not sawing—if you didn't have the butcher cut it, making sure the fat is still connected at the bottom; do not cut it off completely. Fold the fat back and sprinkle the meat generously with the salt and pepper. Replace the fat and place it in a roasting pan. Add 1 1/2 cups of the water and tent it with foil. Bake in a preheated 275°F oven for 4 hours. Place a meat thermometer in the meat, making sure it does not touch a bone. The thermometer will show the baking temperatures so you can roast it from rare, medium, to well done. Remove the foil after roasting for 3 hours. When done, place the roast on a heated platter, skim the fat from the pan and deglaze it with the 1 cup of the water for a broth or gravy. If you prefer gravy, dissolve the cornstarch in the 1/4 cup water and add it to the broth. Cook over medium heat until thickened, approximately 5 minutes. The broth is excellent for stews and soups. Remove the fat from the roast for easy carving.

YIELD: 6 TO 8 SERVINGS

Variations: Rolled Rib Roast: Have the butcher trim and roll the roast, tying it every 2 inches, to form a neat, tight roll. Moisten the outside with a bit of water so the salt and pepper will stick. Bake as instructed above, using a meat thermometer to insure the rare, medium, or well done temperature you want, approximately 3 1/2 hours. This is wonderful for slicing cold.
Barbecued Short Ribs: After cutting out the eye, cut each rib apart, trim some of the fat and brush with your favorite barbecue sauce. Place on a grill or in a preheated 425°F oven in a shallow pan, baking until crisp, approximately 40 minutes.

SAUERBRATEN

Our heritage really shows through in this recipe. It is interesting to see how this dish has remained nearly the same since it came over from Europe in the early 1700s.

1 cup dry red wine
3/4 cup red wine vinegar
1 1/2 cups water
1 medium-size onion, sliced thin
1 teaspoon salt
1 teaspoon whole black peppercorns, broken
1/2 teaspoon whole cloves
2 bay leaves

¹/₄ teaspoon ground ginger
4 pounds beef, top round, rump, or chuck
3 tablespoons vegetable shortening
¹/₂ cup chopped onions
¹/₂ cup grated carrots
¹/₂ cup chopped celery
3 tablespoons all-purpose flour
²/₃ cup water

Combine the wine, vinegar, water, onion, salt, peppercorns, cloves, bay leaves, and ginger in a 2-quart saucepan and bring to a boil. Place the beef in a casserole dish or pot large enough to hold it and the marinade—make sure it is not made of aluminum, as there will be a chemical reaction. Pour the hot liquid over the beef, cover partially with the lid, and refrigerate for 3 days, turning the meat twice each day. When ready to cook the beef, remove it from the marinade and pat dry. Strain the marinade through a double thickness of cheesecloth, discarding the onions and spices. Melt the shortening in a Dutch oven and brown the beef over medium-high heat on all sides. Remove from the pan. Add the vegetables and sauté over medium heat until the onions and celery are clear, about 6 minutes. Add the flour, reduce the heat to low, and stir until the mixture is golden brown and thick, about 10 minutes. Gradually add the reserved marinade and water and bring to a boil over medium heat. Then add the meat, cover, and simmer over low heat for 1 to 1½ hours or until the meat is tender. Remove the meat and slice thin, serving the marinade gravy in a gravy boat. Serve with boiled potatoes, potato dumplings, or potato cakes (page 76).

YIELD: 6 TO 8 SERVINGS

BEEF POT ROAST

Everyone's favorite one-dish meal on a cold day, this recipe may be a bit different in presentation and flavor.

6 slices bacon
4 to 5 pounds beef roast (top round or
    brisket is best)
1 tablespoon chopped fresh parsley
¹/₂ teaspoon coarsely ground black pepper
1 teaspoon salt
¹/₄ teaspoon ground nutmeg
1 teaspoon ground thyme
6 medium-size onions, whole or halved
8 large carrots, cut in 3-inch pieces
8 to 10 medium-size potatoes, peeled and
    quartered
¹/₂ cup sherry or white wine
¹/₂ cup brandy
1 cup water

In a Dutch oven or large kettle, fry the bacon until crisp. Drain it on paper towels and crumble. Over medium-high heat, brown the roast on all sides in the bacon fat, adding the parsley, pepper, salt, nutmeg, and thyme as you turn the beef the first time. When brown, remove the meat and brown the vegetables, then remove half the vegetables to a microwave dish or skillet. Place the roast back in the pot with the remaining vegetables, making sure the meat makes direct contact with the bottom of the pot. Add the sherry or wine, brandy and water, reduce heat to low, cover and simmer for at least 2½ hours, turning the meat and vegetables occasionally to prevent sticking. Pour the gravy into a bowl, skim off the fat, then return it to the pot. Add the other half of the vegetables and simmer over low heat for 30 minutes or until the beef is very tender and all the vegetables are tender. Add ½ cup water during the cooking if the pot roast seems to be drying out or is sticking to the bottom of the pot. The gravy should be thick when served. Carve the roast and place on a heated platter. Arrange the vegetables around the sides of the roast and top with the crumbled bacon.

YIELD: 6 TO 8 SERVINGS

Variations: Pork Pot Roast: Use a pork roast, 4 peeled turnips, 4 potatoes, add 1 teaspoon dry mustard in addition to the herbs, and follow the above recipe.
Beef Pot Roast with Parsnips: Use half potatoes and half peeled parsnips.

SWISS STEAK

Many folks will always prefer their beef well done, but it should be tender and very flavorful. We always canned round steak in quart jars for that moment when we needed a meal in a hurry. It's not hard to do, tastes great, and I think it's easier than making it the usual way. For those of you who still buy a quarter of a side of beef, why not can a few jars of beef for a special occasion?

2 to 2½ pounds round steak, cut 1 inch thick
½ teaspoon ground white pepper
1 teaspoon salt
¼ cup all-purpose flour
1 tablespoon butter
1 tablespoon vegetable oil

2½ cups water or 1¼ cups water and 1¼ cups red wine
2 tablespoons cornstarch

Lightly pepper and salt one side of the steak. Generously dredge in the flour, then pound with a meat mallet or the back of a butcher knife. Turn it over and salt and pepper and pound it again. Heat the butter and vegetable oil in a deep pan or skillet. When very hot, add the steak and brown it on both sides. Pour off the fat, cover the steak with the water, cover the pan, and simmer over low heat for 1½ hours or until tender. Remove onto a heated platter and thicken the pan gravy with the cornstarch, dissolved in ¼ cup of water. Serve the gravy in a boat. Some folks like to leave the steak whole, others cut it into thin slices before serving.

YIELD: 4 TO 6 SERVINGS

PAN-FRIED STEAK

My Dad, Clarence Herr, was known as the steak king to anyone who purchased beef at our butcher shop on the farm. He would cut a small steak from each quarter of beef and fry it for the customer, right in the butcher shop. He used a Coleman burner and an old tin pan. With his usual twinkle, he would warn *"Never"* cook a steak more than 2 to 3 minutes. He scored the fat around the outside of the steak, had the pan as hot as it could get, sprinkled the pan with a bit of salt, waiting until it popped up and down like popcorn, then placed the steak proudly in the pan. As the smoke rolled to the ceiling, he would gently press the fat into the pan, pepper the steak generously, turn it and brown the other side, and look at his watch. "Two minutes—you'll see—now try it." He always won the customer to his side (even those that swore they would never eat anything pink!).

Steaks should be cut at least ¾ inch thick or they'll be hard to keep rare. If you're frying 2-inch-thick steaks, make sure you have a lid tilted over the top of the pan to keep the splattering to a minimum.

STUFFED FLANK STEAK

For steak lovers, this economical meal is sure to please.

2 pounds flank steak, about 1½ inches
thick with pocket cut in
3 tablespoons butter
3 tablespoons chopped onion
½ cup chopped celery with leaves
½ cup grated carrots
½ cup grated raw white or sweet potatoes
1 tablespoon chopped fresh parsley
1 teaspoon salt
½ teaspoon ground black pepper

If your steak does not have a pocket, cut a long slit alongside the steak, cutting ⅔ the way through to the other side. In a Dutch oven or deep sauté pan, melt the butter and sauté the vegetables for approximately 5 minutes over medium heat, then salt and pepper them. Stuff this vegetable mixture into the pocket of steak and close it with skewers. There should be

enough butter left in the pan to brown the steak; if not, add 1 tablespoon vegetable oil and brown the steak on both sides over medium-high heat. Remove, place a baking rack in the pan, and lay the stuffed steak on it. Add enough water to cover the rack but not the steak. Cover, reduce heat to medium low and simmer for 1½ to 2 hours until meat is very tender. If you have a pressure cooker, follow the directions and you'll save a lot of time. Add extra vegetables, if desired, to the pan for the last 40 minutes of cooking. If you want to serve gravy with the steak, check the broth in the pan for seasoning and add extra beef broth if needed. Thicken as for any gravy, adding 2 tablespoons cornstarch dissolved in ¼ cup water to each cup of beef broth. Cook over medium heat until thickened.

YIELD: 6 SERVINGS

CREAMED FRIZZLED DRIED BEEF

One of my favorites, this is as good for light suppers as well as for breakfast. We always brown the flour as we brown the dried beef, giving the dish a rich, nutty flavor.

3 tablespoons butter or margarine
6 ounces thinly sliced dried beef, shredded
1/4 cup all-purpose flour
1 teaspoon chopped fresh chives
1/2 teaspoon chopped fresh parsley
1/8 teaspoon ground white pepper
3 cups milk

Melt the butter in a heavy skillet. Add the shredded dried beef and cook over medium-high heat until golden brown, approximately 3 minutes. Add the flour and seasonings and stir until well blended and flour turns a light brown. Lower to medium heat, then slowly add the milk, stirring constantly until thickened and creamy, approximately 6 minutes. Add more milk if desired. Serve in Toast Cups (page 86), or with toast tips, pancakes, or potato cakes.

YIELD: 4 TO 6 SERVINGS

CITY CHICKEN DRUMSTICKS

When young, tender chickens were only available in the springtime, the creative housewife found many ways to substitute. City chicken was sold in the farmers' markets and butcher shops year-round. It tasted like chicken and at that time veal and pork were cheaper than young chickens. That's hard to imagine now that chicken is so available and reasonably priced.

1 pound lean ground beef
1 pound lean ground pork
1/2 pound ground veal
3 large eggs
1 cup coarsely crushed cracker crumbs
1 1/2 teaspoons salt
1/2 teaspoon ground white pepper
1 teaspoon chopped fresh parsley
2 tablespoons milk
1 cup fresh bread crumbs
6 to 8 wooden skewers
3 to 4 tablespoons vegetable oil

In a large mixing bowl, combine the ground beef, pork, and veal with 2 of the eggs, the cracker crumbs, salt, pepper, and parsley. Using about 1/2 cup of the mixture for each serving, form it into the shape of a drumstick. Combine the remaining egg with the milk in a deep soup bowl and pour the bread crumbs into a deep bowl as well. Roll each drumstick in the egg wash and then into the bread crumbs. Insert a skewer into the base of each drumstick. Heat the oil in a large skillet over medium heat. Fry until golden brown on all sides, cover with a lid, reduce heat to low, and simmer for at least 30 minutes. If the skillet becomes dry on the bottom, add two tablespoons of oil or water to prevent burning. If you prefer to bake the drumsticks, place in a greased 9-by-13-inch baking dish and bake in preheated 350°F oven for 35 minutes. If they are not as brown as you would like, increase the heat to 400°F and bake an additional 10 minutes. Serve as you would fried chicken.

YIELD: 6 SERVINGS

MEAT LOAF WITH SWEET POTATOES

Everyone tries to do something different with this all-time favorite. Hot or cold, this recipe is delicious!

2 pounds ground meat, preferably equal parts of beef, pork, and veal (or turkey)
1 medium-size onion, chopped
½ cup chopped celery
1 tablespoon chopped fresh parsley
2 large eggs, lightly beaten
¾ cup dry bread crumbs
1 teaspoon salt
½ teaspoon ground white pepper
1½ cups cooked, mashed sweet potatoes
¼ cup finely chopped green bell pepper or green onion
¼ cup pure maple or light corn syrup (I use Karo)

Mix ground meats, onion, celery, parsley, eggs, crumbs, salt, and pepper together in large bowl. Place between two large sheets of wax paper and roll into a rectangle about 14″ × 10″. Remove the top paper and spread the

meat with the mashed potatoes. Sprinkle with the chopped pepper or onion or both. Roll the mixture jelly-roll fashion, seal the outside edge, and place in a shallow greased baking pan, seam side down. Bake in a preheated 350°F oven for 45 minutes. Drain off excess fat and drizzle the syrup on top of the loaf. Bake 25 minutes more or until the juices are clear and the loaf is golden brown.

YIELD: 4 TO 6 SERVINGS

Variation: Stuffed Peppers: Clean, core, and seed 6 large green bell peppers, trimming the bottoms enough to make them stand straight in a greased 9-inch square baking dish. Fill the peppers with one recipe of meat loaf. Add ½ cup water to the bottom of the dish, tent with aluminum foil, and bake in a preheated 350°F oven for 45 minutes. Remove the foil and continue baking for another 10 minutes or until lightly browned on top.

LAMB ROAST WITH CRUSTY MINT

Lamb should be basted in crème de menthe, preferably white, to prevent an unusual taste, especially if you do not use an abundance of garlic.

6 to 8 pounds leg, or roast, of lamb
½ cup white crème de menthe (or sherry)
1 clove garlic, minced
1 teaspoon Krazy salt or steak salt (a coarse salt with herbs added)
1 teaspoon coarsely ground black pepper
1 cup water
⅓ cup lemon curd jelly or marmalade
⅓ cup mint jelly
1 teaspoon chopped fresh or dried mint
½ teaspoon chopped fresh or dried marjoram
1 cup fresh bread crumbs
Fresh mint or parsley sprigs for garnish

Moisten roast with crème de menthe, then sprinkle with minced garlic and salt and pepper on all sides. Place on a rack in a roasting pan, add the water to the bottom of the roaster and tent it with aluminum foil. Roast in a preheated 325°F oven for 25 minutes per pound or until meat thermometer registers 145°F (medium rare). Baste with remaining crème de menthe during first hour of roasting. About 30 minutes before the roast should be done, combine the lemon and mint jellies, mint, marjoram, and bread crumbs. Spread the mixture over the roast, patting firmly with the blade of a cold knife. Roast until golden brown. Garnish with fresh mint.

YIELD: 6 TO 8 SERVINGS

Variation: Lamb Chops with Crusty Mint: Use all the above ingredients in ½ measurements and spread over 2 pounds of chops. Place them in a buttered baking dish and bake in a preheated 350°F oven for one hour; then turn and bake until golden brown and crusty, approximately 20 minutes.

LAMB PAPRIKA

I love this for all the extra flavor, plus, it's so easy to prepare.

1 pound lamb, cubed
3 tablespoons all-purpose flour
5 or 6 slices bacon, cut in small pieces
½ cup chopped onion
2 cups diced potatoes (about 4 medium-size)
1 tablespoon paprika
½ teaspoon caraway seeds
¼ teaspoon crushed fresh rosemary
½ teaspoon salt
¼ teaspoon ground white pepper
1 cup diced and drained tomatoes (fresh or canned)
½ cup beef broth
½ cup red wine

Dredge the meat cubes in the flour. In a heavy, deep skillet, sauté the bacon and onion over medium high heat until golden brown. Add the potatoes and floured meat and brown lightly. Sprinkle with paprika, caraway, rosemary, salt, and pepper. Add the tomatoes, broth, and wine, and simmer over medium heat, covered, for 10 minutes. If you prefer, finish cooking in the skillet over medium heat for 30 minutes or place in a 2-quart baking dish and bake in a preheated 375°F oven for 30 minutes. If placed in the oven, it will be drier when served.

YIELD: 6 SERVINGS

BAKED HOME-CURED HAM

Everyone asks why their hams become so salty and dry when they bake them. The answer for keeping a ham moist, mild, and tender is to roast it in water at a low temperature. If the ham is very salty, pour off the water after 2 hours of baking and add fresh water. This gives you the wonderful smoky flavor without all the salt.

12 to 14 pound smoked, home-cured ham
2 cups water

Soak the ham overnight in cold water. When ready to roast, remove the rind and place bone side down in a roaster pan. Add the water, tent with aluminum foil, and bake in a preheated 300°F oven for 2 1/2 hours. Remove and debone. If the broth seems salty, pour it off and add 2 cups fresh water. Put the deboned ham in the water and continue baking for one more hour.

YIELD: 14 TO 18 SERVINGS

HINT: For a smaller ham, the same rule applies since home-cured hams are cured in the same way no matter what size.

SCHNITZ UND KNEPP

Here is a fine example of combining sweet and salty foods together to make a delicious meal.

3 pound smoked ham butt or end
1/2 pound sliced dried apples (the schnitz)
6 cups water
2 tablespoons light brown sugar
1/4 teaspoon ground cloves
1/4 teaspoon ground cinnamon
1 recipe Knepp (page 46)

Place the ham, apples, water, brown sugar, and spices in a 6-quart Dutch oven or heavy kettle. Cover and bring to a boil. Simmer over medium heat for about 1 1/2 hours or until the ham is tender. (If you are using a precooked ham, it will only take 30 to 45 minutes.) Remove the ham from the broth and let cool enough to debone, remove the fat, and cut in bite-size pieces. Prepare the knepp dough. Return the cut meat to the broth and bring to a full boil over medium high heat. Continue with this heat until all the dumplings are added. There must be enough liquid to boil the dumplings, so add extra water if necessary. Drop the dough by tablespoonsful into the boiling broth. Cover with the lid and simmer over low heat for 12 minutes. DO NOT PEEK OR LIFT THE LID! Remove the knepp with a slotted spoon and set aside while pouring the ham and apples into a heated bowl or deep platter. Arrange the knepp around the sides and serve at once.

YIELD: 6 SERVINGS

FRIED HAM SLICES

The best way to have several memorable meals from one home-cured ham is to cut three or four slices, 1 inch thick, from the center of the ham for frying. This leaves the butt end (best for a meal of ham, green beans, and potatoes) for cooking and the other end for roasting. This is the most common practice—the whole ham is roasted only for special occasions.

2 slices of center-cut ham (home-cured is
*   the best), about 1 pound each*
1 tablespoon butter or vegetable oil
1 teaspoon dry mustard (optional)
2 teaspoons light brown sugar (optional)

For gravy, if desired:

1 tablespoon cornstarch
1 cup milk or water
1 teaspoon chopped fresh parsley

Trim the rind from the ham slices. Melt the butter in a large heavy skillet. Sprinkle the slices with the mustard and brown sugar if desired. Place them in the skillet and fry over medium heat until golden brown on each side, about 15 minutes a side. Remove the slices to a heated platter and slice them thin. For gravy, dissolve the cornstarch in the milk and add to the skillet. Reduce heat to low, stir in the parsley and bring to a boil. Make sure all the brownings are loosened from the pan and stir until thickened, about 5 minutes. Serve with biscuits or whole browned potatoes.

YIELD: 4 TO 6 SERVINGS

SOUTHERN STYLE HAM

My mother's cookbook, written by her during her teenage years, gives us one way of retaining the wonderful flavor of home-cured ham without the strong, salty flavor.

1 pound of center cut, home-cured ham, cut
*   about 1 inch thick*
1 teaspoon dry mustard
1/3 cup lightly packed light brown sugar
2 tablespoons (1/4 stick) butter
1 cup milk

Rub the mustard on top of the ham. Place in a 9-by-11-inch baking dish and sprinkle with the brown sugar. Dot with the butter. Pour the milk in the dish and bake in slow, preheated, 325°F oven, for 1 hour. It will develop a browned crust on top which sometimes looks curdled. That's fine, as the milk helps take away the salty taste. Remove the ham to a heated platter. Cut into thin slices.

YIELD: 4 TO 6 SERVINGS

HAM, GREEN BEANS, AND POTATOES

Everyone loves this one-dish meal. During the busy summer harvest days, we counted on this dinner at least once a week.

4 pound butt end of ham
4 cups water
6 to 8 medium-size potatoes, peeled
2 pounds green beans, fresh or frozen
1 teaspoon coarsely ground black pepper

Trim the rind from the ham. Place the ham in a Dutch oven or large kettle, add the water and cook, covered, over medium heat until tender, about 3 hours. Remove the ham and debone. Cut the potatoes in half and add, along with the beans and pepper, to the ham broth. Simmer over medium heat until vegetables are soft, about 30 minutes. Add ham and heat thoroughly.

YIELD: 6 SERVINGS

Variation: Add 2 cups corn kernels, fresh or frozen. This may replace the potatoes or be added in addition to them.

POT PIE

Give me a good, rich broth and some fine meat and I'll assure you a great meal. Pot pie in the Pennsylvania Dutch country is not a baked pie but a slippery dough noodle dish with lots of flavor. Every kind of meat works well in this recipe.

4 to 6 pound roast with bones (ham, pork, chicken, squirrel, rabbit, or beef)
1/2 cup coarsely chopped celery with leaves
2 medium-size potatoes, peeled and thinly sliced
6 cups reserved broth
Pot Pie Squares (page 45)
Fresh parsley sprigs for garnish

Cover meat with water, season, and cook, covered, over medium heat until tender, about 2 hours. Remove and debone, discarding any fat or skin. Cut the meat into bite-size chunks and set aside. Add celery, potatoes, and parsley to 6 cups of the broth and simmer over medium heat. Meanwhile, roll out the pot pie dough 1/8 inch thick and cut it into 2-inch squares. Drop them into the simmering broth only one layer at a time, cooking about 3 minutes before pushing the cooked dough under the broth before dropping in the next layer. If several layers are put in at the same time, they will become thick and doughy. After all the dough is in the broth, add the meat chunks and simmer for 15 minutes more. Garnish with parsley before serving.

YIELD: 6 TO 8 SERVINGS

PORK LOIN ROAST STUFFED WITH DRIED FRUIT

This is a very elegant dish and will make any meal seem special.

4 pounds pork loin, without the bone
1 recipe of Dried Fruit Stuffing (page 134)
1 cup water
1½ teaspoons salt
1 teaspoon ground black pepper
1 teaspoon dry mustard
1 tablespoon light brown sugar
½ cup sherry

Cut the loin lengthwise, about ⅔ the way through, and fill with the stuffing. Tie with cord and skewers to keep the filling inside. Place the water in a roasting pan. Season the loin with the salt, pepper, mustard, and brown sugar and place in the pan. Tent with aluminum foil and bake in a preheated 375°F oven for 2 hours, basting every 30 minutes with the sherry. Remove the foil and reduce the heat to 350°F, baking for another 15 minutes (or turn off the oven and let it stand uncovered for 30 minutes until ready to serve). If using a meat thermometer, let roast reach an internal temperature of 185–190°F. If you have extra filling, bake in a buttered baking dish for the last 15 minutes and arrange around the roast before serving.

YIELD: 6 TO 8 SERVINGS

Variation: Pork Chops with Wine: Use 4 pounds pork chops and season the same as above. Omit the water, fry chops in a large, heavy skillet over medium heat in 2 tablespoons (¼ stick) of butter or oil and baste with the sherry or an equal amount of red or white wine as they are browning, about 35 minutes. Serve the stuffing as a side dish.

WIENER SCHNITZEL

Turkey may be substituted for the veal, but wiener schnitzel and red cabbage are a meal that most of us cannot live without for any length of time.

2 pounds veal cutlets, cut ½ inch thick
½ cup all-purpose flour
1½ teaspoons salt
½ teaspoon freshly ground black pepper
2 large eggs, lightly beaten
1 tablespoon evaporated or whole milk
1 cup dry bread crumbs
½ cup saltine cracker crumbs, rolled fine
¼ cup vegetable oil
Lemon slices and fresh parsley sprigs for garnish

Score the edges of the cutlets with a sharp knife to prevent curling. Pound the cutlets between 2 sheets of wax paper until ¼ inch thick and set aside. Combine the flour, salt, and pepper together on a plate or sheet of wax paper. Mix the eggs and milk together in a shallow dish and combine the bread and cracker crumbs together on a plate or sheet of wax paper. Then, take each cutlet and first generously dredge it in the flour mixture, then dip it in the egg mixture, and finally dredge it in the crumbs until thoroughly coated. Heat the oil in a large, heavy skillet over medium heat and fry the cutlets until golden brown on each side, approximately 3 minutes per side. DO NOT OVERCOOK! Serve on a heated platter and garnish with lemon slices and sprigs of parsley.

YIELD: 4 SERVINGS

BRAISED SWEETBREADS WITH ALMONDS

Sweetbreads are the thymus glands of the calf, steer, or lamb. They come in pairs and the meat is white and very soft. They should be chilled in cold water before and after parboiling to prevent breaking while removing the membrane and veins. One pound of meat will serve three or four, because it is richly flavored. They may be cleaned and parboiled, then frozen for later use. They will keep in the freezer for at least 6 weeks if properly sealed.

2 pounds sweetbreads (about 3 cups cooked and cleaned)
3 cups water
1 teaspoon salt
2 tablespoons cider or white wine vinegar
4 tablespoons (½ stick) butter
½ cup slivered almonds
¼ cup chopped onion
¼ cup all-purpose flour
1 teaspoon dried chervil
1 teaspoon dried marjoram
1 teaspoon celery salt
1 teaspoon ground white pepper
2 cups dry white wine (chicken broth or heavy cream may be substituted)

Rinse the sweetbreads thoroughly in cold water. Place in a large saucepan or kettle with the water, salt, and vinegar. Bring to a boil over high heat, skim, lower the heat to medium low and cover with a lid, simmering the sweetbreads for 20 minutes. Remove with a slotted spoon and plunge into cold water. When cool, remove and discard all the membranes and veins. The meat will be white and semiround, tender balls.

Melt the butter in a large heavy skillet or saucepan and sauté the almonds over medium heat until golden, about 3 minutes. Remove the almonds with a slotted spoon and set aside until ready to serve. Sauté the onion over the same heat in the same pan until golden, about 2 minutes. Add the flour, chervil, marjoram, salt, and pepper, stirring until all the flour is mixed with the butter. Slowly add the wine and whisk until smooth and thickened over medium heat, about 4 minutes. Add the sweetbreads, reduce the heat to low and simmer, uncovered, for another 10 minutes. Top with the almonds and serve with rice or potatoes.

YIELD: 6 SERVINGS

Variation: Substitute 1 cup sliced fresh mushrooms and 1 tablespoon chopped fresh parsley for the almonds, using beef or chicken broth instead of wine.

COOKED BEEF TONGUE

Smoked tongue was considered a delicacy when I was growing up. I can remember all the older folks picking out the sliced, smoked tongue from the platters of cold cuts. I like tongue hot as well as cold and I love it when it is smoked. If you have a smoker or grill, cook the tongue and smoke it for extra flavor. The cooked tongue tastes like a tender beef roast with a very fine texture, so go ahead and try it, you'll find your family will enjoy it.

1½ pounds beef tongue, cleaned
1 green bell pepper, cut in quarters
4 stems celery with leaves, cut in 2-inch pieces
1 tablespoon chopped fresh parsley
½ teaspoon chopped fresh thyme
2 teaspoons salt
1 teaspoon coarsely ground black pepper

Place the tongue in a 6-quart stockpot, add the rest of the ingredients, and cover with water. Bring to a boil over high heat, cover with a lid, and reduce the heat to medium. Cook until the tongue is tender, approximately 3 hours. Let the tongue cool in the broth. Peel off the skin of the tongue when you remove it from the broth. If you prefer the tongue served hot, strain the broth through a double thickness of cheesecloth, slice the tongue, and heat it thoroughly in the broth. To serve it cold, refrigerate and slice thin, serving it with a horseradish sauce or mustard. To smoke the tongue, follow the directions for the smoker, smoking over wet hickory chips for no more than four hours. Refrigerate the smoked tongue, tightly covered, until ready to serve. Freeze the tongue that is left over. It will keep in the freezer for at least six weeks.

YIELD: 6 SERVINGS

STUFFED BEEF HEART

This is so good served cold for picnics, we always make several. They freeze well and are as good hot as cold. This recipe is for one, but you can double or triple it.

3 pounds fresh beef or steer heart
8 cups water
1 teaspoon salt
1 teaspoon ground black pepper
1 tablespoon dried salad herbs
1 teaspoon dry mustard
½ recipe stuffing of your choice (I recommend a Nutty or Herb Stuffing—see the Index)
½ cup sherry, brandy, or grape juice
½ teaspoon Worcestershire sauce (optional)
½ teaspoon soy sauce (optional)
3 tablespoons all-purpose flour

Wash and trim the heart of extra fat and veins. Place in a Dutch oven (a pressure cooker will save time; follow the instructions in the booklet), add the water, salt, pepper, herbs, and mustard. Cook over medium heat, covered, until tender, about 2½ hours. Remove the heart and let cool. Strain the broth through a double thickness of cheesecloth and skim off the fat after the broth has cooled; reserve. Trim off any extra fat now visible and the fiber from the center of the heart. Cut some of the meat out of the center with a sharp knife, chop, and reserve. Stuff the heart whole or cut it in half, lengthwise, and fill each side with stuffing. Place in a greased 9-by-13-inch baking dish and bake in a preheated 375°F oven. Baste with the sherry every 5 minutes until it is all gone and the heart is golden brown, about 15 minutes. Place the heart on a heated platter and keep warm until the gravy is made. Use the reserved broth to deglaze the pan, check for seasonings, and add the Worcestershire and soy sauce, if desired. Remove from the heat, add the flour, and stir until smooth. Return to the stove and cook over low heat for about 4 minutes or until thickened, then add the reserved chopped meat. Serve the gravy in a boat on the side. Slice the meat about 1/4 inch thick and arrange on a heated platter.

YIELD: 6 SERVINGS

SCRAPPLE

Scrapple is finely ground pork cooked with cornmeal and seasonings, then poured into loaf pans, and cooled and refrigerated for several days. Cut into slices, it should be fried on a grill or in a skillet and served crispy on the outside. We always served scrapple for supper, spreading it with applebutter, molasses, or syrup. Everyone else seems to like it best for breakfast, so you decide when to enjoy it.

16 cups water
3 cups finely ground pork or the chopped
*   meat from pork rib rack, heart, or feet*
*   (3 cups pork sausage meat is also fine)*
2 teaspoons salt
2 teaspoons coarsely ground black pepper
1/2 teaspoon dried basil (optional)
Pinch of dried rosemary (optional)
Pinch of ground thyme (optional)
3 1/2 cups cornmeal
2 tablespoons vegetable oil

In a large 6-quart stockpot, combine the water, pork, salt, pepper, and herbs. Bring to a boil, skim, cover, and simmer over medium heat for 3 hours or until the meat falls off the bones. Remove the meat and strain the broth through a double thickness of cheesecloth. Debone and remove all the fat, gristle, and skin. Chop or grind the meat in a food processor or grinder. Skim the fat from the broth, making sure you have 12 cups of broth. If not, add enough water to make 12 cups. Place the broth and meat in a large, heavy saucepan and bring to a boil. Slowly add the cornmeal, continually stirring with a whisk to prevent lumping. Simmer over low heat for 1 hour, stirring frequently with a wooden spoon. The mixture should be thick like mush. Remove from the heat and pour into three greased 8 1/2-by-4 1/2-inch loaf pans. Cool and refrigerate, covered with wax paper, until ready to use. It does not freeze well, but will keep for weeks in the refrigerator. To serve, slice 1/3 inch thick and fry on a grill or in a skillet greased with the vegetable oil over medium heat until golden and crisp, about 3 minutes on each side.

YIELD: THREE 8 1/2-BY-4 1/2-INCH LOAF PANS

SOUSE

Some people call this head cheese. It's great sliced cold with mustard or horseradish sauce.

4 pig's feet, about 2 pounds
2 pork hocks, about 4 pounds
1 pork tongue, about 1 pound
2 teaspoons salt
1/2 teaspoon ground black pepper
1 large onion, quartered
6 whole black peppercorns, cracked
1 teaspoon whole cloves
1 bay leaf
1 tablespoon granulated sugar
1/2 teaspoon salt
3/4 cup cider vinegar

Split the skin and clean the feet thoroughly. Clean the hocks and slit the tongue skin with a sharp knife. Place the feet, hocks, tongue, salt, and pepper in a large stockpot. Add enough water to cover and bring to a boil over high heat. Cover and continue to boil over medium heat for about 1 1/2 hours or until tender. Skim several times until the broth is clear. Remove the meat from the broth and let cool. Discard the skin, fat, and bones. Cut the meat into pieces, set aside. Reduce the broth by boiling it over high heat to one half the amount, strain through a double thickness of cheesecloth, and pour into a large saucepan. Add the onion, peppercorns, cloves, bay leaf, sugar, and salt, and simmer for 10 minutes over medium heat. Strain again and cool enough to skim off the fat. Return to the saucepan and add the vinegar and meat and bring to a full boil over high heat. Remove from heat and pour into two 8 1/2-by-4 1/2-inch loaf pans to cool. Pour just enough liquid into the dishes to cover the meat, as it will gel enough to slice. After it is cool and set, refrigerate for at least one day, covered. Slice 1/3 inch thick and serve chilled.

YIELD: ABOUT 4 POUNDS OR TWO 8 1/2-BY-4 1/2-INCH LOAF PANS

SAUSAGE AND SQUASH STIR FRY

Appealing to the eye and the palate, it is also easy and quick to prepare.

1 pound smoked pork sausage
2 yellow (summer) squash, each about 10 inches long
1 zucchini, about 1/3 pound
1 tablespoon butter
1 teaspoon steak salt
1 teaspoon dried chervil
1/2 teaspoon celery seed
1/2 teaspoon ground white pepper

Slice the sausage about 1/3 inch thick. Slice the squash and zucchini the same size or into thin strips. Melt the butter in a large, heavy skillet or wok and stir fry the sausage over high heat for 5 minutes. Add all the remaining ingredients and continue to stir fry until vegetables are nearly tender and sausage is golden, about 8 minutes. Serve immediately.

YIELD: 4 SERVINGS

PAN-FRIED LIVER AND ONIONS

If you are used to eating liver that has been dredged in flour and fried to death till it's tough, try this recipe. You won't believe liver could be so tender!

3 tablespoons butter
1 cup sliced onions
1½ pounds fresh calf's liver, sliced 1 inch
   thick, skinned
¾ teaspoon salt
¼ teaspoon ground white pepper

Melt the butter in a large, heavy skillet and sauté the onions over medium heat until they are clear and golden around the edges, about 3 minutes. Remove the onions onto a heated platter and increase the heat to high. Add the slices of liver, pressing with a fork to seal in all the juices. Fry until browned, about 2 minutes, sprinkle with the salt and pepper and turn. Fry on other side for 2 minutes, add the onions, and heat through, covering the pan with the lid until heated. Serve immediately. If the liver is left a bit pink it will be more tender.

YIELD: 4 SERVINGS

STUFFED PIG STOMACH
OR FRENCH GOOSE

This is one of my favorite sausage recipes. It looks so pretty when it is cut in thick slices. Although I prefer the real stomach, a roasting bag works quite well.

1 pig's stomach (optional)
2 pounds fresh pork sausage
2 pounds white potatoes, peeled and diced
8 stems celery, sliced crosswise
½ pound carrots, peeled and sliced
3 tablespoons chopped fresh parsley
½ cup chopped onion, (optional)
1 teaspoon salt
½ teaspoon coarsely ground black pepper

Wash the stomach thoroughly. Combine the sausage, vegetables, and seasonings, mixing well. Stuff it firmly into the stomach or an oven roaster bag. Close with skewers and string; if using a bag, pierce a few holes in the top and several on the bottom so the fat will drain out. Place on a rack in a roasting pan and bake in a preheated 350°F oven for about 3 hours or until golden brown. When using a stomach, baste with drippings every half hour. If skin is not browning, increase the oven temperature to 375°F for the last 15 minutes. If using a roasting bag, peel it off. Place on a heated platter and cut into 2-inch slices. It will not fall apart if cut into thick slices. It is delicious when reheated.

YIELD: 6 SERVINGS

Chapter 7

Seafood

DEVILED CLAMS

These are delicious either baked or pan-fried.

12 large clams or 2 cups frozen or canned
  chopped clams with broth
4 large eggs, lightly beaten
1/2 cup chopped onion
2/3 cup chopped celery
1/2 cup chopped green bell pepper
2 tablespoons chopped fresh parsley
1 teaspoon chopped fresh chervil
1/2 teaspoon salt
1/2 teaspoon ground white pepper
4 cups fresh bread crumbs

Scrub the clams and open with a shucking knife, or place in a baking pan. Bake in 300°F oven until shells open enough to remove clam, reserving the broth. Do not bake the clams! Remove the clams from shells and chop up or use the frozen or canned ones. Oil the inside of the scrubbed clam shells. Mix the remaining ingredients together until well blended, then divide among the shells. Place them in a shallow baking pan and bake in preheated 375°F oven until golden brown, approximately 25 minutes. If pan frying, place the filled clam shells upside down in a large, heated and buttered saucepan, and fry, covered, over medium heat until golden brown, approximately 8 minutes.

YIELD: 12 DEVILED CLAMS (I USUALLY SERVE 2 PER PERSON)

BOX PANNED OYSTERS

These are for the true oyster lover.

*3 dozen large shucked oysters with the
   liquor*
3 tablespoons butter
1/4 teaspoon ground white pepper
Dash of paprika
Old Bay (seafood) seasoning (optional)
Chopped fresh parsley for garnish

Check the oysters for shells. In a large, heavy
sauté pan, lightly brown the butter over medium-high heat and add the oysters. Fry only
till the edges curl, about 1 minute. Add the
reserved liquor and seasonings. Heat thoroughly over medium heat and serve immediately in heated bowls with toast tips or crackers. Garnish with parsley.

YIELD: 4 TO 6 SERVINGS

FRIED OYSTERS

Excellent!

*3 dozen large shucked oysters (reserve 1/2
   cup oyster liquor)*
3 cups assorted cracker crumbs
1/4 teaspoon Old Bay (seafood) seasoning
1/4 teaspoon Hungarian paprika
1/2 teaspoon dried dillweed
1/4 teaspoon ground white pepper
1/4 teaspoon red (cayenne) pepper
1 large egg, well beaten
1/3 cup vegetable oil or butter

Check oysters for shells. Combine the crumbs
and seasonings in a medium-size bowl. Combine the beaten egg and oyster liquor in a small
bowl. Roll each oyster in the crumbs, let stand
30 minutes, then dip in the egg liquid. Roll
again in the crumbs and fry both sides over
medium heat in a large, heavy skillet until
golden brown.

YIELD: 4 TO 6 SERVINGS (MY DAD AND GRAND-
FATHER ALWAYS ATE AT LEAST 8 OYSTERS
EACH, SO YOU BE THE JUDGE)

OYSTER PIE

A traditional, favorite one-dish meal served with a salad or relishes. The Shirks prepared this for one of the most memorable dinners we've enjoyed. It is their old family recipe and it deserves special applause.

*3 medium-size potatoes, peeled and sliced
    1/4-inch thick*
1 stem celery, chopped
1 cup water
1 teaspoon salt
*Pastry for a double crust 10-inch pie (page
    149)*
*1 1/2 cups shucked oysters including the
    liquor, about 2 1/2 dozen*
4 large eggs, lightly beaten
1/2 teaspoon ground white pepper
1 tablespoon all-purpose flour
3 tablespoons butter, melted
1 tablespoon chopped fresh parsley

Place the sliced potatoes, celery, water, and 1/2 teaspoon of the salt in a medium-size saucepan. Boil until vegetables are tender, about 10 minutes, over medium heat. Reserve the liquid. Roll out the bottom crust of the pie, fit into a 9-inch pie pan, and puff in a preheated 350°F oven for about 3 minutes to prevent a soggy bottom crust. Check the oysters for shell particles. Blend the oyster liquor with the beaten eggs, the remaining salt, the pepper, and flour. Layer half the potatoes, celery, and oysters onto the bottom crust. Pour in half the egg mixture. Add the rest of the potatoes, celery, and oysters, and pour the remaining egg mixture plus the melted butter and parsley over the top. If there is not enough liquid to cover the vegetables and oysters, use the potato liq-uid to cover. Moisten edges of the bottom crust with the liquid. Cover it with the top crust, piercing it in several places first. Flute the edges, place the pie pan on aluminum foil or a baking sheet and bake in a preheated 350°F oven for 45 minutes or until the juices start to bubble through the edges or vents. Serve hot.

YIELD: ONE 9-INCH PIE OR 4 SERVINGS

SALMON CROQUETTES

My mother, Bertha, and Abe's mother, Elizabeth, both made these quite often. If they were used as an appetizer, they were made smaller. As the main course, they were shaped like large cones and served with a thin white sauce. I like serving them with a wine-caper sauce.

*1 pound fresh salmon, filleted and poached
    (canned salmon may be substituted)*
2 tablespoons finely chopped onion
*1 tablespoon minced fresh dill or 1/2
    tablespoon dried*
*1 teaspoon minced fresh basil or 1/2
    teaspoon dried*
1 teaspoon seasoned salt
1/4 cup evaporated milk or whole milk
3 large eggs, lightly beaten
2 tablespoons (1/4 stick) butter, melted
1 1/2 cups fresh bread crumbs
3 tablespoons vegetable oil
1/2 cup dry white wine
1 tablespoon capers
Fresh dill sprigs or lemon slices for garnish

Remove any skin or small bones from the salmon. Flake the fish with a fork in a large mixing bowl. Combine it with the onion, dill, basil, salt, milk, beaten eggs, butter, and 1 cup of the bread crumbs. Cover with plastic wrap and refrigerate for 30 minutes. Form into balls, cones, or patties and roll in the remaining bread crumbs. Heat the oil in a large, heavy skillet over medium-high heat and fry the croquettes until golden brown on all sides, about 10 minutes altogether. Remove them from the skillet, then add the wine and capers and deglaze the pan. Pour the sauce over the top of the croquettes before serving. Garnish with sprigs of dill or lemon slices

YIELD: ABOUT 12 TWO-INCH BALLS, 4 SERVINGS

SHAD AND ROE
BAKED AND FRIED

Shad is a strong-flavored fish, the roe very mild and delicious, especially when fried with bacon. The old-fashioned way of baking shad was to use the whole fish and bake at 350°F for 3 to 4 hours. They say the bones, at least the small ones, would then be soft enough to eat. I have not found that to be true, so I have the fish filleted. It saves time in the oven and they are just as tasty.

Shad:

6 to 8 slices bacon
3 pounds shad fillets
1 teaspoon salt

1/2 teaspoon ground white pepper
Thin slices of lemon or lime

Roe:

3 pairs shad roe
1/4 cup all-purpose flour
1/2 teaspoon salt
1/2 teaspoon ground white pepper
6 slices bacon
Lemon wedges

Place 2 or 3 slices of the bacon in the bottom of a buttered baking pan, add the fillets, sprinkle them with the salt and pepper, and top with slices of lemon and the remaining bacon. Bake in a preheated 400°F oven for 30 minutes. The fillets should be golden brown on the top but flake when you pierce them with a fork.

Separate the pairs of roe by cutting the fiber that holds them together. Shake the roe in a paper bag with the flour, salt, and pepper until coated. Wrap the roe halves in bacon and place them in a large skillet. Slowly heat the skillet until the bacon has warmed enough to fry the roe; cover the skillet partially while you do this, as roe has a tendency to splatter. Fry until golden over medium-high heat, about 8 minutes for each side. Serve with lemon wedges or a special vinegar, such as Celery Vinegar on page 206.

YIELD: 6 SERVINGS

Variation: Shad Stuffed with Spinach: Spread the spinach stuffing used to stuff tomatoes (recipe on page 81) between the fillets. Bake one hour in a preheated 400°F oven or until golden on top and flaky on the bottom.

TROUT CAMERON ESTATE STYLE

Simon Cameron, native of Lancaster County and first Secretary of War for Abraham Lincoln, used the fresh springs of Donegal to nurture the trout he brought to the area. The Cameron Estate was his summer residence and is now a beautiful country inn with the streams stocked with lots of trout. This recipe honors him for his great contribution to our area.

1 trout or 2 fillets, about 14 ounces
Flour for dredging
1 large egg, slightly beaten
1 teaspoon water or milk
Pecan Breading (page 135)
2 tablespoons butter (¼ stick) or vegetable oil
Dash of ground white pepper
⅓ cup dry white wine
1 tablespoon fresh lemon juice
1 teaspoon capers
Lemon slices and watercress for garnish

You may want to use trout that are boned and beheaded, but if you are catching your own, give my way a try. Don't remove the fins or the head until the fish is cooked. At that point, a fork inserted under the backbone will be all that's needed to neatly fillet the fish in a matter of seconds.

Dredge the trout in flour, then dip in the egg wash made from the beaten egg and water. Dredge trout in pecan breading. Heat the butter or oil over medium-high heat in a large sauté pan or skillet and place the trout skin side up. Season lightly with pepper and salt if desired. Sauté until edges start to curl, then flip over and cook until the fish flakes when a fork is inserted at thickest part. Gently remove fish onto heated platter. Add the wine, lemon juice, and capers to the pan brownings. Deglaze the pan and pour the sauce over the fish or serve on the side. Garnish with lemon slices and watercress.

YIELD: 1 SERVING

Variation: Use this recipe for any mild, fresh fish. Two tablespoons chopped scallions may be added when deglazing pan.

Chapter 8

Sauces, Dressings, and Stuffings

GRAVY

Gravy may be made from any broth or a combination of broth, brownings from the roast, and milk. Cornstarch may be substituted for flour as a thickener.

2 cups broth
1/2 cup water
3 1/2 tablespoons all-purpose flour or
*   cornstarch*
Season to taste with salt, ground black or
*   white pepper, chopped fresh parsley, or*
*   paprika*

If you want to make gravy from a roast, pour all the drippings into a bowl. Skim and discard the fat. Heat the pan over medium heat and deglaze with the water. Scrape and stir with a wooden spoon until all the brownings are loos-

ened. Reduce the heat to low and whisk in the flour, stirring until all the lumps are dissolved. Slowly add the broth and whisk until velvety smooth, about 5 minutes. Season to taste. Serve piping hot.

YIELD: 2 1/2 CUPS

BROWNED BUTTER

I like to make a large amount at one time because it will keep, covered, in the refrigerator for at least two weeks. All I have to do is spoon it onto any hot vegetable and the butter melts into the vegetables. And mashed potatoes are heavenly when topped with browned butter.

¼ pound (1 stick) butter or margarine

Melt the butter in a 1-quart saucepan over medium heat. After it has melted, stir constantly until the butter begins to turn a nutty, golden brown, approximately 4 minutes. Remove from the heat immediately, before it burns. It will have what some call a spicy taste. This is caused by the browning of the milk particles in the butter. Spoon a small amount over hot vegetables before serving. Cover the remaining butter and refrigerate until ready to use. The dark particles will settle to the bottom, so when spooning the cold butter, make sure you touch the bottom of the pan for all the good parts.

YIELD: ½ CUP

CLARIFIED BUTTER

Clarified butter will keep for at least a week if stored, covered, in a cool place or in the refrigerator.

¼ pound (1 stick) butter

Place the butter in a deep saucepan and cook over medium heat until it foams. Remove it from the heat and skim the foam from the top. The clear yellow liquid is the clarified butter. Carefully pour it off from the solids and the milky liquid at the bottom of the pan.

YIELD: ABOUT ½ CUP

WHITE SAUCE

Thin:

1 tablespoon butter or vegetable shortening
1 tablespoon all-purpose flour
1 cup milk
¼ teaspoon salt
Dash of freshly ground black or white pepper

Medium:

2 tablespoons (¼ stick) butter or vegetable shortening
2 tablespoons all-purpose flour
1 cup milk
¼ teaspoon salt
Dash of freshly ground black or white pepper

Thick:

3 tablespoons butter or vegetable shortening
3 tablespoons all-purpose flour
1 cup milk
¼ teaspoon salt
Dash of freshly ground black or white pepper

In a 1-quart saucepan, melt the butter over medium heat. Gradually add the flour, stirring with a whisk until it becomes a smooth paste, approximately 2 minutes. Gradually add the milk, stirring constantly until thickened. Add salt and pepper and reduce the heat to very low. Stir for at least one minute before adding to the prepared dish.

YIELD: 1 CUP

HOLLANDAISE SAUCE

When serving hollandaise sauce, it must be kept warm, not hot, as the sauce will break (curdle). If that happens, add another egg yolk and beat the sauce vigorously.

2 large egg yolks
1 tablespoon white wine
1/2 cup Clarified Butter (page 124)
2 drops Tabasco sauce
2 tablespoons fresh lemon juice
1/8 teaspoon salt
1/8 teaspoon ground white pepper

In the top of a double boiler, beat the egg yolks and wine together thoroughly as the water below heats up. Do not allow the water to boil. If you are not using a double boiler, beat the yolks and wine in a bowl set in a pan of near-boiling water. Be careful not to cook the yolks—just heat them—always beating with a wire whisk. When the egg yolks are warm, slowly add the clarified butter, mixing all the time, until smooth and thickened, approximately 1 1/2 to 2 minutes. Gradually whisk in the Tabasco, lemon juice, salt, and pepper. As soon as it is thick and creamy, remove from the heat. Keep warm, but not hot, until ready to serve.

YIELD: 3/4 CUP

TOMATO SAUCE

The Dutch like their tomato sauce sweet, and either chunky or smooth, and often serve it with mashed potatoes.

3 tablespoons butter or margarine
1/2 cup chopped onion
1/3 cup all-purpose flour
1/2 teaspoon salt
1/2 teaspoon ground black pepper
1 to 2 tablespoons light brown sugar
1 tablespoon chopped fresh parsley or 1
*   teaspoon dried*
3 cups diced or pureed (depending on
*   preference), peeled tomatoes, fresh or*
*   canned (with juice)*
Croutons, toasted crackers, or hardboiled
*   eggs slices for garnish*

Melt the butter in a large saucepan over medium heat. Sauté the onion until golden, then add the flour. Stir until smooth and add the salt, pepper, brown sugar, parsley, and tomatoes. Cook over medium-low heat until thick, about 12 minutes. When ready to serve, garnish with croutons, toasted crackers or hardboiled egg slices.

YIELD: 4 CUPS

Variation: Add 1 chopped green bell pepper and sauté with the onion.

MUSHROOM-HERB SAUCE

This sauce is perfect over beans, peas, or nearly everything.

1/4 cup chopped onion
2 tablespoons (1/4 stick) butter
1 1/4 pounds mushrooms, sliced
1 large egg yolk, beaten with fork
1 teaspoon ground white pepper
1/2 teaspoon salt
1 teaspoon celery salt
1 teaspoon dried parsley flakes
1/2 teaspoon dried tarragon
1/4 teaspoon dried dillweed
1 cup half and half (milk may be substituted)
1/2 cup dry white wine

In a saucepan or skillet, sauté the onions in the butter over medium-high heat until clear, then add the sliced mushrooms. After evaporating almost all the mushrooms' liquid, stir in the beaten yolk, pepper, salt, and herbs. Reduce heat to medium. Slowly add the cream, stirring with a wooden spoon until slightly thickened. Gradually add the wine and heat thoroughly. Serve over vegetables or in a sauce boat on the side.

YIELD: 2 CUPS

WINE SAUCE

This is delicious served over puddings and cakes.

10 tablespoons butter, (1 1/4 sticks) at room temperature
3 cups confectioners sugar
1/4 teaspoon salt
3/4 cup boiling water
2/3 cup white wine or sherry
1 teaspoon ground nutmeg
1/4 teaspoon ground cinnamon

Place the butter, sugar, and salt in a large mixing bowl and beat vigorously until light and fluffy. Slowly add the boiling water to mixture, beating rapidly until very creamy. Gradually add the wine, nutmeg, and cinnamon, beating thoroughly. It should look milky white, if beaten properly. Set the bowl over very hot water, either in a saucepan or the bottom of a double boiler is fine, and keep hot until ready to serve—do not boil.

YIELD: ABOUT 4 CUPS

HINT: If you have sauce left over, refrigerate it covered. Reheat it on top of a double boiler, whipping constantly with a wire whisk. It will keep at least 2 weeks if properly covered.

STRAWBERRY-RHUBARB SAUCE

This is a great sauce to serve with fresh strawberries or puddings. Fill baked meringues with a combination of fresh fruit and sauce to make an elegant dessert.

1 pound fresh rhubarb
⅓ cup granulated sugar
1¼ cups frozen strawberries or 1½ cups
   sliced fresh strawberries
2 tablespoons fresh lemon juice
⅓ teaspoon ground nutmeg
3 drops red food coloring
3 tablespoons arrowroot or cornstarch
6 tablespoons water

Wash and cut off the leaves (they are poisonous) and stem ends of the rhubarb. Cut into ½-inch pieces. Place the diced rhubarb, sugar, and strawberries in a food processor or blender. Chop fine and pour into a 1½-quart saucepan. Add the lemon juice, nutmeg, food coloring, arrowroot, and water, stirring until completely dissolved. Bring to a boil and cook over medium heat, stirring until thickened, about 10 minutes. Cool and refrigerate, covered, until ready to serve.

YIELD: 2½ CUPS

FRESH FRUIT GLAZE

This is a perfect glaze for all fresh, uncooked fruits. While cornstarch has a tendency to gel and turn cloudy, arrowroot remains clear. The most economical way to buy arrowroot is to order it from your grocery store buyer in large ½-pound boxes. The major companies package it in large boxes for commercial restaurant use and will sell it to the grocery buyers by special order. It keeps at least a year if stored with the lid sealed.

1 tablespoon arrowroot
½ cup water
⅓ cup granulated sugar
1 teaspoon fresh lemon juice (optional)
Dash of ground nutmeg (optional)
Drop of food coloring (optional)

Blend all the ingredients together, except the food coloring, in a 1-quart saucepan and bring to a boil over medium-high heat. Reduce heat to low and simmer until thickened, approximately 3 minutes. Add the food coloring if desired, stir until blended, and cool before adding to fruit.

YIELD: ABOUT 1 CUP

HARD SAUCE

Especially good on plum pudding or warm gingerbread, many folks serve it on top of any warm pudding. It can be poured into a fancy mold, kept hard in a cool place, and then dipped in warm water for a few seconds to loosen before unmolding into a pretty glass dish for serving.

¼ pound (1 stick) butter, at room temperature
2 cups confectioners sugar
¼ teaspoon salt
1 teaspoon vanilla extract
Dash of ground nutmeg
⅓ cup brandy or rum or 2 to 3 tablespoons rum flavoring

Place the butter, sugar, and salt in a large mixing bowl and beat until light. Slowly add in the vanilla, nutmeg, and brandy. Beat until fluffy. Pour into a 3-cup mold or dish. It can be refrigerated, covered, for at least 3 weeks. Spoon over any warm pudding or cake.

YIELD: ABOUT 2 CUPS

LEMON-LIME SAUCE

A little goes a long way. Adding rum makes this a delightful sauce for gingerbread or plum pudding.

1½ cups granulated sugar
¼ pound (1 stick) butter
¼ teaspoon salt

1 large egg, lightly beaten
1 lemon, juiced and rind grated
1 lime, juiced and rind grated
¾ teaspoon ground nutmeg
¼ cup boiling water

Cream the sugar, butter, and salt together in a large mixing bowl until fluffy. Gradually add in the beaten egg, juice and grated rind of the lemon and lime, nutmeg, and water, beating thoroughly. Heat in the top of a double boiler over simmering water, stirring frequently, until sauce is clear and thickened a bit, about 20 minutes. Serve warm.

YIELD: 2 CUPS

Variation: For lemon-rum sauce, omit lime juice and rind. Add ½ cup light rum just before serving.

CHOCOLATE SYRUP

Make a full recipe of this because it keeps, refrigerated, for a long time.

1 cup unsweetened cocoa
4 cups (2 pounds) granulated sugar
1 teaspoon salt
6 cups water
2 tablespoons arrowroot, dissolved in ¼ cup water
1 tablespoon vanilla extract

Sift the cocoa, sugar, and salt together in a large mixing bowl. Put in a 5-quart kettle and gradually whisk in the water over medium heat. Bring to a boil, stirring constantly. As it comes to the boil, mix in the arrowroot and cook for 5 minutes, until thickened. Remove from the heat and stir in the vanilla. Store in airtight jars and refrigerate.

YIELD: AT LEAST 1½ QUARTS

COOKED DRESSING

This is an old-fashioned dressing that was always used in salads. The only problem in serving this dressing is that it becomes watery if it stands too long (more than two hours). It is important to stir the salad or pour off the excess liquid and toss before serving. It is the original dressing used for chicken, turkey, or ham salad.

3 tablespoons granulated sugar
1 tablespoon butter, melted
1 teaspoon all-purpose flour
1 teaspoon dry mustard
¼ teaspoon ground turmeric
½ teaspoon salt
1 large egg, lightly beaten
1 cup milk, scalded
½ cup cider vinegar

Combine sugar, melted butter, flour, mustard, turmeric, and salt in a small saucepan. Whisk in the beaten egg and gradually add the hot milk. Place on the stove over medium heat. When hot, briskly beat in the vinegar, stirring until thickened. Remove from heat and cool. If using for potato or macaroni salad, add to the salad while warm so the flavor permeates the entire salad. If using with apples, add minutes before serving.

YIELD: ABOUT 2 CUPS

FRUIT DRESSING

This is a perfect touch for molded salads.

½ cup granulated sugar
1½ tablespoons arrowroot or cornstarch
1 cup pineapple juice
2 large eggs, slightly beaten
¼ teaspoon ground nutmeg
1 cup heavy cream

In a small saucepan, combine the sugar and arrowroot with the pineapple juice until thoroughly blended. Gradually mix in the beaten eggs and nutmeg. Bring to a boil over medium heat and stir until thickened, about 5 minutes. Remove from heat, cool, and refrigerate until ready to serve. Whip the cream until it forms soft peaks and fold into the sauce. Serve with or pour over fresh fruit or molded salad.

YIELD: ABOUT 3 CUPS

Variation: Substitute any fruit juice for the pineapple juice.

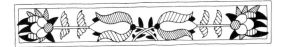

HONEY-FRUIT DRESSING

Although this is super for all fruits, it is especially great when poured over berries (wineberries, blueberries, raspberries, and strawberries, in particular) and served in peeled fruit halves.

¾ cup sour cream
3 tablespoons honey
½ teaspoon grated orange rind
½ teaspoon grated lime rind
½ teaspoon grated lemon rind
1 tablespoon fresh orange juice
1 tablespoon fresh lime juice
1 tablespoon fresh lemon juice
⅛ teaspoon ground nutmeg
⅛ teaspoon salt
Fresh mint leaves for garnish

Combine all the ingredients thoroughly and chill for at least an hour. Pour over the top of fruit slices or berries, reserving a little extra dressing to serve on the side. Garnish with fresh mint sprigs.

YIELD: 1 CUP

HORSERADISH DRESSING

The secret to making your own horseradish is to grind it with a fan behind you to blow away the strong odor and prevent the eyes from watering. Today it is still available in the local farmers' markets and is well worth the money.

1½ cups sour cream
¼ cup grated fresh horseradish
2 tablespoons fresh lemon juice
1 tablespoon Worcestershire sauce
3 tablespoons granulated sugar
1 tablespoon chopped fresh chives
½ teaspoon dry mustard
½ teaspoon coarsely ground black pepper
1 teaspoon salt

Blend all the ingredients thoroughly and chill. Will keep, in an airtight container, for at least a week.

YIELD: 2 CUPS

CREAMY SWEET-SOUR DRESSING

Everyone asks for this recipe. It is so simple, yet so great, you'll make lots at a time and store it in the refrigerator. Just shake it up when you are ready to serve and it will taste better than any "bought" dressing.

½ cup cider vinegar or white wine vinegar
⅔ cup granulated sugar
¾ cup evaporated milk
½ teaspoon salt

*Several dashes of freshly ground black
  pepper*
1/2 teaspoon celery seed
*1 tablespoon chopped fresh or dried herbs
  (parsley, rosemary, chives, thyme, etc.)*

Blend all the ingredients thoroughly until the
sugar is dissolved. Cover and refrigerate at
least 30 minutes. This will keep, tightly covered, for at least one week.

YIELD: ABOUT 2 CUPS

BEER BATTER

This batter is excellent for deep frying vegetables, fish, or edible flowers. It is very light.

3/4 cup all-purpose flour
1/4 teaspoon salt
1 1/2 teaspoons baking powder
1/4 teaspoon ground white pepper
2 tablespoons milk
1/2 cup beer
1 large egg

Mix all the batter ingredients together in a
blender or mixer. Cover and chill for at least
30 minutes—it is even better if you can refrigerate it overnight.

YIELD: ABOUT 1 1/2 CUPS

APPLE STUFFING

This stuffing is great with pork chops, lamb, or
any type of fowl.

6 slices bacon
1/2 cup chopped celery
1/4 cup chopped onion
1/4 cup chopped fresh parsley
1/2 cup granulated sugar
*4 cups cored and diced apples (peeled if
  desired)*
1 cup finely crushed saltine crackers

Fry the bacon in large saucepan or skillet. Remove the bacon when crisp and drain on paper
towels. Break into bits. Sauté the celery, onion,
and parsley for several minutes in the bacon fat
over medium heat, then remove to a large
bowl. Put the sugar in the skillet, add the
apples, and saute in the bacon fat over medium
heat until the edges of the apples are golden
and nearly soft, about 3 minutes. Add the
bacon bits, celery mixture, and crackers and
blend thoroughly. Stuff in meat or fowl or
bake in a 2-quart buttered baking dish for 30
minutes in a preheated 350°F oven.

YIELD: ABOUT 7 CUPS OR ENOUGH TO STUFF
AN 8-POUND BIRD, 6 PORK CHOPS, OR A
CROWN ROAST OF LAMB

OYSTER STUFFING

As a child, I would read the menu served at the White House on Thanksgiving day. It always included oyster stuffing. When oysters are plentiful or you want to really celebrate, try this with turkey, chicken, or pheasant.

1/3 cup chopped celery
1/4 cup chopped onion
1/4 cup water
4 cups fresh bread cubes
2 large eggs, lightly beaten
1 teaspoon Old Bay (seafood) seasoning
1/2 teaspoon ground white pepper
1 cup shucked oysters with liquor (about 1 1/2 dozen)
1/2 cup half and half, milk, or evaporated milk

Cook the celery, onion, and water in a small saucepan over medium heat for 3 minutes, or until the liquid has evaporated. Remove from heat. Check the oysters for shells. Place the bread, beaten eggs, celery mixture, seasonings, oysters, and cream in a large mixing bowl and blend thoroughly. Pour into a greased 2-quart baking dish or stuff into the roast or fowl. If baking separately, bake in a preheated 350°F oven, lightly tented with aluminum foil, for 30 minutes or until golden brown.

YIELD: ABOUT 6 CUPS OR ENOUGH TO STUFF A LARGE (12-POUND) TURKEY OR 2 CHICKENS OR 2 PHEASANTS

Variation: Clam and Oyster Stuffing: Add an additional cup of bread cubes or broken crackers and 1 cup chopped or whole shucked clams (be sure to check for shells).

SALSIFY STUFFING

Folks will be certain they are eating oysters, so don't tell them they're not! We usually serve this with roast duck or roast turkey. Why not try it with beef or pork roasts cut with pockets? Fill with the stuffing for an elegant dinner, or serve it as a side dish.

2 pounds salsify (oyster plant)
1 teaspoon salt
4 cups water
3 tablespoons butter or margarine
1/3 cup chopped celery
1/3 cup chopped onion
1/2 teaspoon Old Bay (seafood) seasoning
1/2 teaspoon dried dillweed
2 cups bread cubes
1 cup broken crackers or oyster crackers
2 large eggs, lightly beaten
3/4 cup milk
1/2 teaspoon salt
1/2 teaspoon ground black pepper
1 tablespoon fresh lemon juice

Scrub and boil salsify in the salt and water, covered, over medium-high heat until tender, about 20 minutes. Drain, peel, and cut the salsify into 1/2-inch thick slices. Melt the butter in a deep, heavy saucepan and sauté the celery and onion for 3 minutes over medium heat. Remove from the heat and add all the other ingredients. Toss lightly until completely blended. Pour into a buttered 2-quart casserole or baking dish and bake in a preheated 350°F oven for 35 to 40 minutes or until golden brown.

YIELD: ABOUT 4 CUPS OR 6 SERVINGS

ALMOND STUFFING

This is very rich and nutty—perfect with small birds or veal.

3 slices bacon
1 cup chopped celery
1/3 cup slivered almonds
1/2 teaspoon salt
1/2 teaspoon ground white pepper
1 tablespoon chopped fresh parsley
1 cup fresh bread crumbs
1/2 cup light cream or half and half

Fry the bacon in a large, heavy skillet until crisp. Remove bacon, drain on paper towels, then crumble. Sauté the celery, almonds, salt, pepper, and parsley in the bacon grease over medium heat until the almonds are golden, about 5 minutes. Stir in the bread crumbs and cream. Remove from the heat and spoon into a buttered 1-quart baking dish. Bake in a preheated 350°F oven for 25 to 30 minutes or until it pulls away from the sides of the baking dish. If using some for stuffing birds, bake the remainder in a small baking dish for the last 10 minutes.

YIELD: ABOUT 3 CUPS OR ENOUGH TO STUFF 1 CHICKEN, 2 GAME HENS, OR 4 QUAIL

CORNBREAD-BACON STUFFING

This stuffing will make you yearn for the country, or at least a vacation in the country. It tastes great with any kind of poultry or game or pork roast.

6 slices bacon
1/2 cup chopped onion
1 cup chopped celery
2 tablespoons chopped fresh parsley
1 1/2 cups chicken broth
3 cups Cornbread cut into cubes (page 140)

Fry the bacon in a large, heavy skillet until crisp. Remove bacon, drain on paper towels, and crumble. Drain all but 2 tablespoons of the bacon grease. Sauté the onion, celery, and parsley in the fat over medium heat until the onion is clear, about 5 minutes. Add the broth, cornbread cubes, and crumbled bacon, and mix thoroughly. Pour into a buttered baking pan and bake in a preheated 350°F oven for 35 minutes or until it pulls away from the sides of the baking pan.

YIELD: 4 SERVINGS OR ENOUGH TO STUFF A ROASTER CHICKEN OR 2 GAME HENS

CHESTNUT STUFFING

Chestnut trees were everywhere until the blight of the early 1900s. Since then they have become quite a delicacy. Available, canned, from France, they are expensive but worth every penny. If you are lucky enough to find them in the markets, enjoy them with any kind of poultry. To prepare the raw ones, make a slit on the side of the shell, cover with water and boil for 15 minutes. Peel and remove the paper-thin skin while warm.

3 cups boiled or canned chestnuts, drained
4 tablespoons (1/2 stick) butter, melted
1/4 cup light cream or milk
1/2 cup finely broken saltine crackers
1/2 teaspoon salt
1/2 teaspoon coarsely ground white pepper

Coarsely chop the chestnuts in food processor or blender. Add all the other ingredients and blend thoroughly. Pour into a buttered 2-quart casserole and bake in a preheated 350°F oven for 25 minutes or until it pulls away from the sides of the baking dish.

YIELD: 6 SERVINGS OR ENOUGH TO STUFF A 10- TO 12-POUND TURKEY, 1 ROASTER CHICKEN, OR SEVERAL GAME HENS

DRIED FRUIT STUFFING

Every good homemaker had dried fruit to use as snacks, for baking, and just because she couldn't throw anything away. Today they are

easily available and as popular as ever. Serve this instead of a starch with pork, ham, wild game, or turkey.

2 tablespoons (1/4 stick) butter or margarine
1 cup chopped celery
1/2 cup chopped onion
1 teaspoon salt (optional)
1 teaspoon ground black pepper
1 teaspoon chopped fresh chervil
1 teaspoon chopped fresh parsley
1 cup chopped dried fruit
2 cups fresh bread crumbs
1 1/3 cups apple wine or juice

Melt the butter in a large, heavy skillet and sauté the celery and onion over medium heat until clear, about 5 minutes. Add the salt, pepper, chervil, parsley, dried fruit, crumbs, and wine. Stir until blended thoroughly. Pour into a buttered 2-quart baking dish and bake in a preheated 350°F oven for about 30 minutes or until it pulls away from the sides of the baking dish or pan.

YIELD: 4 SERVINGS, ABOUT 4 CUPS, OR ENOUGH TO STUFF A LARGE BIRD OR SEVERAL GAME HENS

RAISIN-PECAN STUFFING

This can be a great side dish or substitute for a vegetable. Pork, poultry, and seafood dishes are complemented when served with this stuffing.

4 tablespoons (½ stick) butter or
    margarine
1 cup chopped celery
1 cup chopped onion
6 cups fresh bread cubes
1 teaspoon salt
¼ teaspoon ground black pepper
1 teaspoon dried or fresh grated orange
    rind
1 cup raisins
1 cup broken pecans
½ cup chopped fresh parsley
½ cup white wine or apple juice

Melt the butter in a large, heavy skillet and
sauté the celery and onion over medium heat
until the onion is clear, about 6 minutes. Add
the bread cubes, salt, pepper, grated rind, raisins, pecans, parsley, and wine. Heat thoroughly, then pour into a buttered 2½-quart
baking dish. Bake in a preheated 350°F oven
for 30 minutes or until golden brown and pulls
away from the sides of the baking dish.

YIELD: 6 SERVINGS, ABOUT 6 CUPS. ENOUGH
TO STUFF A SMALL TURKEY OR ROASTER
CHICKEN, DUCK, OR SEVERAL GAME BIRDS

MOIST BREAD STUFFING

Whether you call it dressing, filling, or stuffing, this is the old standby.

6 cups fresh bread cubes, half brown bread,
    half white bread
3 large eggs, lightly beaten
Pinch of saffron threads
1 cup milk

½ cup chopped celery
⅓ cup chopped onion
1 teaspoon salt
½ teaspoon ground black pepper
4 tablespoons (½ stick) butter, melted

Place bread cubes in a large bowl. Pour the
beaten eggs over them. Crush the saffron and
sprinkle over bread. Add all the other ingredients and toss gently as you would a salad, not
pressing the cubes together. Spoon into a
greased baking pan or dish and bake in a preheated 350°F oven for 30 to 35 minutes or
until golden brown on top. This freezes well
after baking and will keep at least 6 weeks if
properly wrapped or covered.

YIELD: 6 SERVINGS. ENOUGH TO STUFF A 10-
POUND TURKEY, 2 PHEASANTS, 2 CHICKENS,
OR 4 GAME HENS

PECAN BREADING

This is an excellent breading for seafood or
chicken. Make it ahead and store in an air-tight
container in the refrigerator. It will keep for at
least 4 weeks.

1 cup fresh bread crumbs
1 cup cornmeal
1 cup pecans

Place everything in a food processor or blender
and blend until the pecans are finely ground.
Store in refrigerator or freezer until needed.

YIELD: 3 CUPS

Chapter 9

Breads, Biscuits, Buns, and Muffins

WHITE BREAD

Bread baking is one of the most satisfying and rewarding things you can do in the kitchen. It's fascinating to watch the rising, fun for children, and irresistible when taken from the oven. Better yet, the kitchen smells WONDERFUL!

2 packages dry granular yeast or 2 yeast
  cakes
1/4 cup lukewarm water
Pinch of granulated sugar
2 cups milk, scalded
1 1/2 tablespoons granulated sugar
2 teaspoons salt
3 tablespoons butter
2 large eggs, lightly beaten
7 cups sifted all-purpose flour
1 teaspoon butter

Proof the yeast by combining it with the lukewarm water and pinch of sugar. If it foams, it is active and ready. Cool the milk to lukewarm, place in a large mixing bowl, and add the sugar, salt, and butter. Slowly add the yeast mixture, the beaten eggs and about 2 cups of the sifted flour. Cover with a damp cloth and let rise until double, about 30 minutes, in a warm, draft-free area. Then, punch down the dough and add the remaining flour, kneading until the dough is smooth and elastic. Place in greased bowl and let rise again until double, about 30 minutes, in a warm, draft-free place. Knead or punch down the dough to remove all the air bubbles. Cut into thirds and form into 3 loaves. Place the loaves in greased 9-by-5-by-3-inch loaf pans. Cover and let rise again until double. Bake in a preheated 375°F oven for 35 minutes. The loaves are fully baked when they sound hollow when tapped. Lightly butter the

tops, remove from the pans immediately and serve warm or at room temperature. If freezing, place the loaf in a plastic bag while slightly warm to insure that it retains all its moisture when thawed.

YIELD: THREE 9-BY-5-BY-3-INCH LOAVES

Variations: Herb Bread: Add your favorite chopped fresh herbs, approximately ¼ cup, with the last addition of flour. Fresh dill, chives, parsley, chopped scallions, and oregano are some of my favorites, but try your own combination.
Whole-wheat Bread: Substitute whole or cracked wheat flour (stone-ground flour is best, if available) for half of the white flour. Use only 1 egg and add ¼ cup honey when stirring in the egg.

OLD-FASHIONED OATMEAL BREAD

I receive letters from all over the country praising this bread recipe. A friend, Blanche, shared this with me many years ago and it remains the best ever.

1¾ cups boiling water
1 cup rolled (quick-cooking) oats
5⅓ tablespoons (⅔ stick) butter or
    margarine
½ cup table molasses (golden, barrel, or
    King Syrup), do not use baking molasses
1 tablespoon salt
2 packages dry granular yeast or 2 yeast
    cakes
¼ cup lukewarm water
Pinch of granulated sugar
2 large eggs, lightly beaten
6 cups sifted all-purpose flour

Combine the boiling water, rolled oats, butter, molasses, and salt in a large mixing bowl. Cool to lukewarm. While cooling, proof the yeast by adding it to the lukewarm water with the sugar. If it foams, it is active. Add to the lukewarm oat mixture and blend well. Gradually stir in the eggs and flour. The dough will be stickier than regular bread dough. Pour into a greased bowl, cover with a damp cloth and place in the refrigerator for at least 2 hours or until needed. Remove the chilled dough and knead about 2 minutes to remove air bubbles. Divide into two and shape into loaves on a well-floured surface. Generously grease two 8½-by-4½-inch pans and sprinkle extra rolled oats around their bottoms and sides (the extra oats are optional but give the bread a special look). Place the loaves into the greased pans.

Cover with a damp cloth and let rise in a warm, draft-free place until double in bulk, approximately 2 hours. Bake in a preheated 375°F oven for 45 to 50 minutes or until done. The bread should pull away from the sides of the pan. Remove from pans at once and serve warm.

YIELD: TWO 8½-BY-4½-INCH LOAVES

POTATO BREAD

This bread is filled with nutrition and flavor.

2 packages dry granular yeast or 2 yeast
*   cakes*
¼ cup lukewarm water
Pinch of granulated sugar
2 cups cooked mashed potatoes (save the
*   water they were cooked in)*
1 cup potato water or lukewarm water
1 cup milk, scalded
1½ tablespoons salt (more or less as
*   desired)*
3 tablespoons butter
2 tablespoons light brown sugar
2 tablespoons granulated sugar
2 large eggs, lightly beaten
5½ to 6 cups sifted all-purpose flour
1½ tablespoons butter, melted

Proof the yeast by dissolving it in the lukewarm water with the pinch of sugar; if it foams, it is active. Combine the mashed potatoes, potato water, milk, salt, butter, sugars, and beaten eggs in a large mixing bowl. Stir in the yeast mixture and 2 cups of the flour. Knead on a floured board or counter until smooth. Cover with a damp cloth and place in a warm, draft-free area until double in bulk, approximately 30 minutes. Punch down and add the remaining flour. Knead until smooth and elastic. Put in a well-greased bowl, turning the dough so it is greased on all sides. Cover with a damp cloth and let double again, approximately 30 minutes. Divide into three parts and form into loaves. Place the loaves in 3 well-greased 8½-by-4½-inch loaf pans and bake in a preheated 375°F oven for 45 to 50 minutes or until done. The bread should pull away from the sides of pan and sound hollow when tapped with fingers. Brush the tops of the loaves with butter for a soft, shiny look and remove from pans immediately.

YIELD: THREE 8½-BY-4½-INCH LOAVES

CORNBREAD

My family often serves warm cornbread and fresh, pitted and sweetened, sour cherries with milk or cream as a luncheon dish. When we bake it with floured fruit, we call it "corn-pone." So versatile, cornbread can be made in cake pans, muffin tins, or the iron molds resembling ears of corn. After one day, cornbread makes an excellent stuffing, or when dried, the crumbs are very flavorful for topping vegetables.

1½ cups cornmeal
1 cup all-purpose flour
¼ cup lightly packed light brown sugar
1 teaspoon salt
2 teaspoons baking soda
¼ pound (1 stick) butter, or half butter
  and half margarine, melted
2 large eggs, lightly beaten
1 cup milk
½ cup sour cream

Sift the cornmeal, flour, brown sugar, salt, and baking soda together. Place the butter and eggs in a large mixing bowl. Alternately mix in the flour mixture, milk, and sour cream, beating until just blended. Do not overbeat. Pour into a greased 9-inch square cake pan or molds.

Bake in a preheated 375°F oven for about 30 minutes or until a toothpick, when inserted into the thickest part of the bread, comes out clean. Cool slightly before removing from the pans. If using cast-iron molds, invert on cooling rack.

YIELD: 9-INCH SQUARE PAN, 18 MUFFINS, OR 24 GEMS FROM IRON MOLDS

Variation: For cornbread cubes, cut cornbread into 1-inch squares and place on cookie sheets. Bake in a preheated 275°F oven for about 12 minutes. These freeze well.

BUTTERMILK BISCUITS

These biscuits are as light as feathers. If you do not have buttermilk, add 1 tablespoon cider vinegar to 1 cup milk.

2 cups all-purpose flour
1 tablespoon granulated sugar
4 teaspoons baking powder
½ teaspoon salt
½ cup vegetable shortening
1 large egg, lightly beaten
⅔ cup buttermilk

Sift the flour, sugar, baking powder, and salt together in a large mixing bowl. Cut in the shortening with a fork or pastry blender. Stir in the egg and buttermilk, mixing thoroughly. Knead lightly on a floured surface and pat or roll to about ¾-inch thickness. Cut into desired shapes, flouring the cutter each time after cutting. Place on an ungreased baking sheet and bake in a preheated 400°F oven for 12 to 14 minutes or until golden brown. Serve warm.

YIELD: 16 BISCUITS

Variation: Brush the tops with melted butter and sprinkle with cinnamon sugar.
Cheese Biscuits: Add 1 cup grated Cheddar to the batter.

1–2–3–4 BISCUITS

My mother told me I could bake these as soon as I could count. They are so easy and good, you'll try them too.

2 cups all-purpose flour
4 teaspoons baking powder
1/2 teaspoon salt
3 tablespoons vegetable shortening
1 cup milk

Sift the dry ingredients into a large bowl. Cut in the shortening with a pastry blender or your hands until you have fine crumbs. Pour in the milk and stir until well blended. Turn dough onto a floured surface, knead for one minute and roll or pat to about 3/4 inch thick. Cut with a floured cutter and place on an ungreased baking sheet. Bake in a preheated 400°F oven for 12 to 15 minutes or until lightly brown on top. Serve warm. (Brush the tops with butter if desired.)

YIELD: 16 BISCUITS

GRAHAM ICE BOX ROLL

A perfect dessert to make and store in the refrigerator for "spur of the moment" entertaining.

24 graham crackers (3-inch square)
1 cup coarsely chopped or broken nuts
1 cup chopped dates
1/4 teaspoon salt
3 cups miniature marshmallows or 20
*   regular ones cut in small pieces*
1/2 cup milk
1 cup Whipped Cream (page 170; optional)

Roll the crackers between 2 sheets of wax paper to make fine crumbs (a food processor works well). The reason I use crackers instead of packaged crumbs is because crumbs tend to be drier. Reserve about 1/3 of the crumbs for coating the finished roll. Combine the crumbs, nuts, dates, salt, and marshmallows in a large mixing bowl. Moisten with milk and stir until blended. Form into a roll about 3 to 3 1/2 inches in diameter, packing firmly. Roll in the reserved crumbs and wrap tightly in plastic wrap. Chill in the refrigerator for several hours or until needed. To serve, cut into 1-inch slices and top with whipped cream.

YIELD: 6 TO 8 SERVINGS

MOTHER'S ICE BOX ROLLS

Mother often served these instead of bread when she entertained. They're great!

1 package dry granular yeast or yeast cakes
2 tablespoons lukewarm water
Pinch of granulated sugar
1 cup boiling water
¼ cup granulated sugar
½ teaspoon salt (less if desired)
1 tablespoon vegetable shortening
1 large egg, lightly beaten
2½ cups all-purpose flour
1 tablespoon butter or vegetable shortening

Proof the yeast by dissolving it in the lukewarm water and adding the pinch of sugar. If it foams, it's active and ready. Mix the boiling water with the sugar, salt, and shortening in a large mixing bowl. Let cool to lukewarm and add the yeast mixture and beaten egg. Gradually stir in the flour until well blended. Do not knead. Turn into a large, greased bowl, cover with a damp cloth and refrigerate overnight or for at least 4 hours. With buttered hands, mold the dough into balls and place in greased muffin pans. Cover with a damp cloth and let stand in a warm, draft-free area until doubled, approximately 2 hours. Bake in a preheated 400°F oven for 12 to 15 minutes. Brush the tops with the butter or shortening and remove from the pans immediately. If freezing, place in heavy plastic bags and freeze while still warm.

YIELD: 15 TO 17 ROLLS

GRACE'S MUFFINS

Grace Knepper of Somerset County, Pennsylvania, gave lots to her church and community but she was best known for the food she prepared for family and friends. These muffins were one of her favorites—the recipe was adapted continuously to take advantage of the bounty of every season.

2 cups sifted all-purpose flour
1 teaspoon salt
1 tablespoon granulated sugar
4 teaspoons baking powder
1 large egg, lightly beaten
1 cup milk or water
¼ cup vegetable shortening, melted

Sift the dry ingredients together and blend lightly with the liquid and the beaten egg. Fold in the melted shortening and stir until just blended, about 30 seconds. *Do not* overblend. Fill well-greased muffin cups half full and bake in a preheated 400°F oven for 20 minutes or until lightly browned on top.

YIELD: 12 TO 16 REGULAR-SIZE MUFFINS OR 24 MINI MUFFINS

Variations: Blueberry: Add 1 scant cup of blueberries, washed, drained, and dredged in flour. Sprinkle 1 tablespoon of sugar over the berries if they are not sweet.

Cheese: Add 4 tablespoons grated Cheddar cheese and a dash of paprika. Top the muffins with grated cheese.

Cranberry: Add 1 cup cranberries, washed, stemmed, dredged in 2 tablespoons flour and 3 tablespoons granulated sugar.

Date: Add ½ cup finely cut dates and 1 teaspoon vanilla extract.

Holiday: Add ½ cup mixed candied fruit, ¼ cup currants, and ¼ cup chopped pecans.

BRAN MUFFINS

These are popular everywhere and it seems each area has a special name for them. Nevertheless, a cookbook shouldn't be without them.

½ cup boiling water
½ cup 100% Natural Bran Cereal
¼ cup vegetable shortening
¾ cup granulated sugar
1 large egg, lightly beaten
1 cup buttermilk
1¼ cups unsifted all-purpose flour
1¼ teaspoons baking soda
¼ teaspoon salt
1 cup All Bran

Pour the boiling water over the bran and let stand. In a large mixing bowl, cream the shortening and sugar together. Add the eggs, buttermilk, and then the 100% Natural Bran. Mix the flour, soda, salt, and All Bran together in another large mixing bowl. Next add the 100% Natural Bran mixture all at once. Fold only until the dry ingredients are just moistened. Let stand for at least 30 minutes. Fill greased muffin tins ⅔ full and bake in a preheated 400°F oven for 15 to 20 minutes or until golden brown on top. Bake only as many as you need for a serving. Refrigerate the remainder of the batter and add your favorite extras. This batter keeps for weeks if tightly covered.

YIELD: 15 MUFFINS

Variations: Add ⅓ cup raisins, chopped nuts, or dried fruits to the batter before baking.

STICKY BUNS

These are beautiful and dainty if made very small, but most people go wild when they get the chance to sink their teeth into a great big one! The Pennsylvania Dutch call these *Schneckenhaus'ln* (little snail houses) because they look like snails.

1 recipe Basic Sweet Dough (page 191)
4 tablespoons (½ stick) melted butter or
*   margarine*
½ cup lightly packed light brown sugar
1½ teaspoons ground cinnamon
2 tablespoons granulated sugar
⅓ cup light corn syrup (I use Karo)
½ cup coarsely chopped English walnuts or
*   pecans*
½ cup seedless raisins

Divide the dough in half and roll out into rectangles about 13 by 9 inches. Combine the melted butter, brown sugar, cinnamon, granulated sugar, and corn syrup. Spread over the dough and sprinkle with the chopped nuts and raisins or have one with nuts and the other with raisins. Roll up jelly-roll fashion and cut into 1½-to-2-inch thick slices. Place on a greased baking pan or sheet or in greased muffin cups. Cover and let rise in a warm, draft-free place until almost double, about 30 minutes. Bake in a preheated 350°F oven for 25 minutes or until golden brown. Turn upside down onto wax paper immediately after removing from the oven. This gives the syrup a chance to run around the sides of the buns.

YIELD: 12 LARGE, 18 MEDIUM-SIZE, OR 24 TINY BUNS

HOT CROSS BUNS

Historic Donegal Presbyterian Church, founded before 1721, serves a lovely breakfast after the Easter Sunrise Service. We all look forward to the tasty hot cross buns served with the traditional baked ham and eggs and all the trimmings. The congregation enjoys sharing this day with visitors, so if you are in the area, do make plans to join us at Donegal. You are always welcome.

1 teaspoon ground cinnamon
¼ teaspoon ground cloves
1 cup dried currants
½ cup finely cut candied citron
1 recipe Basic Sweet Dough (page 191)

1 large egg, lightly beaten
2 cups sifted confectioners sugar
¼ cup milk
1 teaspoon vanilla extract
Pinch of salt

Mix the cinnamon, cloves, currants, and citron together until blended, then add to dough. After first rising, shape the dough into round buns and place them in two well-greased 13-by-9-by-2-inch pans. Cover lightly and let rise until double, about 45 minutes. Brush the tops with the beaten egg. Make a cross on each bun with a sharp knife. Bake in a preheated 400°F oven for 20 minutes. While buns are baking, combine the sugar, milk, vanilla, and salt until well blended. Remove the buns to a cooling rack and brush the cross markings with the confectioners sugar mixture. Serve warm.

YIELD: 36 BUNS

CORNMEAL MUSH

The Pennsylvania Dutch often serve hot mush with milk and sugar as a light meal. They always make a large amount so they may enjoy "fried mush" the following day. While the mush is hot, it is poured into a buttered loaf pan, usually a 9-by-3-inch bread pan to cool. When cold, it is sliced into ½-inch thick slices, dredged lightly in all-purpose flour (about ½ cup), and fried in oil or butter over medium heat for about 6 minutes on each side or until it is crisp and golden brown. Served with molasses or maple syrup, it is excellent for a hot breakfast or brunch.

1½ teaspoons salt
2½ cups cornmeal
½ cup all-purpose flour
2 cups cold water
6 cups boiling water

Combine the salt, cornmeal, and flour in a large mixing bowl. Whisk in the cold water, mixing until smooth and thoroughly blended. Pour the boiling water into the top of a large double boiler and slowly whisk in the cornmeal mixture over simmering water set over medium heat. Stir until all lumps are dissolved. Continue to cook over medium heat for at least one hour, stirring every 15 minutes. Reduce the heat to low and continue cooking slowly for another 1½ hours, stirring every 30 minutes. Serve the hot mush in deep soup bowls with milk and granulated sugar for pouring over the top, as you would serve oatmeal. To make mush for frying, pour the hot mush into a buttered 9-by-3-inch loaf pan to cool.

YIELD: 6 SERVINGS

SOFT PRETZELS

Making your own pretzels is a real labor of love. It can also be an excuse for a party. Why not have a get-together and let guests twist their own? There are many legends about the pretzel but I like the one that claims they were a monk's gift to the children for learning their prayers. They really taste best when taken right from the oven, or at least kept warm until served. Salted or unsalted, they're enjoyed by most folks with a mustard or cheese spread for dipping.

½ cup warm water (105°F to 115°F)
1 package (1 tablespoon) dry yeast
1 cup milk
¼ cup honey or granulated sugar
4 tablespoons (½ stick) butter or vegetable
    shortening, at room temperature
1 large egg, separated
1 teaspoon salt
4½ to 5 cups all-purpose flour
8 cups water
8 tablespoons baking soda
¼ cup coarse salt (optional)

Place warm water in a small bowl and add the yeast. Let stand for about 10 minutes until it foams. Stir until dissolved and pour into a large mixing bowl. Add the milk, honey, butter, egg yolk, and salt. Slowly add the flour until the dough is stiff enough to knead. Place on a floured surface and knead by pressing the heel of your hand into the dough and rolling it over again and again for about 5 minutes. Cover with a towel and let the dough rise on the board for one hour. Pinch off dough the size of golf balls. Roll with the palms of your hands into strips about 18 inches long and ½ inch thick. Twist each into a shape and place on a tray. Preheat the oven to 425°F. Bring the water and baking soda to a boil in a large stainless steel saucepan or kettle (the baking soda will stain an aluminum pan) over high heat. Drop three pretzels at a time into the boiling water, making sure they do not touch each other, boiling for about ½ minute over high heat—be careful, they will become soggy if overcooked. Remove the pretzels with a slotted spoon and place them on greased cookie sheets. When all are cooked, lightly beat the egg white and 1 tablespoon water together with a fork. With a pastry brush, cover the top of each pretzel with the egg white mixture. Sprinkle with a small amount of coarse salt, if desired, and bake for 13 to 15 minutes or until golden brown. Remove from the oven and cool slightly on baking racks or linen towels. For reheating, tent with foil and warm in a preheated 350°F oven for 6 minutes.

YIELD: 18 FOUR-INCH PRETZELS OR 24 THREE-INCH PRETZELS

Chapter 10

Cobblers, Pies, Cakes, and Icings

APRICOT COBBLER

This is the kind of fruit cobbler I make most often. My family used this recipe for the first sour cherries and followed through the year with every kind of fresh fruit in season. We always served it in bowls with plenty of fresh, sweetened milk.

Fruit mixture:

1/2 to 3/4 cup granulated sugar
1 tablespoon cornstarch
1 cup boiling water or canned fruit juice, such as apricot, peach, or pineapple
3 cups apricot halves (canned or fresh)
1 tablespoon butter
1/4 teaspoon ground cinnamon
1/8 teaspoon ground nutmeg

Pastry:

1 cup all-purpose flour
1 tablespoon granulated sugar
1 1/2 teaspoons baking powder
1/2 teaspoon salt
3 tablespoons butter, melted
1/2 cup milk

Mix the sugar and cornstarch together and add to the water or juice in a large, heavy saucepan. Bring to a boil and simmer over medium heat 1 minute. Add the fruit, butter, and spices, stirring until heated through, about 5 minutes. Pour into a buttered 1 1/2-quart baking dish. Sift the flour, sugar, baking powder, and salt together in a large mixing bowl. Beat in the butter and milk until well blended. Spoon the batter over the fruit and bake in a preheated

400°F oven for 30 minutes or until golden on top. Serve hot or warm.

YIELD: 4 TO 6 SERVINGS

HINT: Any type of canned or fresh fruit can be substituted, if you make sure the pits are removed.

PEACH COBBLER

Use any fruit you choose, but this is the old-fashioned style cobbler.

Pastry:

3½ cups all-purpose flour
1 teaspoon salt
1 teaspoon baking powder
¼ pound (1 stick) butter or margarine
½ cup vegetable shortening
½ cup cold water

Fruit mixture:

8 peaches, or 4 cups, halved, pitted, peeled,
*   and sliced ⅓ inch thick*
⅛ teaspoon ground cinnamon
⅛ teaspoon ground nutmeg
½ cup granulated sugar
½ cup lightly packed light brown sugar
2 tablespoons (¼ stick) butter, melted

Cut the flour, salt, baking powder, butter, and shortening together in large mixing bowl until it forms fine crumbs. Add the water gradually until the dough is moistened and can be formed into a ball. Roll out ⅛ inch thick—

enough to top the cobbler—and set aside. Roll out the rest of the dough about ¼ inch thick and place on an ungreased cookie sheet. Cut it into 2-inch squares and bake in a preheated 350°F oven for 8 to 10 minutes. Do not let them brown.

In a greased 9-by-13-inch cake pan or baking dish, place several of the squares of dough. Combine the peaches with the cinnamon, nutmeg, and sugars. Layer the peaches and the dough squares, ending with peaches. Dribble with the melted butter and top with the unbaked crust. Slit or cut a design into the crust to allow steam to escape. Bake in a preheated 350°F oven for 1 hour or until the filling bubbles around the edges. Serve warm with milk, sweetened if desired.

YIELD: 4 TO 6 SERVINGS

Variation: Use any type of fruit, peeled or unpeeled, with pits removed.

BASIC PIE DOUGH

I like to make a large quantity of these crumbs. I only use the amount I need for the day by adding the water and refrigerate the rest. Usually the amount of crumbs you can hold in both hands together is enough for one crust. These crumbs will keep in refrigerator for at least 4 weeks if tightly covered.

½ cup fresh lard or vegetable shortening
4 tablespoons (½ stick) butter
¾ teaspoon salt
2½ cups all-purpose flour
About ⅓ cup ice water

Put shortening, butter, salt, and flour into a large bowl. Cut with a pastry blender or rub with your hands until they are fine crumbs. Carefully dribble water evenly over the crumbs with one hand while tossing the crumbs lightly with the other. Use only enough water to hold the dough together. As the dough becomes moist, gently press it to the side of the bowl. The less it is handled, the flakier it will be. If you are using a food processor, add the water cautiously, watching for the moment it starts to form a ball. Generously flour the board or counter, making sure the top and bottom of the dough are floured. Pat the edges of the dough before rolling (this will prevent an uneven crust when baking). Roll out the dough about ⅛ inch thick, moving the rolling pin lightly until the round crust is about an inch larger than the pie pan. Place the dough in the pan, cutting off any excess dough. Crimp the edges with your fingers or a pastry crimper.

If making patty shells, roll out the dough into a large rectangle. Use a 3-inch round cutter to cut the circles of pastry. Press each circle gently into a muffin cup. Crimp the edges in your favorite fashion.

If making pastry squares, roll out the dough onto a large cookie sheet. Cut the dough with a crinkle cutter in the form of squares or diamonds.

Keep the pieces of excess dough in plastic wrap, keeping it moist until you are ready to roll it out. Do not use the dough over and over again or it will become dry and tough.

To bake the pie or patty shells, prick the dough four or five times with a fork to prevent it from shrinking while baking. Bake in a preheated 350°F oven for approximately 10 minutes for a prebaked shell or 20 minutes for a fully baked shell. If the pastry puffs during baking, gently press the bubbles with the back of a soup or serving spoon. Before removing the baked shells from the oven, check for any trace of fat bubbles. If you find any, bake a bit longer or until they disappear. Fully baked shells must be dry, light golden, and flaky.

To bake pastry squares, set in the oven until they puff and are golden brown. They should be crisp and flaky.

YIELD: ENOUGH DOUGH FOR TWO 9-INCH PIE SHELLS, ONE DOUBLE CRUST OR 10 PATTY SHELLS

BAKING POWDER CRUST

This crust is really flaky and great for meat pies or apple dumplings.

2½ cups all-purpose flour
2 tablespoons baking powder
1 teaspoon salt
4 tablespoons (½ stick) butter or
    margarine
¼ cup lard or vegetable shortening
1 cup milk

Blend flour, baking powder, salt, butter, and shortening with pastry blender or with the hands. Gradually add the milk until it forms a soft ball. Roll out a bit thicker than regular pie dough on a well-floured board.

YIELD: ENOUGH DOUGH FOR TWO 9-INCH PIE CRUSTS OR TO COVER A 9-BY-13-INCH BAKING DISH

AMISH VANILLA PIE

Abe's mother, Elizabeth, makes the best vanilla pies. Even though they are Mennonites, the recipe is still the same. It is one of the dessert favorites here at Groff's Farm Restaurant because it is lighter than shoo-fly pie—more like pecan pie without the nuts. While you're at it, make two—they freeze well.

1 cup table molasses (golden, barrel, or
    King Syrup—do not use baking molasses)
½ cup granulated sugar
1 large egg, slightly beaten

2 tablespoons all-purpose flour
½ teaspoon salt
2 cups hot water
1 teaspoon vanilla extract
2 unbaked 9-inch pie shells

Crumb topping:

1 cup granulated sugar
¼ pound (1 stick) butter
2 cups all-purpose flour
½ teaspoon baking soda
½ teaspoon cream of tartar

Combine the molasses, sugar, egg, flour, and salt in a 1-quart saucepan and mix well. Gradually add the hot water and cook over medium heat until thickened about 6 minutes, stirring constantly. Remove from the heat and add the vanilla. Cool and pour into the unbaked pie shells.

To make the crumb topping, mix all the ingredients together in a large bowl, cutting with pastry blender or rubbing by hand until the mixture forms fine crumbs. Divide them in half, spreading evenly over each pie. Bake in preheated 375°F oven for 10 minutes. Then reduce the heat to 350°F and bake about 30 minutes or until the center doesn't shake when jiggled. Serve warm or at room temperature.

YIELD: TWO 9-INCH PIES

MILK PIE

This pie was always eaten as a snack because it was made with the dough left over from making several pies. Some called it sugar pie,

Johnny pie, or, I suppose, the name of any child enjoying it.

1/2 cup all-purpose flour
3/4 cup granulated sugar (less if desired)
1 cup milk
1/2 cup half and half
1 unbaked 9-inch pie shell
1 tablespoon butter, melted
Several dashes of ground cinnamon and
   nutmeg

Combine the flour and sugar. Gradually whip in the milk and cream until smooth. Pour into the pie shell, dribble the top with the melted butter and sprinkle with the cinnamon and nutmeg. Bake in preheated 350°F oven for about one hour, or until the center is set and doesn't shake when the pie is jiggled. Serve warm.

YIELD: ONE 9-INCH PIE

CHOCOLATE CREAM PIE

Cream fillings are great because you can put some in a bowl to serve separately, and fill a baked shell with the other half.

1/2 cup unsweetened cocoa
1/2 cup boiling water
4 tablespoons (1/2 stick) butter, melted
1 cup granulated sugar
1/3 cup cornstarch
1/4 teaspoon salt
3 cups milk, warmed
1 large egg, lightly beaten
1 teaspoon vanilla extract
2 baked 9-inch pie shells
Whipped Cream (page 170) or shaved milk
   or dark chocolate for topping

Stir the cocoa into the boiling water until it's a smooth paste. Stir about 3 tablespoons of the melted butter into cocoa mixture. Combine the sugar, cornstarch, and salt in a 2-quart saucepan. Slowly add the warm milk and stir until blended. Add the cocoa mixture and beaten egg. Cook over medium-low heat, stirring constantly until thick but not boiling. Remove and add the rest of the melted butter and the vanilla. Pour into baked pie shells. When cool, pipe edge with whipped cream or top with shaved chocolate.

YIELD: TWO 9-INCH PIES OR 5 CUPS

Variation: Chocolate Pudding: Follow the above recipe but use 1/4 cup cornstarch. When done, pour into dish and top with whipped cream or shaved chocolate.

APPLE PIE

There are so many ways to serve apple pie that I'll leave it up to your own creative mind. We enjoy deep-dish apple pie with milk as a summer meal, but who could refuse a piece of apple pie with coffee in the morning? It sure beats eating filled doughnuts for breakfast.

Unbaked top and bottom crust for 9-inch
  pie (page 149)
½ cup granulated sugar
3 tablespoons all-purpose flour
⅓ teaspoon salt
½ teaspoon ground cinnamon
¼ teaspoon ground nutmeg
3½ to 4 cups sliced tart apples (Stayman,
  Granny, or Smokehouse), cored, peeled,
  and sliced
½ teaspoon grated lemon rind
1 tablespoon fresh lemon juice
½ cup sour cream or milk
2 tablespoons (¼ stick) butter, melted

Roll out the bottom pie crust, fit into a 9-inch pie pan, and trim the edges without crimping. Puff in a preheated 350°F oven for 5 minutes or until the dough puffs (do not fully bake!) to prevent a soggy crust. Remove from the oven immediately. Combine the sugar, flour, salt, cinnamon, and nutmeg and toss with the sliced apples. Add the lemon rind, lemon juice, and sour cream, stirring until well blended. Pour into the shell, roll out the top crust, and slit it with your own design to let the steam escape. Moisten the edges of the bottom crust with milk or water. Place the top crust over the pie and crimp the edges together to seal. Bake in a preheated 350°F oven for 50 minutes. Increase the heat to 375°F and let bake another

10 minutes or until golden on top. Some of the juice should bubble through the slits and around edges. Serve warm or cold.

YIELD: ONE 9-INCH PIE

LEMON MERINGUE PIE

This is my favorite pie. As a child I really thought the meringue was magic, as it always had a few drops of gold on top, formed by the sugar melting when baked in the meringue. Later I found out it was caused by the pie "weeping" and considered undesirable by professional bakers. You couldn't make me believe that, because I liked it when a bit of the sticky meringue would stick to the tip of my nose as I was eating a big, high piece of pie.

¼ cup cornstarch
2 cups water
1 cup granulated sugar
3 large eggs, separated
Grated rind and juice of 2 lemons
1 tablespoon butter
¼ teaspoon salt
1 baked 9-inch pie shell
1 recipe Great Meringue (page 170)

Dissolve the cornstarch in ½ cup of the water. Pour the rest of the water into the top of a double boiler and bring to a boil over boiling water. Add the dissolved cornstarch and sugar, bring to a boil, and cook over medium heat until thickened, about 10 minutes, stirring constantly. Beat the egg yolks lightly with a fork, add in several tablespoons of the cornstarch mixture, and beat until well blended. Then add the beaten eggs to the cornstarch mixture and cook together over medium heat for 2 minutes. Remove from the heat and add the lemon rind and juice, butter, and salt, blending well. Cool to lukewarm while making the meringue and pour into the baked pie shell. Spread the meringue evenly over the filling, touching all around the edges. Swirl and peak with the back of a spoon. Place on the middle rack under a preheated broiler and broil for a few seconds, only enough to brown the peaks a light gold. Let cool to room temperature.

YIELD: ONE 9-INCH PIE

BANANA CREAM PIE

Abe can make one of these pies disappear in the blink of an eye—I guess that's why our grandsons call the dessert cart "Pop's Cart."

2 cups milk
²⁄₃ cup granulated sugar
½ teaspoon salt
3 tablespoons cornstarch
3 large eggs, separated
1½ tablespoons butter
1 teaspoon vanilla extract
1½ cups sliced bananas
1 tablespoon fresh lemon juice
1 baked 9-inch pie shell
1 recipe Great Meringue (page 170)

Scald 1½ cups of milk on top of a double boiler over simmering but not boiling water. Combine sugar, salt, and cornstarch with the

remaining milk and stir until dissolved. Add this to the hot milk and bring to a boil over boiling water; lower heat to medium and cook until thickened. Beat the egg yolks lightly with a fork, then add several tablespoons of the milk mixture and beat into the yolks until well blended. Add the eggs to the milk mixture and cook together over medium heat for 2 minutes. Remove from the heat and stir in the butter and vanilla. Toss the sliced bananas with the lemon juice to keep them from getting brown. Spread a thin layer of the filling in the bottom of the pie shell, then the sliced bananas. Top with the rest of the filling and let cool while making the meringue. Top with the meringue and slip under a preheated broiler until gold. Let cool and enjoy!

YIELD: ONE 9-INCH PIE

Variation: Coconut Cream Pie: Follow the above recipe but omit the lemon juice and bananas. Use 1¼ cup shredded coconut instead, folding it in with the butter and vanilla.

MONTGOMERY PIE

Historic Donegal Presbyterian Church could not have their traditional "Donegal Day" without serving this pie. Now that Abe and I are members of Donegal, we're often asked to bring some of them for the picnic. It's similar to shoo-fly pie, but with a gooey lemon bottom and white cake top.

2 unbaked 9-inch pie shells

Bottom:

Grated rind and juice of 1 lemon
½ cup granulated sugar
½ cup table molasses (golden, barrel, or King Syrup), not baking molasses
1 large egg, lightly beaten
1 tablespoon all-purpose flour
1 cup boiling water

Top:

1 cup granulated sugar
¼ cup vegetable shortening
1 large egg
1½ cups all-purpose flour
2 teaspoons baking powder
½ teaspoon salt
½ cup milk

Combine all the ingredients for the bottom part of the pies in a 1-quart saucepan and bring to a boil over medium heat, stirring until thickened, about 10 minutes. Cool a bit, then pour into the pie shells. For the top part, cream the sugar and shortening together in a large mixing bowl until fluffy. Add the egg and beat thoroughly. Sift the flour, baking powder, and salt together in a medium-size bowl and add to the egg batter alternately with the milk until well blended. Spoon the batter evenly over the lemon filling and bake in preheated 350°F oven for 45 minutes or until the center does not shake when the pie is jiggled. Serve warm or at room temperature.

YIELD: TWO 9-INCH PIES

RAISIN PIE

Known as "funeral pie" because it was always served to the mourning family and friends after the church service, it most often was made with a latticed top or crumb topping which I thought was too sweet. This recipe is more like a custard, a bit tart and wonderful with a dollop of whipped cream.

1 cup red wine (white will do)
1½ cups seedless raisins
4 tablespoons (½ stick) butter
¾ cup granulated sugar (less if desired)
3 large eggs, lightly beaten
1 teaspoon grated lemon rind
1 tablespoon fresh lemon juice
¼ teaspoon salt
1 teaspoon vanilla extract
1 unbaked 9-inch pie shell

In a saucepan, heat the wine, then add the raisins and let them soak until plump. Cream the butter and sugar in a mixing bowl. Beat in the eggs, lemon rind and juice, salt, and vanilla. The batter may look a bit curdled, but don't worry. Add the raisins and wine, mixing well. Puff the unbaked pie shell by placing it in the oven as you are preheating it to 325°F for approximately 6 minutes. As soon as it puffs, remove it (this will keep the crust from getting soggy) and pour the batter in. Bake in the preheated oven for 50 minutes or until the filling is set. Cool before serving, room temperature is best.

YIELD: ONE 9-INCH PIE

CHERRY CRUMB PIE

Everyone loves our crumb pies and this one is no exception.

1 cup granulated sugar, less if desired
3 tablespoons arrowroot or cornstarch
½ cup water or liquid from canned
  cherries
1 teaspoon fresh lemon juice
½ teaspoon ground cinnamon
2½ cups pitted cherries, fresh, frozen, or
  canned
1 unbaked 9-inch pie shell (puffed in the
  oven for a few minutes; see page 149)
1½ tablespoons butter, melted
½ recipe Crumb Topping (page 171)

Combine the sugar, arrowroot, and water in a saucepan, stirring until dissolved. Bring to a boil and stir over medium heat until slightly thickened, about 3 minutes. Remove from the heat and add the lemon juice, cinnamon, and cherries. Pour into the pie shell and dribble the top with the melted butter. Sprinkle the filling with the crumb topping and bake in a preheated 350°F oven for 45 to 50 minutes or

until the juice starts to bubble through the topping.

YIELD: ONE 9-INCH PIE

Variation: Blueberry Crumb Pie: Substitute blueberries for the cherries and add ½ teaspoon ground nutmeg.

MINCEMEAT PIE

My family had mince pie fall, winter, and spring. We ate it hot for dessert and cold for breakfast. It makes sense to enjoy this as a snack, too, for it is very nutritious. I took the flavor for granted until I tried other people's mincemeat. This is mincemeat with lots of beef. You also must realize that the plain people do not believe in drinking socially, but many of them use liquor in cooking certain important dishes. It really isn't as good without the spirits. Also, make sure you use light table molasses, not baking molasses. Baking molasses is dark, nearly black, and has a strong sulphur taste.

Mincemeat freezes well, so it's best to make a lot at a time.

To make a mincemeat pie:

Pastry for two 9-inch crusts (page 149)
2½ cups mincemeat (see next page)
½ cup red wine or whiskey

Fill the unbaked crust with mincemeat, pour the wine over it, and top with the crust. Seal, slit vents in the top crust, and bake in a preheated 350°F oven for 45 minutes or until the juice bubbles out of the slits on top.

Mincemeat:

2½ pounds lean ground beef
4 cups dried apples, soaked in 3 cups water
 overnight
2½ pounds fresh apples (Stayman,
 Winesap, Smokehouse, or Jonathan),
 peeled, cored, and quartered
2 lemons, quartered and seeded
½ pound raisins
½ pound currants, or more raisins if
 unavailable
1½ cups lightly packed light brown sugar
2 cups table molasses (golden, barrel, or
 King Syrup), not baking molasses
½ cup cider vinegar
1½ cups heavy red wine
½ teaspoon ground cinnamon
½ teaspoon freshly grated nutmeg
½ teaspoon ground cloves
¼ teaspoon ground mace

Cook the meat in a large, heavy skillet over medium heat, breaking it up with a wooden spoon, until all traces of pink are gone, but before it begins to brown. Drain off the fat. Coarsely chop the soaked apples, fresh apples, and lemons, rind and all, in a food processor or grinder. In a large stock pot combine all the ingredients and bring to a boil. Simmer for at least 30 minutes over low heat, stirring occasionally to prevent sticking. It should be the consistency of thick chutney. If you are canning some of this, ladle into hot, sterilized jars and seal immediately with new lids and seals. If you are freezing it, cool first then freeze.

YIELD: ABOUT 16 CUPS

SHOOFLY PIE

This has got to be the best-known pie of the Pennsylvania Dutch.

1 (9-inch) unbaked pie shell

Crumb Topping:

1 cup unsifted flour
½ cup lightly packed light brown sugar
¼ cup vegetable shortening

Liquid Bottom:

1 teaspoon baking soda
1 cup boiling water
1 cup golden table molasses
¼ teaspoon salt

Put the unbaked pie shell in a preheated 350°F oven for about 5 minutes to prevent the bottom from getting soggy. Combine the topping ingredients in a bowl and cut together with a pastry blender or rub with your fingers until the mixture forms fine crumbs. Set aside. Dissolve the baking soda in the water in a large mixing bowl. Add the molasses and salt and blend well. Pour this into the pie shell and sprinkle evenly with the crumb topping. Bake in a preheated 375°F oven for 10 minutes, then reduce the temperature to 350°F and bake for another 30 minutes, or until set (when the pie is given a gentle shake, the top remains firm). Serve warm with whipped cream or ice cream.

YIELD: ONE 9-INCH PIE

PUMPKIN CHIFFON PIE

This is a very light and mild-flavored pumpkin pie.

1 unbaked 10-inch pie shell
1¼ cups cooked pumpkin, drained
3 large eggs, separated
¾ cup lightly packed light brown sugar
1 tablespoon cornstarch
½ teaspoon salt
⅛ teaspoon ground ginger
⅛ teaspoon ground cloves
¼ teaspoon freshly grated nutmeg
¾ teaspoon ground cinnamon
1¼ cups milk, scalded
¼ cup granulated sugar

Put the unbaked pie shell in a preheated 350°F oven for 5 minutes or until the dough puffs (do not fully bake it!) to prevent a soggy crust. Remove from the oven immediately. Put the pumpkin in a large mixing bowl. Beat in the egg yolks, brown sugar, cornstarch, salt, and spices. Gradually stir in the scalded milk, mixing until blended. Whip the egg whites with the sugar in a large mixing bowl until stiff, then fold into the pumpkin mixture. Pour into the pie shell and bake in a preheated 400°F oven for 10 minutes. Reduce the heat to 350°F and continue baking 35 to 40 minutes longer or until the center does not shake when the pie is jiggled. Cool and serve with ice cream or whipped cream.

YIELD: ONE 10-INCH PIE

GOLD CAKE

I often thought my mother made angel food cakes because we used the yolks for noodles, but looking back, I know she loved to bake and we loved to eat all her cakes, especially her gold cake. Frosted with seafoam icing, it seems light. When frosted with chocolate or caramel icing, it is especially rich.

8 tablespoons (1 stick) butter or half
*   margarine and half vegetable shortening*
1½ cups granulated sugar
8 large egg yolks
2¼ cups cake flour
3 teaspoons baking powder
½ teaspoon salt
1 cup milk
½ teaspoon lemon extract
½ teaspoon vanilla extract
Frosting of your choice (see Index)

Cream the butter and sugar together in a large mixing bowl until light and fluffy. Add the yolks and beat thoroughly. Sift the flour, baking powder, and salt together onto a plate or sheet of wax paper. Return to the sifter and sift again. Gradually add the flour mixture and milk alternately to the egg batter and blend until smooth. Stir in the extracts and pour the batter into two greased and floured 9-inch cake pans. Bake in a preheated 350°F oven for 25 to 30 minutes or until a toothpick inserted in the middle of the cake comes out clean. Cool a few minutes before inverting on cooling racks. Frost with your favorite frosting.

YIELD: TWO 9-INCH LAYERS OR ONE 9-BY-13-INCH CAKE

Variation: Orange or Mandarin Orange Cake: Follow above recipe, using 2 teaspoons baking powder and 1 teaspoon baking soda and substituting ½ cup of orange juice for the milk and ½ teaspoon grated orange rind for the vanilla extract. Frost with: Orange Cream Frosting (see page 169).

CRUMB CAKE

To most folks, this would seem to be a coffee cake. To the Pennsylvania Dutch it is a dessert, served right from the oven with canned or poached peaches, pears, or apricots. The fruit is served on the side and the juice is poured over the cake—Wow!

4 cups all-purpose flour
12 tablespoons (1½ sticks) butter or vegetable shortening
2½ cups lightly packed light brown sugar
1 teaspoon ground cinnamon
1 teaspoon ground cloves
2 teaspoons baking soda
1½ cups buttermilk

Blend the flour, butter, sugar, and spices together with a pastry blender or your hands in a large mixing bowl until it makes fine crumbs. Reserve 1½ cups of the crumbs for the topping. Dissolve the soda in the buttermilk and mix with the remaining crumbs until well blended. Pour into 2 greased 9-inch cake pans or one 9-by-11-inch pan and top with the reserved crumbs. Bake in a preheated 350°F oven for 35 to 40 minutes. Do not overbake but it should not shake in the middle when jiggled. Remove and serve warm right from the pan.

YIELD: TWO 9-INCH ROUND CAKES OR ONE 9-BY-11-INCH CAKE

DATE AND NUT CAKE

My Aunt Elizabeth made the best desserts but rarely gave the recipes to strangers, much less tell the real "secrets." I hope you'll enjoy this as much as we do, for it sure brings back memories of great family dinners and celebrations. This is a heavy, moist cake, much like a fruitcake. In her handwriting the recipe says, "Its flavor improves if allowed to stand for a time (Forget you have it)." Later she told me it was because she stored it in the basement (where it was soaked in elderberry wine) for several days or weeks.

¼ pound (1 stick) butter or margarine
1 cup granulated sugar
4 large eggs, separated
1 cup all-purpose flour
2 teaspoons baking powder

1/2 teaspoon salt
1 pound walnuts, chopped
1 pound dates, pitted and chopped
1 teaspoon vanilla extract
Fruit wine or sherry for soaking (optional)

Cream the butter and sugar together in a large mixing bowl until fluffy. Gradually add the egg yolks, beating until light. Sift together the flour, baking powder, and salt. Reserve 1/4 cup of the flour mixture to dredge the nuts and dates. Add the rest of the flour to the egg mixture, beating thoroughly. Fold in the dredged nuts and dates and the vanilla. Beat the egg whites until stiff in a large mixing bowl and fold into the batter. Pour into a greased 9-by-5-by-3-inch loaf pan and bake in a pre-heated 300°F oven for 1 1/2 hours. Insert a wooden skewer into the middle; if it comes out clean, the cake is done. Invert and cool on a cooling rack. When cool, wrap in a piece of cheesecloth or a napkin soaked with wine and place in a plastic container with the lid covered tightly. Every day or two, add a bit more sherry. After 2 weeks, refrigerate, tightly covered, until ready to use.

YIELD: ONE 9-BY-5-BY-3-INCH LOAF CAKE

Variation: Fruit Cake: Use 1/2 pound candied fruit and only 1/2 pound chopped dates.

SAFFRON CAKE

Thelma and Bill Smith are special friends. Bill makes the nicest cookie cutters and Thelma gave me this recipe. She writes it this way:

"We lived in a town that was mostly English and Welsh. The tradition at Christmas was to have and visit friends, neighbors, and relatives. Each visit you always served tea, cookies, and the special treat, Saffron Cake. At Christmas time the druggist would make sure he had plenty of saffron because at that time saffron was sold by weight. Today I can only buy saffron at one food store in our area (Wind Gap, Pa.) and believe it or not, Betty, I must go to the office and they have it in their safe. I, also, must depend on the spice company to put up enough to make it a delicious cake."

2 cups granulated sugar
1/2 pound (2 sticks) butter, at room temperature
3 large eggs, lightly beaten
2 tablespoons grated lemon rind
1 tablespoon baking powder
1/2 teaspoon salt
3 cups all-purpose flour
1/2 dram of saffron threads steeped in 1 scant cup of boiling water for 30 minutes
1 cup raisins
1 cup currants (If currants are not available, substitute white raisins)

In a large mixing bowl, cream the sugar and butter together until light and fluffy. Slowly add the eggs until well blended. Add lemon rind. Sift the baking powder, salt, and flour together. Mix flour and saffron water alternately into the creamed mixture until thoroughly combined. Fold in the raisins and currants. Pour into two greased 9-by-5-by-2 3/4-inch loaf pans. Bake in a preheated 350°F oven for 25 minutes. Reduce heat to 325°F and bake another 25 minutes or until a skewer comes out clean when inserted into the middle of the cake. Cool and store in a cool place, wrapped in wax paper, until ready to serve. Slice in very thin slices as this is a very flavorful cake.

YIELD: TWO 9-BY-5-BY-2¾-INCH LOAVES

COCONUT CAKE

This is the cake we looked forward to enjoying especially at Easter. Grandma loved her sweets and so did we.

5⅓ tablespoons (⅔ stick) butter
⅓ cup vegetable shortening
1 cup granulated sugar
3 large eggs, separated
2½ cups sifted cake flour
2¼ teaspoons baking powder
½ teaspoon salt
⅔ cup milk
1 teaspoon vanilla extract
Boiled Frosting (page 168)
1½ cups shredded coconut

Cream the butter and shortening together in a large mixing bowl. Gradually beat in the sugar, creaming until very light. Add the egg yolks one by one, beating well after each addition. In another bowl, sift the flour, baking powder, and salt together three times. Alternately blend the dry ingredients and milk into the creamed mixture. Beat until smooth, then add the vanilla. Beat the egg whites until stiff but not dry, then fold them into the cake batter, blending but not beating. Pour the batter

into two greased and floured 9-inch layer cake pans and bake in a preheated 375°F oven for approximately 30 minutes or until a toothpick inserted into the cake's center comes out clean. Remove and cool a few minutes. Invert on racks until completely cooled. Cut each layer in half horizontally and frost, generously adding coconut on top of each layer of icing, making sure you have plenty of coconut for the outside of cake.

YIELD: TWO 9-INCH ROUND LAYERS

MORAVIAN SUGAR CAKE

Well-kept secret recipes must be shared before they're lost. Thanks to several ladies of the church, this recipe has been saved for the enjoyment of future generations and those who may never have the opportunity to visit Bethlehem or Lititz, where it is traditional.

1 cup cooked mashed potatoes (save ¼ cup
    of the water the potatoes were cooked in)
1 cup granulated sugar
1 package active yeast
¼ pound (1 stick) butter
¼ cup lard or vegetable shortening
1 teaspoon salt
2 large eggs, lightly beaten
5 to 5½ cups sifted all-purpose flour

For the holes:

4 tablespoons (½ stick) butter
1 cup light brown sugar (do not pack down
    when measuring)

If you start with raw potatoes, dice 3 medium potatoes and cook in just enough water to cover over medium heat until soft. Drain, reserving 1/4 cup of the water, and mash until the lumps disappear. Add the sugar to the potatoes and beat until fluffy. Dissolve the yeast in the lukewarm potato water. To be sure the yeast is active, add a pinch of sugar. If it foams, the yeast is good.

Slowly cream together the butter, lard, salt, eggs, yeast, and potato water until well blended. Gradually add the flour, kneading with the dough hook of a mixer, until the dough is smooth and elastic. If kneading by hand, work the dough be pressing down with the heel of your hand, pushing the dough back and forth, folding it, and pressing it again and again until all the air bubbles are removed and the dough is smooth and elastic. It should pull away from the sides of the bowl and look like satin—it should not look dry. Turn the dough into a greased bowl, turning it so all the sides are greased. Cover with a clean, damp cloth and let rise in a warm, draft-free area until doubled in size. Knead for a minute, then divide evenly between four greased 6 1/2-by-10-inch pans. Cover with the same cloth and let rise again for one hour. Break the butter into tiny pieces and punch them into the cakes in rows with your fingertips. Press the brown sugar into the same holes, sprinkling the remainder over the tops. Bake in a preheated 350°F oven for 20 to 25 minutes or until golden brown and crusty on top and the cake pulls away from the sides of the pan. Serve warm.

YIELD: FOUR 6 1/2-BY-10-INCH CAKES

SHELLBARK (HICKORY NUT) CAKE

Shellbarks are so unique to this area that few people know how wonderful they are. Known as hickory nuts, these nuts are larger, the shell harder, than the small hickory variety. They grew wild, but the best varieties were nurtured by many who couldn't survive winter without them. Only folks that know their worth can find them in the farmers' market—and are happy to pay the price.

4 large egg whites
1/4 teaspoon cream of tartar
1 cup granulated sugar
5 1/3 tablespoons (2/3 stick) butter or margarine
1 3/4 cups cake flour
1/2 teaspoon salt
3 teaspoons baking powder
1/2 cup milk
1 teaspoon vanilla extract
1/4 cup all-purpose flour
1/2 cup chopped shellbarks (other nuts may be substituted)
Your favorite frosting, or dust with sifted confectioners sugar
Extra shellbark halves for topping

In a large mixing bowl, beat the egg whites until foamy, add the cream of tartar, and beat until they start to form peaks. Gradually add 1/2 cup of the sugar and beat until the whites hold firm but not dry peaks. Set aside. Cream the butter and the remaining sugar until light in a large mixing bowl. Sift 1 1/2 cups of the flour, the salt, and baking powder together. Blend the flour mixture and milk alternately with the butter-sugar mixture. When thoroughly blended, add the vanilla, then dredge the nuts in the remaining flour and add to the batter, folding in gently. Fold in the egg whites and pour batter into two greased and floured 8-inch cake pans. Bake in a preheated 350°F oven for about 25 to 30 minutes. Insert a toothpick in the center of the cake; if it comes out clean, it is done. Remove from the oven and cool a few minutes before inverting on cooling racks. Frost with your favorite frosting, topping with extra nuts.

YIELD: TWO 8-INCH LAYER CAKES

Variation: White Cake: Use 1¾ cups cake flour and omit the nuts. I recommend butter cream frosting, chocolate, or cream cheese frosting.

SPICE CAKE

With a cream cheese frosting (page 171), this is hard to beat.

6 tablespoons vegetable shortening
6 tablespoons (¾ stick) margarine
¾ cup firmly packed light brown sugar
4 large eggs
2¼ cups cake flour
1 cup granulated sugar
1 teaspoon baking powder
1 teaspoon baking soda
½ teaspoon salt
½ teaspoon ground nutmeg
½ teaspoon ground cloves
1 teaspoon ground cinnamon
1 cup buttermilk or thick milk (add 1 tablespoon fresh lemon juice or vinegar to whole milk)
1 teaspoon vanilla extract
Frosting or confectioners sugar

Cream the shortening, margarine, and brown sugar together in a large mixing bowl. Beat until light and fluffy. Gradually add the eggs and beat until light and smooth. Sift the flour, sugar, baking powder, baking soda, salt, and spices together. Add gradually, alternately with the buttermilk to the creamed mixture until well blended. Add the vanilla, blend, and pour into one 9-by-13-inch or two 9-inch round greased and floured cake pans. Bake in a preheated 350°F oven for 30 to 35 minutes for 2 pans or 40 to 45 minutes for one large pan. The cake is done when a toothpick, inserted in the middle of the cake, comes out clean. Frost with your favorite frosting or sift confectioners sugar over the top.

YIELD: ONE 9-BY-13-INCH CAKE OR TWO 9-INCH ROUND LAYERS

BUTTERSPONGE CAKE

Because it is so light, this cake is perfect for use as a shortcake with fresh fruit. It is also great when iced with Caramel Icing (page 170).

4 large eggs
1½ cups granulated sugar
1½ cups all-purpose flour
1 teaspoon baking powder
Pinch of salt
⅔ cup milk
2 tablespoons (¼ stick) butter
1 teaspoon vanilla extract

Cream the eggs and sugar together in a large mixing bowl until light and foamy. Sift together the flour, baking powder, and salt in another bowl. In a small saucepan, heat the milk and the butter. Alternately mix the hot milk and butter and sifted flour into the creamed mixture. Add vanilla and mix until well blended. Pour the batter into a greased and floured 9-by-13-inch cake pan and bake in a preheated 350°F oven for 45 minutes or until a toothpick inserted into the center of the cake comes out clean. Remove from the oven and cool a few minutes before inverting onto a rack.

YIELD: ONE 9-BY-13-INCH CAKE OR TWO 8-INCH ROUND LAYERS

FLAME CAKE

Today this cake is known as red velvet, but years ago, it was called flame cake. No matter what name we give it, everyone loves it.

½ cup vegetable shortening
1½ cups granulated sugar
2 large eggs
1 teaspoon salt
1 teaspoon vanilla extract
2 teaspoons unsweetened cocoa
¼ cup red food coloring
1 teaspoon baking soda
1 teaspoon cider vinegar
2¼ cups flour, sifted
1 cup buttermilk
1 recipe Butter Frosting (page 168) or
  Cream Cheese Frosting (page 171)

Cream the shortening, sugar, and eggs together in a mixing bowl until fluffy. Blend in the salt and vanilla. Slowly add the cocoa and food coloring, mixing until well blended. Dissolve the baking soda in the vinegar, then add to the cake mixture. Alternately blend the flour and buttermilk into the cake mixture, beating until thoroughly mixed. Pour the batter into a greased 8½-by-11-inch cake pan and bake in a preheated 350°F oven for 25 to 30 minutes or until a toothpick inserted in the center of cake comes out clean. Remove from the oven and let cool in the pan for a few minutes before turning it onto a cooling rack. If you are planning on icing the cake and serving in the pan, there is no need to invert. Ice with the traditional butter frosting or cream cheese frosting.

YIELD: ONE 8½-BY-11-INCH CAKE OR TWO 8-INCH ROUND LAYERS

GINGERBREAD CAKE

I love this cake right from the oven with a nice lemon-rum sauce or warm applesauce (see page 51).

6 tablespoons (¾ stick) butter or margarine
6 tablespoons vegetable shortening
1 cup lightly packed light brown sugar
3 large eggs, lightly beaten
1 cup buttermilk or thick milk (add 1 tablespoon lemon juice or vinegar to whole milk)
1 teaspoon salt
1 teaspoon baking soda
1 teaspoon ground cinnamon
1 teaspoon ground ginger
1 teaspoon ground nutmeg
3 cups all-purpose flour
1 cup table molasses (golden, barrel, or King Syrup), not baking molasses

Cream the butter and shortening and brown sugar together in a large mixing bowl until fluffy. Gradually add eggs and buttermilk, beating until well blended. Sift the salt, soda, spices, and flour together and add alternately with the molasses to the egg mixture. When the batter is smooth, pour it into a greased and floured 9-by-13-inch cake pan and bake in a preheated 350°F oven for 50 minutes or until a toothpick, when inserted in the center of cake, comes out clean. Let cool in pan, cutting into large squares for serving.

YIELD: ONE 9-BY-13-INCH CAKE

LEMON CHIFFON CAKE

This is a great cake to serve plain with fresh fruit. For cooler weather, serve this cake with a lemon-lime sauce (see page 128).

2¼ cups sifted cake flour
1½ cups granulated sugar
1 tablespoon baking powder
1 teaspoon salt
½ cup vegetable oil
6 large eggs, separated
⅔ cup cold water
2 teaspoons vanilla extract
1 tablespoon fresh lemon juice
Grated rind of 1 lemon
½ teaspoon cream of tartar
Confectioners sugar

Sift the flour, sugar, baking powder, and salt together in a large mixing bowl. Make a well in the center of the dry ingredients with a wooden spoon. Add, in the following order, the oil, egg yolks, water, vanilla, lemon juice, and rind. Stir with a spoon until the batter is smooth. In another large mixing bowl, beat the egg whites with the cream of tartar until stiff peaks form. Pour the batter over the egg whites in a gentle stream, then fold in very gently with a rubber spatula. Pour the batter into an ungreased, footed 10-inch tube pan 4 inches deep. Take a table knife and, starting in the center, by the tube, cut several circles in the batter around the pan until you reach the outer edge. This will puncture the air bubbles and prevent holes in the finished cake. Bake the cake in a preheated 375°F oven, on the middle rack, for 55 minutes, then lower the heat to 350°F and bake 12 minutes longer. Turn the cake pan upside down to cool, but do not remove the cake from the pan for at least 1 hour. If the pan does not have feet, place center tube over a funnel or catsup bottle. Dust the top of the cake with confectioners sugar before serving.

YIELD: ONE 10-INCH CAKE

PLUM-CHEESE SQUARES

Very rich, tart, and crunchy, these squares are perfect for dessert or tea.

For the pastry:

1½ cups all-purpose flour
½ cup granulated sugar
1 teaspoon salt
½ pound (2 sticks) butter or margarine
2 large egg yolks or 1 whole egg
1 teaspoon cider vinegar
¼ cup water

For the plum-cheese filling:

4 cups pitted plums
1 cup granulated sugar
½ teaspoon ground cinnamon
½ teaspoon ground nutmeg
8 ounces cream cheese, at room temperature
3 large eggs, lightly beaten
¾ cup sour cream
1 teaspoon vanilla extract
1 teaspoon fresh lemon juice
1 teaspoon grated lemon rind

If you are using a food processor for the pastry, combine all the ingredients and pulse in the processor until it forms a ball in the bowl. Press gently into a 9-by-13-inch cake pan. To make by hand, combine the flour, sugar, and salt together in a large mixing bowl. Cut in the butter with a pastry blender or rub the dry ingredients and butter together with your hands until they form fine crumbs. Combine the yolks, vinegar, and water together in another bowl and gradually add to the crumbs, tossing them lightly until fully moist. Press evenly into the pan. Bake in a preheated 350°F oven for 15 minutes. Cool a few minutes, then add the plums. Combine ⅓ cup of the sugar, the cinnamon, and nutmeg together in a small bowl and sprinkle over the plums. Bake another 15 minutes at 350°F. Meanwhile, beat the cream cheese, eggs, sour cream, the remaining sugar, vanilla, and lemon juice and rind together in a large mixing bowl until smooth and creamy. Pour the cheese mixture over the plums and bake 40 to 50 minutes longer. The cake is done when the center does not shake when pan is jiggled. Cut into small squares when cold.

YIELD: ONE 9-BY-13-INCH CAKE

ANGEL FOOD CAKE

There seemed to be a contest among all our family bakers to see how high and fine-textured their angel food cakes could be. It has a lot to do with the beating and blending of the egg whites. When I gave this recipe to our son to make for the first time, he read it hurriedly; thinking 1 cup egg whites meant beaten, he used two egg whites and beat them until stiff, making one cup. Of course, the cake was one inch high and looked more like a torte shell. It also taught me the importance of writing precisely what I mean in recipes!

1 cup sifted cake flour
1 cup granulated sugar, less 1 tablespoon
1 cup egg whites (usually the whites of 10
  large eggs), at room temperature
¾ teaspoon cream of tartar
¼ teaspoon salt
1 teaspoon vanilla extract

Sift the flour and half the sugar together onto a plate or piece of wax paper. Gently pour it back into the sifter and sift again. Place the egg whites in large mixing bowl and whip until foamy, about 1 minute. Add the cream of tartar and whip until they form moist, stiff peaks, about 4 minutes. The beaten egg whites should be very shiny and, when lifted, stand straight up. Using the wire whip of a mixer or a hand whisk, slowly fold in the flour mixture alternately with the rest of sugar, adding about 2 tablespoons at a time until it is all folded in. Scrape down the sides of bowl, then add the salt and vanilla, folding just until all traces of flour are gone. If you are folding in with a spatula or hand whisk, fold in a slow circular motion—do not beat. Gently pour or spoon the batter into an ungreased 10-inch tube pan. Use a long knife to circle the batter; starting in the center, around the tube, circle several times, ending at the outside edge of the pan to pop any large air bubbles. Place the pan in the middle rack of a preheated 375°F oven and bake for 40 to 45 minutes. Insert a long wire or wooden skewer in the center of the cake; if it comes out clean the cake is done. Remove and invert immediately. If the pan does not have "feet," place the center of the pan over the neck of a bottle or an upside-down funnel. Leave in the pan until ready to frost. Frost with a light icing or sprinkle with confectioners sugar.

YIELD: ONE 10-INCH CAKE

BLUEBERRY CAKE

This is a small cake, just enough for one meal, served with mounds of freshly picked berries.

½ cup vegetable shortening
1¼ cup granulated sugar
1 large egg
2½ cups all-purpose flour
2½ teaspoons baking powder
½ teaspoon salt
¾ cup milk
1¼ cups fresh blueberries

Cream the shortening and 1 cup of the sugar together in a large mixing bowl. Add the egg and beat well. Sift the flour, baking powder, and salt together in a medium-size mixing bowl; reserve ½ cup to dredge the blueberries. Alternately mix the milk and the flour mixture, into the creamed mixture gradually. Beat until the batter is smooth. Dredge the berries in the remaining flour and fold into the batter until all traces of the flour are gone. Sprinkle the top of batter with the remaining ¼ cup sugar. Pour into a greased and floured 9-inch square baking pan and bake in preheated 350°F oven for 40 to 45 minutes or until a toothpick inserted in its center comes out clean.

YIELD: ONE 9-INCH SQUARE CAKE

BUTTERMILK CHOCOLATE CAKE

We've served this cake ever since we started serving meals in our home, now known as Groff's Farm Restaurant. We frost the cakes with butter cream or caramel icing and serve it in small pieces with cracker pudding at the beginning of the meal so everyone will make enough room for dessert later on.

2 cups lightly packed light brown sugar
8 tablespoons (1 stick) butter or half margarine or vegetable shortening
2 large eggs
¾ cup buttermilk
½ cup unsweetened cocoa
½ cup strong coffee, boiling hot
1 teaspoon baking soda
1 teaspoon cider vinegar
½ teaspoon salt
1 teaspoon vanilla extract
2½ cups sifted all-purpose flour

Cream the sugar and butter together in a large mixing bowl until fluffy. Add the eggs one at a time, beat a minute, then add the buttermilk. Put cocoa in a small bowl and add the coffee to it slowly, stirring constantly to prevent lumping. Add this to the creamed mixture, beating until well blended. In a small bowl, moisten the baking soda with the vinegar, then add to the creamed mixture. Stir in the salt and vanilla. Gradually add the flour, beating until smooth. Pour the batter into a greased and floured 9-by-13-inch cake pan. Bake in preheated 350°F oven for 45 minutes or until a toothpick, inserted in the center of the cake, comes out clean. Cool and frost with your favorite icing. I like caramel, myself (see page 170).

YIELD: ONE 9-BY-13-INCH CAKE OR TWO 9-INCH ROUND LAYERS

BUTTER FROSTING

One of the quickest and easiest frostings, this can be prepared in minutes. It keeps for a week or two in the refrigerator if it is tightly covered.

3 tablespoons butter, at room temperature
1 tablespoon heavy cream
1½ cups confectioners sugar
Pinch of salt
½ teaspoon vanilla extract

Cream all the ingredients together in a large mixing bowl until light and fluffy. Spread on cake.

YIELD: ENOUGH TO ICE ONE 9-BY-13-INCH CAKE

HINT: This recipe should be doubled to frost a 3-layer 9-inch cake.

Variations: Add 1 ounce melted milk or dark chocolate or 1 tablespoon grated orange rind and 1 tablespoon orange juice, omitting the vanilla, or 1 tablespoon grated lemon rind and 1 tablespoon fresh lemon juice, again omitting the vanilla.

BOILED FROSTING— SEVEN MINUTE ICING

Perfect, light, and airy, this is the one we use for coconut layer cakes.

1½ cups granulated sugar
½ cup water
⅛ teaspoon cream of tartar
2 large egg whites
½ teaspoon vanilla extract

Combine the sugar, water, and cream of tartar in a heavy saucepan. Stir together, then bring to a boil over high heat without stirring again until it reaches 242°F on a candy thermometer or spins a thread. Meanwhile beat the egg whites in a bowl until they hold soft peaks. Beat about 3 tablespoons of the hot sugar syrup into the whites until blended. Gradually add the rest of the syrup, beating steadily until the frosting stands in soft peaks, approximately 6 minutes. Add the vanilla and continue to beat until stiff enough to frost the cake. If frosting is too sugary, add a few drops of lemon juice.

YIELD: ENOUGH FROSTING FOR A TWO-LAYER CAKE

Variation: Sea Foam Frosting: Follow the above recipe, using ¾ cup granulated sugar and ¾ cup lightly packed light brown sugar instead of 1½ cups granulated sugar.

MARSHMALLOW FROSTING

This is an excellent frosting for layer cakes.

1½ cups granulated sugar
½ cup water
1 cup marshmallows
3 large egg whites
Pinch of salt
¾ teaspoon vanilla extract

Combine the sugar and water in a heavy sauce-pan. Bring to a boil over high heat, not stirring, until the syrup reaches 242°F on a candy thermometer or spins a thread. Remove from the heat and add the marshmallows, stirring until melted. Beat the egg whites until they form soft peaks, then slowly pour the syrup into the whites, beating constantly until thoroughly blended. Add the salt and vanilla and beat until cool enough to spread. Frost cake immediately.

YIELD: ENOUGH FROSTING FOR A TWO-LAYER CAKE

ORANGE CREAM FROSTING

1 tablespoon grated orange rind
1 teaspoon grated lime or lemon rind
¼ cup fresh orange juice
1 tablespoon fresh lime or lemon juice
1 pound confectioners sugar (about 3½
  cups sifted)
4 tablespoons (½ stick) butter or
  margarine, at room temperature
1 large egg yolk
Pinch of salt

Combine the orange and lime rinds with the juices. Let stand together while you sift the confectioners sugar. Cream the butter until light and fluffy. Gradually add the egg yolk and salt and blend thoroughly. Slowly add about one cup of the sifted sugar, the rind and juice mixture, then slowly beat in the rest of the sugar. When blended, beat vigorously until light and fluffy and easy to spread.

YIELD: ABOUT 2½ CUPS OR ENOUGH TO FROST A LARGE LAYER CAKE

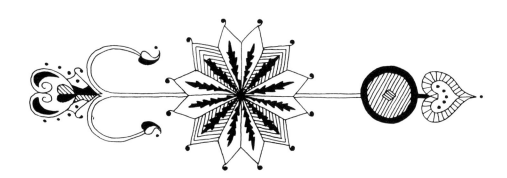

CARAMEL ICING

This icing is especially good on chocolate cake but my mother always added milk to thin it enough to spread on her white layer cakes.

1/4 pound (1 stick) butter
1 cup lightly packed light brown sugar
1/4 cup evaporated milk
Pinch of salt
2 cups confectioners sugar
1/2 teaspoon vanilla extract

Melt the butter in a saucepan, add the brown sugar, and bring to a boil over medium heat. Reduce heat to medium-low for 2 minutes, stirring constantly. Remove from the heat and add the milk and salt. Return to the stove and bring to a full boil over medium heat. Remove from the heat and let cool until lukewarm. Gradually beat in the confectioners sugar and vanilla, beating until the icing is thick enough to spread.

YIELD: ENOUGH ICING FOR A 13-BY-9-INCH CAKE OR 2-LAYER CAKE. RECIPE SHOULD BE DOUBLED FOR A 3-LAYER 8-INCH CAKE.

WHIPPED CREAM

It doesn't take long to whip cream if the bowl and beaters are thoroughly chilled in the freezer before you start.

1 cup heavy cream
2 tablespoons granulated sugar
1/2 teaspoon vanilla extract

Pour cream into a large, chilled mixing bowl. Beat with an electric mixer on medium-high speed until it forms soft peaks, about 2 minutes. Gradually add the sugar and vanilla and continue beating until it forms firm peaks.

YIELD: 2 CUPS

Variation: Maple Whipped Cream: Add 1/4 cup pure maple syrup to the cream and omit the sugar and vanilla.
Spiced Whipped Cream: Place 1 teaspoon curry powder and 1/2 teaspoon ground nutmeg in a small skillet or saucepan and heat over low heat, stirring constantly with a wooden spoon until slightly dark, about 2 minutes. Cool. Fold into whipped cream.

GREAT MERINGUE

This makes a fine, high meringue, thanks to my friend Marion Cunningham and *The Fannie Farmer Baking Book*!

2/3 cup egg whites (about 6 large egg whites)
1/2 cup granulated sugar
1/3 teaspoon cream of tartar
1/4 teaspoon salt

Combine all the ingredients in a large mixing bowl. Place over a pan of hot water and stir briskly until the mixture feels slightly warm to the back of your hand or finger, about 15 seconds. Remove the bowl from the water and beat with a mixer on high speed until the meringue holds firm peaks, about 1 1/2 minutes.

Do not overbeat or the meringue will be dry and hard to spread.

YIELD: ENOUGH TO COVER A 9-INCH PIE

BROILED ICING

Mother Groff often broiled this icing on a yellow cake for quick entertaining.

4 tablespoons (½ stick) butter, melted
5 tablespoons evaporated milk
⅓ cup firmly packed light brown sugar
½ cup coconut (medium shred)

In a small mixing bowl, combine all the ingredients thoroughly. Spread on the warm cake. Do not remove the cake from the pan. Place the cake on the medium rack of the oven. Broil 6 minutes or until the icing bubbles and is golden brown.

YIELD: ENOUGH TO ICE ONE 13-BY-9-INCH CAKE

CREAM CHEESE FROSTING

This is easy to make and especially good on fruit and nut cakes.

3 ounces cream cheese
6 tablespoons butter (¾ stick), at room temperature
1 cup confectioners sugar
1 teaspoon vanilla extract

Beat all the ingredients together in a large mixing bowl until satin-smooth. Frost cake when cool.

YIELD: ENOUGH TO FROST ONE 9-BY-13-INCH CAKE OR TWO 9-INCH LAYERS

Variation: Chocolate Cream Frosting: Add 1 square unsweetened chocolate (1 ounce) or 2 tablespoons unsweetened cocoa powder to the above recipe.

BASIC CRUMB TOPPING

Make a lot of these crumbs (they're great for fruit pies, especially blueberry and cherry) and refrigerate them in an airtight container. It saves lots of time later and they'll keep for at least 4 weeks.

3 cups all-purpose flour or 2 cups flour and 1 cup fresh bread crumbs
12 tablespoons (1½ sticks) butter or margarine, at room temperature
½ cup granulated sugar
½ teaspoon salt

Cut all the ingredients together with a pastry blender, by hand, or with a food processor until the crumbs are very fine. Sprinkle evenly, ½ inch thick, over the top of a pie filling before baking.

YIELD: ENOUGH FOR FOUR 9-INCH PIES

Chapter 11

Puddings, Cookies, Candies, and Other Pennsylvania Dutch Treats

APPLE MERINGUE PUDDING

This is not just another applesauce. It is a wonderfully light and airy pudding. Granny Smith, Greening, or summer Rambo apples are especially good.

12 tart cooking apples, peeled and cored
1 cup water
6 large eggs, separated
2/3 cup granulated sugar
2 tablespoons (1/4 stick) butter
1/2 teaspoon ground nutmeg
1/2 teaspoon ground cinnamon
1/2 teaspoon lemon extract
1/2 teaspoon almond extract
1/3 teaspoon salt

Meringue:

1/3 teaspoon cream of tartar
1/4 cup granulated sugar
1/2 teaspoon lemon extract
Ground nutmeg or cinnamon, or cinnamon
   sugar for garnish

Place the apples and water in large saucepan and cook, covered, over medium heat until soft, about 10 minutes. Puree in a food processor, food mill, or blender, then transfer to a large mixing bowl. Beat the egg yolks lightly with a fork and add to the apples, along with the sugar, butter, nutmeg, cinnamon, extracts, and salt. Beat thoroughly and pour into a buttered baking dish or pan. Bake in a preheated

375°F oven for 12 minutes. While baking the apples, whip the egg whites and cream of tartar into soft peaks. Slowly add the sugar and lemon extract and beat until it forms stiff peaks. Remove the pan from the oven only long enough to spread the meringue on top. Cut through the pudding with the blade of a table knife to make sure some of the meringue gets into the apples. Swirl the meringue with the tip of the blade and place in the oven until golden brown, about 15 minutes. Be careful not to burn the top. Turn off the oven and let stand for another 10 minutes. Remove from the oven and cool a bit before serving. Sprinkle with nutmeg or cinnamon or cinnamon sugar. This is good served warm or cold.

YIELD: ABOUT 3 CUPS

BREAD PUDDING

Everyone loves this bread pudding. It's delicious with a lemon sauce.

6 cups bread cubes or slices without crusts,
    cut into large pieces
¾ teaspoon ground nutmeg
½ teaspoon ground cinnamon
½ cup raisins
3 cups milk
3 tablespoons butter
3 large eggs, lightly beaten
½ cup granulated sugar
¼ teaspoon salt
1 teaspoon vanilla extract
¼ cup slivered blanched or toasted
    almonds (optional)

Place bread cubes or pieces in a buttered 7-by-11-inch or 9-inch square baking dish or pan. Combine the nutmeg, cinnamon, and raisins, and sprinkle evenly over the bread. Heat the milk in 1½ quart saucepan over medium-high heat. Add butter. Combine eggs, sugar, and salt, and stir into the milk until completely dissolved. Add the vanilla, then slowly pour the milk mixture over the bread. Let stand for 15 minutes or until the bread absorbs the liquid. Top with the almonds, if desired. Bake in a preheated 325°F oven for 1 hour or until golden colored and a knife, inserted in the center, comes out clean. Serve warm with or without sauce.

YIELD: 6 SERVINGS

INDIAN PUDDING

The American Indian has given us so many wonderful corn dishes, this being one of them. It's great served with Whipped Cream (page 170) or Hard Sauce (page 128).

½ cup cornmeal
2 cups milk, scalded
1 tablespoon butter
¼ cup table molasses (golden, barrel, or
    King Syrup), not baking molasses
⅔ cup raisins
1 large egg, lightly beaten
2 tablespoons granulated sugar
½ teaspoon salt
¼ teaspoon ground ginger
¼ teaspoon ground cinnamon
2 cups milk

Stir the cornmeal into the hot milk with a whisk, stirring until smooth. Add the butter, molasses, raisins, egg, sugar, salt, ginger, and cinnamon. Blend thoroughly and let stand until it thickens, about 5 minutes. Pour into a buttered 1-quart baking dish. Top with 2 cups milk. Bake in a preheated 300°F oven for 2 hours or until set. Serve warm.

YIELD: 6 SERVINGS

VANILLA CREAM PUDDING

This is often served with fresh or canned fruit, layered if you wish, for a beautiful dessert. It also makes the perfect filling for Cream Puffs (see the recipe on page 191).

¾ cup granulated sugar
6 tablespoons all-purpose flour
¼ teaspoon salt
2 cups milk
2 tablespoons (¼ stick) butter
2 large eggs, lightly beaten
1 teaspoon vanilla extract

Combine the sugar, flour, and salt in a small bowl. Scald milk in a large, heavy saucepan and gradually pour in the sugar mixture, stirring constantly over medium heat until thickened, about 5 minutes. Add the butter and stir. Remove a small amount of the thickened filling and pour it over beaten eggs. Mix together, then pour into the filling, simmering over low for 5 more minutes. Remove from the stove and add the vanilla. Cool (place wax paper on top to prevent the top from drying) and serve.

YIELD: ABOUT 3 CUPS OR ENOUGH TO FILL 1 DOZEN LARGE CREAM PUFFS

MARSHMALLOW PUDDING

Even though there aren't any marshmallows in this pudding, it tastes and looks as though there are. Children and adults alike love it.

1 quart milk
3 tablespoons cornstarch
½ cup milk
¼ teaspoon salt
¾ cup granulated sugar (less if desired)
1 teaspoon butter
2 large egg whites, stiffly beaten
1 teaspoon vanilla extract
2 ounces (2 squares) unsweetened chocolate
Whipped Cream for topping (page 170; optional)

Scald the quart of milk in a 2-quart saucepan. While heating it, combine the cornstarch, milk, salt, and sugar. Add to the scalded milk, reduce the heat to low, and cook until thickened, about 10 minutes. Stir in the butter and divide the pudding into 2 equal parts. Cool for several minutes, then fold the beaten egg whites and ½ teaspoon of the vanilla into one part. Stir the melted chocolate and the remaining vanilla into the other half. Spoon alternate spoonsful into a chilled mold. Chill, covered with wax paper or plastic wrap, until firm, at least 2 hours. Unmold by dipping the mold in warm water for about 15 seconds. Place a serving plate on top of the mold and quickly turn it upside down. Leave the mold in place and refrigerate for a few minutes to keep the pudding from weeping. Remove the mold and top the pudding with whipped cream if desired.

YIELD: 6 SERVINGS

RHUBARB-ORANGE PUDDING

This was one of the first fresh puddings of the season. Now rhubarb is available almost all year round.

4 oranges, 3 cups peeled, seeded, sliced, and quartered with a sharp knife (about 3 cups)
6 stems rhubarb, trimmed and cut in 1-inch cubes (about 4 cups)
Juice of 1 lemon
½ cup water
½ cup granulated sugar
¼ teaspoon salt
5 tablespoons tapioca
½ cup orange juice
1 cup apple wine or light white wine
Several drops of red food coloring (optional)
2 or 3 dashes of ground nutmeg
Grated orange rind for garnish

Place the oranges and rhubarb in a heavy 2-quart saucepan and add the lemon juice, water, sugar, salt, and tapioca. Bring to a boil and simmer over low heat for 5 minutes, stirring occasionally. Add the orange juice and apple wine. Cook till thickened, approximately 6 minutes. Stir in the food coloring and nutmeg, then remove from the stove and let cool for at least 10 minutes. Pour into a serving bowl. When ready to serve, garnish with curls of orange rind or fresh flowers.

YIELD: 6 SERVINGS

CARAMEL PUDDING

Most people think of this as butterscotch pudding. It's a far cry from the boxed kind. It is so smooth and creamy, I guess that's why it's Abe's favorite.

2 tablespoons (1/4 stick) butter
1 cup lightly packed light brown sugar
1/2 teaspoon salt
3 cups milk
1 tablespoon all-purpose flour
2 1/2 tablespoons cornstarch
2 large eggs, lightly beaten
1 teaspoon vanilla extract

Melt the butter in a heavy skillet or large saucepan. Add the brown sugar and salt, stirring constantly over medium-high heat until it caramelizes, about 5 minutes—be careful not to burn it. Remove from the stove and slowly mix in 2 cups of the milk. Return to the stove and heat to near boiling over medium heat, stirring constantly. Combine the flour and cornstarch and stir in; then slowly add the remaining cup of milk. Reduce heat to low and cook until thickened and smooth. Remove a few tablespoons of the pudding, and stir them into the beaten eggs; then return the mixture to the pudding. Cook another 2 minutes, being careful not to let it boil. Remove from the heat and stir in the vanilla. To prevent a skin from forming on top, lay wax paper over it. Serve warm or cold.

YIELD: 6 SERVINGS

RICE PUDDING

Everyone asks why my rice pudding is so creamy. When you start with natural rice and cook it slowly, you'll understand why the extra effort is worth it.

1 cup long-grain rice
2 cups water
1/2 teaspoon salt
6 cups milk
1/4 pound (1 stick) butter or margarine
1/2 teaspoon salt
1/4 cup granulated sugar
2 large eggs, beaten
1 teaspoon vanilla extract

Place the rice, water, and salt in a medium-size saucepan and boil over medium heat for 15 minutes. Drain. In a heavy saucepan or on top of a double boiler over simmering water, heat the milk, butter, and salt until the butter melts. Add the rice and simmer over low heat, lightly covered, for 1 1/2 hours, stirring often to prevent sticking. Then, combine the sugar and beaten eggs thoroughly and slowly blend in with the rice. Continue to simmer until thickened but not boiling, about 15 minutes. Remove from heat and add the vanilla or any other flavorings you desire. Serve warm or chilled.

YIELD: 6 SERVINGS

Variations: For different flavors, add in 1 tablespoon fresh lemon juice, 1 cup raisins, or several dashes of ground cinnamon at the same time you add the sugar and eggs.

GLORIFIED RICE

Everyone's favorite pudding, this was often called heavenly rice. A special family dinner or church social was not complete without it. It's pretty, light, and always popular with all ages.

2 cups (20-ounce can) pineapple tidbits
1/4 cup granulated sugar
2 cups cooked long-grain rice (soft but not mushy)
24 marshmallows or 2 cups of miniature marshmallows
1 cup heavy cream, whipped to firm peaks
Maraschino cherries and pecan halves or chopped nuts for garnish

Drain the pineapple and combine it with the sugar. Stir until the sugar dissolves and add to the rice in a large mixing bowl. Fold in the marshmallows and let stand for at least 1 hour. Before serving, fold in the whipped cream until blended. Garnish with cherries and nuts. Chill until ready to serve.

YIELD: 6 SERVINGS

CRANBERRY CRUMBLE

The apples keep this dessert from being too tart.

Bottom part:

1 cup uncooked oatmeal
1 cup lightly packed light brown sugar
1/2 cup all-purpose flour

1 teaspoon ground cinnamon
6 tablespoons (3/4 stick) butter
3/4 cup chopped English walnuts

Top:

8 ounces cream cheese
1/2 cup firmly packed light brown sugar
3 tablespoons cornstarch
1/4 teaspoon salt
2 1/2 cups cranberries, fresh or frozen
3 apples, cored, peeled, and sliced
1/4 cup orange juice

Blend all the ingredients for the bottom part together in a large mixing bowl, rubbing with your hands until they form large crumbs. Reserve half and press the other half of the crumbs into a buttered 9-inch baking pan or dish. Bake in a preheated 350°F oven for 15 minutes. Set aside. Beat or stir the cream cheese until smooth and creamy and spread in the bottom of the baked shell. Combine the brown sugar, cornstarch, and salt together in a large mixing bowl. Toss the cranberries and sliced apples in the orange juice, then add to the brown sugar mixture. Mix thoroughly and spoon onto the cream cheese. Top with the reserved crumbs. Bake in a 350°F oven for 45 minutes or until golden brown. Cool and serve chilled.

YIELD: 6 SERVINGS

Variations: Rhubarb-Strawberry Crumble: Substitute 3 cups coarsely chopped rhubarb and 2 cups sliced strawberries for cranberries and apples.
Blueberry Crumble: Substitute 4 cups blueberries for the cranberries and apples and add

½ teaspoon ground nutmeg, ½ teaspoon grated lemon rind, and 1 tablespoon fresh lemon juice to the above recipe.

Peach Crumble: Substitute 4 cups sliced peaches for the cranberries and apples. Add ½ teaspoon ground cinnamon, ½ teaspoon ground nutmeg, 1 teaspoon each of grated orange and lemon rind, and 1 teaspoon fresh lemon juice to the above recipe.

FRUIT AND NUT COOKIES

Barb's great-grandmother from Somerset County made these cookies for her friends and family, using their own homemade maple sugar. Today, her family enjoys these cookies most during the holidays.

1 cup lightly packed maple sugar or light
* brown sugar*
¼ pound (1 stick) butter
3 large eggs, lightly beaten
½ cup table molasses (golden, barrel, or
* King Syrup), not baking molasses*
2½ cups all-purpose flour
1 teaspoon ground nutmeg
½ teaspoon ground cloves
1 teaspoon ground cinnamon
½ teaspoon ground ginger
1 teaspoon baking soda dissolved in ½ cup
* boiling water*
1 cup raisins
1 cup chopped dates
1 cup chopped nuts

Cream the sugar and butter together in a large mixing bowl until light and fluffy. Gradually

add the eggs and molasses, beating thoroughly. Sift the flour, nutmeg, cloves, cinnamon, and ginger together in another bowl. Add the flour mixture to the creamed mixture alternately with the soda water until the batter is smooth and creamy. Fold in the raisins, dates, and nuts. Chill the dough for at least one hour. Drop by spoonful onto a greased cookie sheet about 2 inches apart. Bake in a preheated 350°F oven for 10 to 12 minutes or until a mark is not left in the center of the cookie when lightly touched with your finger. Cool on a clean linen towel. Store in an airtight container. They taste better if stored for at least a day or two.

YIELD: ABOUT 4 DOZEN 2-INCH COOKIES

ICE-BOX NUT COOKIES

Delicious and old-fashioned, these cookies are good anytime.

2 cups lightly packed light brown sugar
½ cup lard or vegetable shortening
¼ pound (1 stick) butter
2 large eggs, lightly beaten
3½ cups sifted all-purpose flour
1 teaspoon baking soda
½ teaspoon salt
1 teaspoon vanilla extract
1 cup broken or coarsely chopped nuts

In a large mixing bowl, cream the brown sugar, lard, and butter together until light and fluffy. Gradually add the beaten eggs, combining thoroughly. Sift the sifted flour, baking soda, and salt together in another bowl, then slowly add to the creamed mixture. Add the vanilla, beat thoroughly, then fold in the nuts. Form the dough into a roll about 2 inches in diameter, wrap in plastic wrap, and freeze for at least 1 hour. When hard, slice about ¼-inch thick and place on a greased cookie sheet. Bake in a preheated 350°F oven for about 6 minutes or until golden brown—watch them carefully, they burn easily.

YIELD: ABOUT 5 DOZEN 2-INCH COOKIES

PEPPERNUTS OR SOFT SUGAR CAKES

We always put a raisin in the middle of these delightfully soft cookies. Those who liked to "dunk" their cookies left them on a plate overnight, uncovered, so they would get a bit dry. The next morning they would dunk them in hot chocolate or coffee.

¼ pound (1 stick) butter
2 tablespoons (¼ stick) margarine
1⅓ cups granulated sugar
2 large eggs
¾ cup buttermilk
1 teaspoon baking soda, dissolved in 1
*   tablespoon boiling water*
1 teaspoon vanilla extract
3 cups all-purpose flour
1 teaspoon baking powder
½ teaspoon ground nutmeg
¼ teaspoon salt
¼ cup raisins

Cream the butter, margarine, and sugar together in a large mixing bowl until light and fluffy. Beat in the eggs, one at a time, beating lightly. Add the buttermilk, dissolved soda, and vanilla, mixing thoroughly. Sift together the flour, baking powder, nutmeg, and salt in another bowl. Gradually add to the creamed mixture and beat until well blended. Refrigerate dough for 30 minutes. Drop the batter by teaspoonful onto a greased baking sheet, spacing them at least 2 inches apart. Place a raisin in the center of each and bake in a preheated 350°F oven for 15 minutes or until light brown. Test bake only one at first; if it is too thin, add a bit more flour to the batter. They will spread out, but should not be really thin.

YIELD: ABOUT 36 2-INCH COOKIES

RAISIN-FILLED COOKIES

A year round favorite, these cookies are made in large quantities in order to have enough to dunk in coffee after they become a bit dry. During the holidays or for special occasions, dates and figs were used instead of raisins and they were cut into fancy shapes.

Dough:

¾ cup granulated sugar
½ cup vegetable shortening, at room
*   temperature*
1 large egg
2½ cups sifted all-purpose flour
¼ teaspoon salt

2 teaspoons baking powder
¼ cup milk
1 teaspoon vanilla extract

Filling:

2 teaspoons all-purpose flour
½ cup granulated sugar (less if desired)
1 cup water (or part apple cider or sweet red or white wine)
1½ cups raisins, or part chopped dates and figs
½ teaspoon grated lemon rind
1 tablespoon fresh lemon juice
½ teaspoon ground nutmeg

Cream the sugar and shortening together in a large mixing bowl until light and fluffy. Beat in the egg. Sift the sifted flour, salt, and baking powder together in another bowl. Add to the creamed mixture alternately with the milk until well blended. Mix in the vanilla and chill, covered, until cold, about 1 hour. For the filling, combine all the ingredients in a large saucepan and bring to a boil, cooking over medium heat, about 5 minutes or until thickened. Cool filling thoroughly. Roll the chilled dough very thin on a floured board. Cut in rounds (2½ to 3 inches) or fancy shapes and place on

a greased cookie sheet about 1 inch apart. Spoon a small teaspoonful of filling in the center of each cookie. Cut the tops for each cookie with same cutter, only cut out the center of each with a small cutter or thimble to allow the filling to show through. Before putting the tops on each, moisten the edges of the bottom cookie with a wet finger or pastry brush. Place the top on each and crimp with the prongs of a fork to seal. Bake in a preheated 350°F oven for 15 minutes.

YIELD: ABOUT 3 TO 4 DOZEN, DEPENDING ON THE SIZE OF THE CUTTER

SAND TARTS

Our friend Elwood Grimm makes the best sand tarts in the world, using his father's recipe. For over 60 years Elwood has been making the traditional family specialty. He claims the cookies taste better when the dough is mixed with warm hands instead of a mixer. I believe him—you may want to try it, too.

2 cups (1 pound) confectioners sugar
½ pound (2 sticks) butter, at room temperature
3 large eggs, lightly beaten
4 cups all-purpose flour, sifted
1 teaspoon vanilla extract
1 large egg, well beaten
½ cup granulated sugar
1½ teaspoons ground cinnamon
½ cup finely chopped pecans or English walnuts

Cream the sugar and butter together in a large mixing bowl, beating vigorously with one hand until smooth, light, and creamy. Stir in the eggs, slowly, until well blended. Stir in the flour with a wooden spoon or by hand until thoroughly blended. Add the vanilla and mix well. Chill, covered, for several hours. Roll a small amount of dough at a time, keeping the remainder of the dough cold. Roll the dough very thin, ⅛ to ¼ inch thick, using very little flour on a board. Cut out the cookies with a cutter and place on a greased cookie sheet. Brush with a bit of the beaten egg, top with sugar, cinnamon and nuts. Bake in a preheated 350°F oven on the middle rack until golden brown, about 7 minutes. Watch them closely to make sure they don't burn. Grease the sheet each time after removing the baked cookies. Remove and cool on clean linen towels. These cookies taste better after being stored in airtight containers for a day or two.

YIELD: ABOUT 9 TO 10 DOZEN 2-INCH COOKIES

SPRITZ COOKIES

Children love to decorate these cookies. Whatever the occasion, these cookies are always appreciated.

1¼ cups confectioners sugar
½ pound (2 sticks) butter, at room temperature
2 large egg yolks
2½ cups all-purpose flour
½ teaspoon baking powder
⅛ teaspoon salt
1 teaspoon almond extract
1 teaspoon vanilla extract
Few drops of food coloring (optional)
Various toppings: chopped nuts, sprinkles, colored sugar (see Hint below)

Cream the sugar and butter together in a large mixing bowl until light and fluffy. Slowly add the egg yolks, beating thoroughly. Sift the flour, baking powder, and salt together in another bowl. Gradually add the flour to the creamed mixture, beating until smooth. Add the extracts and blend. Remove the amount of dough that you want for plain vanilla cookies if you plan on adding food coloring to some of the dough. Add the food colorings to the remaining batches of dough. Wrap each color dough in plastic wrap and chill thoroughly, at least one hour. When chilled, shape a ball of dough into the size of a cookie press tube. Fill the tube and press into desired shapes. Press onto an ungreased cookie sheet, at least one inch apart. Decorate with topping of choice. Bake in a preheated 375°F oven for 8 to 10 minutes or until set but not brown. Remove from the cookie sheet immediately and place on clean linen towels to cool.

YIELD: ABOUT 6 DOZEN COOKIES

HINT: To make your own colored sugar, place ½ cup of granulated sugar in a clear plastic bag. Add a few drops of food coloring and shake vigorously until evenly colored. Place in a dry, warm area to dry for about 10 minutes. Stir and store in airtight container.

BLACK WALNUT BARS

The Blum family of York County shared this recipe with my family when I was a little girl. Even though I hated gathering and shelling the walnuts (they make your hands really black), enjoying these walnut bars made it all worthwhile.

Bottom layer:

1 cup lightly packed light brown sugar
½ pound (2 sticks) butter or ½
  margarine, ½ butter
1½ cups all-purpose flour

Top layer:

2 cups lightly packed light brown sugar
4 large eggs, well beaten
2 teaspoons vanilla extract
½ teaspoon salt
2 tablespoons all-purpose flour
½ teaspoon baking powder
3 cups chopped black walnuts (English
  walnuts or pecans may be substituted)

Cream the sugar and butter together in a large mixing bowl until well blended. Stir in the flour thoroughly. Spread evenly in a greased 9-by-13-inch baking pan. Bake in a preheated 350°F oven for 5 minutes. It will look bubbly with holes all over, but that is fine. Let cool while making the top layer. For the top, cream the brown sugar and eggs together in large mixing bowl until light and fluffy. Add the vanilla. Sift the salt, flour, and baking powder together in another bowl and add to the egg mixture. Fold in the nuts and pour over the baked bottom layer. Return to the oven and bake at 350°F for 20 minutes or until light brown on top and firm to the touch. Cool and cut into bars. Do not cut them too thin or they will crumble. These keep well if stored in an airtight container.

YIELD: 3 TO 4 DOZEN 1-BY-2-INCH BARS

DATE-FIG BALLS

These are best if eaten within a day or two. Otherwise the cereal loses its crunchiness.

¼ pound (1 stick) butter or margarine
1 cup granulated sugar, less if desired
2 large eggs, lightly beaten
½ cup chopped dates
½ cup chopped figs or raisins
2½ cups Rice Krispies
⅓ cup chopped nuts
⅓ cup shredded coconut

Melt the butter in large, heavy saucepan. Add the sugar, eggs, dates, and figs. Bring to a boil over medium heat, stirring constantly with a wooden spoon to prevent scorching. Cook slowly until thickened, about 6 minutes. Remove from the heat and let cool to lukewarm. Fold in the Rice Krispies and nuts. Form into small balls and roll in coconut. Cool on wax paper and store in an airtight container.

YIELD: ABOUT 5 DOZEN COOKIES

MERINGUES

Instead of filling pie shells with fruit, make light and fluffy meringues, any size, and fill them with fresh fruit, pudding, or fruit sauce. The meringues may be made the day before, stored in airtight containers, and filled at the last minute.

3 large egg whites (about ½ cup), at room temperature
⅓ teaspoon cream of tartar
¾ cup granulated sugar
⅛ teaspoon salt
½ teaspoon vanilla extract

Place the egg whites and cream of tartar in a large mixing bowl and beat with a wire whisk beater or regular beater until frothy. Gradually add the sugar, by tablespoonsful, to the egg whites while beating on high speed. Add the salt and vanilla and beat until the whites hold firm peaks, approximately 1½ minutes. Do not overbeat or the meringue will be dry and hard to work with. Preheat the oven to 275°F. Line a baking sheet with parchment paper. With the tip of a knife, draw the size circles you prefer the meringues to be when finished. Spoon the meringue into a large pastry bag fitted with a large star tip. Starting in the center of each circle, pipe the meringue in a continuous spiral, filling in each circle. Pipe a ring of meringue on the top edge of each circle. If you want meringue stars for topping, pipe them on the parchment, too. Bake for 45 minutes or until very light gold and firm to the touch. They may crack a bit, but that makes them pretty. Peel off the parchment and let cool completely before storing. If you live in a dry climate, the meringues will stay crisp and fresh longer at room temperature in an airtight container. If it is damp or humid, it is best to freeze them and crisp them in a warm 150°F oven for 10 minutes before filling. Fill with your favorite filling or fresh fruit with fruit glaze.

YIELD: TWO 9-INCH ROUNDS OR SIX 3½-INCH ROUNDS

CARAMEL CORN

I could eat popcorn every day, but this is my favorite way to make it. This keeps well in an airtight container, so make a lot at a time.

1 cup granulated sugar
¼ cup lightly packed light brown sugar
6 tablespoons light corn syrup (I use Karo)
1½ teaspoons cider vinegar
6 tablespoons water
½ teaspoon salt
2 tablespoons (¼ stick) butter
½ teaspoon baking soda
½ teaspoon vanilla extract
1 cup salted or dry roasted peanuts (optional)
14 cups popped corn

Combine the sugars, syrup, vinegar, and water in large, heavy saucepan. Bring to a boil and cook over medium heat, brushing the sides of the pan with a wet pastry brush, until syrup reaches 290°F on a candy thermometer (the soft crack stage), about 12 minutes. If you do not have a candy thermometer, drop a bit of the syrup in cold water. It should turn *hard* and crack into pieces. Stir in the salt and cook over medium-high heat until it reaches the hard crack stage or 300°F on the thermometer, about 3 minutes. If you do not have a thermometer, drop a few drops of the syrup in more ice water; it should turn brittle at once. Remove from the heat and stir in the butter, baking soda, and vanilla until well blended. Add the nuts to the popcorn if desired and spread the popcorn evenly in two buttered 9-by-13-inch baking pans. Pour the syrup over all the popcorn and mix until all the kernels are coated. Bake in a preheated 200°F oven for 1 hour, stirring every 15 minutes. Cool on sheets of wax paper and store in airtight containers.

YIELD: OVER 14 CUPS

CANDIED APPLES

Red candied apples are usually sold at the popcorn stands at fairs, carnivals, or any outdoor festival. The more familiar recipe is the caramel apple, plain or rolled in nuts or shredded coconut. This is easy to make since all you have to do is melt caramels and dip the apples in the mixture and add sticks. The candied apples take time and are most enjoyed by children who don't mind getting their faces sticky.

6 small apples, suitable for eating on a
  stick (McIntosh, Jonathan, Red
  Delicious, Stayman, Winesap, or
  Baldwin are best)
6 popsickle sticks

¾ cup red cinnamon candies (sometimes
  called red hots, imperials, or hearts)
¼ cup granulated sugar
½ cup boiling water
¼ teaspoon fresh lemon juice
Few drops of red food coloring (optional)

Wash and dry the apples and insert the sticks into the stem end of each. Apples should be room temperature to prevent moisture from forming inside the taffy. Mix the rest of the ingredients together and cook over medium heat in a small saucepan until it reaches 300°F on a candy thermometer (the softball stage) or when you drop a few drops in cold water, the syrup gets hard and cracks immediately, about 12 minutes. It takes a while to reach this stage but it occurs quickly, so do not leave the area while the syrup is boiling. As it nears the 280°F mark, watch closely as it may burn if you do not take it off the heat. Quickly dip each apple into the hot syrup, covering it completely, and place it on a greased cookie sheet to dry. Store on wax paper in a dry area. If they are stored in a moist or refrigerated area, they will weep and become sticky.

YIELD: 6 CANDIED APPLES

CLEAR TOY CANDIES

I remember the clear toys we made that were molded in many shapes, such as reindeer, trains, animals, ships, birds, and, most of all, children with their favorite toys, standing proudly in clear or tinted colors on tables, plates, or centerpieces. We made the same candy during the rest of the year, but during the holidays, the molds were a very special part of the celebration. The rest of the year we called it hard candy, but during special occasions we molded it to represent the season. Today, the molds are very expensive and sought after because they are no longer available or are only found in antique shops. The funny thing is, the recipe was the same, just the addition of food coloring for the holidays made them look different. As children, we were sure they tasted different, too.

To purchase reproduction molds, write to Albert C. Dudrear, 125 East Philadelphia Street, York, PA 17403.

2 cups granulated sugar
⅔ cup light corn syrup (I use Karo)
1 teaspoon cider vinegar
⅔ cup water
Few drops of yellow, red, or green food coloring
1 teaspoon oil of peppermint or spearmint extract (optional)

Oil the molds or shallow cake pans or muffin tins with olive or vegetable oil. Combine the sugar, corn syrup, vinegar, and water together in a deep saucepan. Stir until the sugar is completely dissolved. Bring to a boil over high heat. Do not stir the mixture during cooking.

Place a candy thermometer in the syrup and boil until it reaches 290°F. Add the food coloring and any flavoring. Remove from heat and pour into molds. Do not scrape the sides of the pan or you will get sugar crystals in the candies. If you pour it into flat pans, score it before it cools or break into pieces after it is dry. Store in a cool, dry place in an airtight container.

YIELD: ABOUT 1½ POUNDS

BEST AND EASIEST CANDY

Everyone makes this candy and it is fun to see how each family presents it. Some cut it into bars, some into squares, but the taste is still the same—delicious!

Equal amounts of marshmallows, melted chocolate (milk or dark chocolate), and roasted almonds

Stir all the ingredients together and pour into a baking dish or onto a cookie sheet about 1½ inches thick. When cooled, cut as desired and wrap in clear plastic wrap or wax paper.

YIELD: DEPENDS ON VOLUME OF INGREDIENTS

HINT: Any type of roasted nut is good in this recipe.

MORAVIAN MINTS

These mints are an important traditional treat. They are not hard to make after you see someone make them, but try them the second time before you give up. They are crunchy, not creamy like buttercream mints. If you do not have the old molds, don't worry. Pour them into the new plastic molds or even drop them on a lightly oiled cookie sheet, using 1/2 teaspoon syrup per mint.

2 pounds confectioners sugar
1/2 cup plus 2 tablespoons water
Few drops of red, yellow, or green food
*   coloring*
1/2 teaspoon oil of wintergreen, peppermint,
*   or spearmint extract*

Place some water in the bottom of a double boiler and bring to a boil. Place the sugar and water in the top part of the boiler and stir over medium-high heat every five minutes for approximately 30 minutes (it will develop a crust on the top between stirrings). When the sugar is dissolved but still runny, and reaches 180°F

on a candy thermometer, pour 1/2 teaspoon of the mixture onto a plate. If it hardens and doesn't run all over the plate, add the coloring and flavoring, and cook till it reaches 190°F, about 5 minutes. Stir completely and remove from heat. Pour into molds or spoon about 1/2 teaspoonful for each mint onto buttered or oiled cookie sheets. Do not scrape the mixture from the sides of the pan or the mints will contain crystallized sugar. When dry, store in an airtight container between sheets of wax paper. The mints will be thin and crunchy. They are best when stored in a cool, dry place.

YIELD: 1 1/2 POUNDS

VANILLA PULL TAFFY

Pulling taffy is especially fun during the cold winter months. The main reason for making it during the cold weather is because the taffy is very warm during pulling. Although it can be done alone, it is much more fun when made with a friend. Our youth group at church often planned a "taffy pull" for at least thirty children. The real competition was to see who could get their taffy white and smooth first. The screams of pleasure were as exciting as the best of summer games.

1 cup water
1 1/2 cups light corn syrup (I use Karo)
2 1/2 cups granulated sugar
3 tablespoons butter
1/4 teaspoon salt
1 tablespoon vanilla extract

Butter the sides of a 3-quart stainless steel saucepan or kettle. Add the water, syrup, and sugar, stirring with a wooden spoon until the sugar is dissolved. Bring to a boil over medium-high heat without stirring. Place a candy thermometer in the syrup and continue to boil until the syrup reaches 256°F, approx. 25 minutes. Add the butter and salt and continue cooking till it reaches 262°F, about 2 minutes. Remove from the heat and pour into an oiled or buttered shallow pan or buttered marble slab or counter. When cool enough to handle, butter or oil your hands and pull the sides of the taffy toward the middle. Add some of the vanilla, work the taffy for about a minute, and add the remaining vanilla. Continue pulling the taffy until it is creamy white and lukewarm. Keep your hands buttered to prevent the taffy from sticking to them. When cool, twist into strands of taffy. Place on a buttered counter, cut into 1-inch pieces with oiled scissors, and let dry or wrap in wax paper or plastic wrap. Store in airtight containers.

YIELD: 2 POUNDS

PEANUT BRITTLE

Everyone loves this brittle, and when wrapped in a fancy box, it's really special.

2 cups granulated sugar
3 cups light corn syrup (I use Karo)
¼ teaspoon salt
3 cups unroasted peanuts
1 teaspoon baking soda

In a heavy 10-inch skillet (an iron skillet is best) pour the sugar in a circle. Add the corn syrup and salt to the center and place over medium heat. As the syrup begins to boil, add the raw peanuts and cook for an 8 additional minutes. Reduce the heat to low and cook another 15 minutes or until the syrup reaches 300°F on a candy thermometer, stirring constantly. Then remove from the stove and stir in baking soda. Butter a cookie sheet or marble slab and pour out the brittle evenly. As it begins to set, score it with a sharp knife dipped in cold water. Break the brittle into pieces when it is dry and cool. Store in dry, airtight container.

YIELD: ABOUT 2 POUNDS

HINT: Any type of nut may be substituted for the peanuts.

MAPLE FUDGE

The Pennsylvania Dutch of Somerset County always give this as their special treat for any occasion. We cannot include all the ways they use maple syrup, but they pour it over everything from waffles to ice cream. Making the syrup takes many hours and the final product is truly an act of love.

½ cup sweetened condensed milk diluted
    with ½ cup water or 1 cup heavy cream
    or half and half
1 cup lightly packed light brown sugar
¾ cup pure maple syrup
Pinch of salt
1 teaspoon butter
1 teaspoon vanilla extract
¾ cup pecans, broken into small pieces

Place diluted milk, sugar, syrup, and salt in a heavy saucepan. Stir until blended and heat slowly till boiling, stirring constantly. Boil over high heat without stirring until syrup reaches 238 degrees, the soft ball stage, when a drop of syrup dropped in cold water forms a soft ball. Remove the pan from the heat; add the butter, but do not stir it in. Cool to lukewarm, then beat with a mixer until creamy and thick. Add the vanilla and nuts. Work with your hands (warm hands make the fudge smoother) until very smooth and creamy. Spread in buttered 8-inch square pan, cut into small squares, and let cool.

YIELD: ABOUT 1 POUND

MARSHMALLOWS

Often known as "poor man's candy," this is fun to make and gets loads of raves.

6 tablespoons unflavored gelatin
⅔ cup water
3 cups granulated sugar
¾ cup light corn syrup (I use Karo)
¾ cup water
4 large egg whites
⅓ teaspoon cream of tartar
½ teaspoon salt
2 teaspoons vanilla extract
2 tablespoons cornstarch
1 cup confectioners sugar or 2 to 3 cups
    toasted shredded coconut

Mix the gelatin with the ⅔ cup water in a small bowl to soften. In a heavy 3-quart saucepan combine the sugar, syrup, and ¾ cup water. Bring to a boil, stirring with a spatula to get all the crystals from the sides of the pan only one time. Continue to boil over medium-high heat, undisturbed, till the syrup reaches 240°F on a candy thermometer. Remove the pan from the heat and stir in the gelatin (it will seem solid but will melt the minute it hits the hot syrup). Transfer the mixture to a bowl and beat with a mixer until fluffy. Beat the egg whites until nearly stiff in a large mixing bowl. Gradually add the cream of tartar and salt. Beat until very stiff. Slowly add the gelatin mixture and continue beating until it is very thick and stringy, approximately 15 to 20 minutes. Beat in the vanilla and cornstarch. Generously oil an 11-by-13-inch baking pan and dust it with a small amount of confectioners sugar. Pour the mixture into the pan and dust with a bit of confectioners sugar. Let stand uncovered for several hours. Cut into 1-inch squares and roll in sifted confectioners sugar or toasted coconut. (Dip the knife in hot water first for easy, clean cutting.)

YIELD: 2 POUNDS

CREAMY NO-COOK FUDGE

You can make this one in a hurry.

8 ounces cream cheese
¼ cup condensed milk
2 tablespoons (¼ stick) butter
2 or 3 ounces (2 or 3 squares) unsweetened chocolate, melted, or ½ cup unsweetened cocoa
2 cups confectioners sugar
1 teaspoon vanilla extract
½ teaspoon salt
1 cup chopped nuts (optional)

Combine all the ingredients but the nuts in a large mixing bowl. Beat until creamy, about 15 minutes. If too dry, add a small amount of milk to moisten. Remove from the bowl, add the nuts, and work with your hands until very creamy, about 10 minutes. If you knead the fudge on a clean kitchen counter or marble slab, it will take longer, about 20 minutes. Press into a lightly buttered 8-inch pan and score with an attractive pattern. Chill and cut when firm.

YIELD: ABOUT 1½ POUNDS

WHOOPIE PIES

If you want these to last for any length of time, you have to wrap and freeze (or hide) them. They always seem to disappear before your eyes.

1 cup vegetable shortening or margarine
2 cups granulated sugar
2 large eggs
3½ cups all-purpose flour
1 cup unsweetened cocoa
2 teaspoons salt
2 teaspoons baking soda
1 cup buttermilk or milk soured with 1 tablespoon vinegar
1 cup hot coffee or water

Filling:

2 large egg whites
1 tablespoon vanilla extract
¼ cup milk
2 cups confectioners sugar
¼ cup all-purpose flour
1 cup vegetable shortening
¼ pound (1 stick) butter

Cream the shortening and sugar together in a large mixing bowl. Beat in the eggs, one at a time. In another bowl, sift the flour with the cocoa, salt, and baking soda. Gradually add this to the creamed mixture alternating with the buttermilk. Mix in the hot coffee. Drop the batter in teaspoonsful onto greased cookie sheets, spacing them about 3 inches apart. Bake in a preheated 375°F oven for 8 minutes. Store on wax paper until all the cookies have been baked. For the filling, beat the egg whites until fluffy. Gradually beat in the vanilla, milk, sugar, and flour. Add the shortening and butter and beat until very fluffy. Take one cookie and place a generous tablespoon of filling on the flat side. Top with another cookie; they should look like yo-yos. These freeze well if wrapped individually.

YIELD: ABOUT 48 TO 60 WHOOPIE PIES

CREAM PUFFS

These are one of the best "fund raisers" for 4-H and high school band projects. I like them filled with Vanilla Cream Pudding (see page 175), but when they're made very small and filled with ham or chicken salad, they're great for parties.

1 cup water
¼ pound (1 stick) butter
¼ teaspoon salt
1 cup all-purpose flour
4 large eggs

Put the water in a heavy saucepan and bring to a boil over medium-high. Add the butter and salt. When melted, add the flour and stir briskly with a wooden spoon. Reduce heat to medium-low and continue to cook, stirring constantly, until mixture leaves the sides of pan, about 5 minutes. Remove from the heat, cool for 5 minutes, then beat in the eggs, one at a time until the batter is smooth and well mixed. Drop by spoonsful onto a greased baking sheet or muffin pans, shaping the batter to a point. Place about 2 inches apart. Bake in a preheated 425°F oven for 15 minutes, reduce to 350°F and continue baking for 25 to 30 minutes longer. Cool and fill with your favorite filling. Pierce a hole in the side of the cream puff and pipe the filling in with a large pastry tube or split half way around and fill with a small spoon.

YIELD: 12 TO 15 CREAM PUFFS

BASIC SWEET DOUGH

I love to use this recipe to make all kinds of party breads.

2 packages dry granular yeast or 2 yeast
  cakes
½ cup lukewarm water
Pinch of granulated sugar
1 cup milk, scalded
⅓ cup granulated sugar
1 teaspoon salt
2 large eggs, lightly beaten
4 tablespoons (½ stick) butter
4 tablespoons (½ stick) margarine
5 cups sifted all-purpose flour

Proof the yeast by combining the yeast with the lukewarm water and pinch of sugar. If it foams, it is active and ready. Put the milk, sugar, and salt in a large mixing bowl and stir until the sugar is dissolved. Cool to lukewarm, then add the yeast mixture, beaten eggs, butter, and margarine. Gradually add flour, kneading with the dough hook of a mixer or by hand on a lightly floured surface for approximately 5 minutes or until the dough is smooth and elastic; it should not stick to the bowl or board. If it does, add a bit more flour. Turn the dough into a greased bowl, turning it so all sides are greased. Cover with a clean, damp cloth and let rise in a warm, draft-free area until doubled in bulk, about 1 hour. Knead on a lightly floured surface for a minute to remove all air bubbles. When smooth, cover and let rise again until almost double, about 30 minutes. Shape as desired and bake as particular recipe indicates.

YIELD: 1 LARGE PAN OF ROLLS OR 1 COFFEE CAKE

RAISED DOUGHNUTS

Doughnuts are to the Pennsylvania Dutch as bagels are to New Yorkers, and they aren't just for breakfast anymore. The Dutch like to dunk them in coffee or, for the children, hot chocolate after they are a day old.

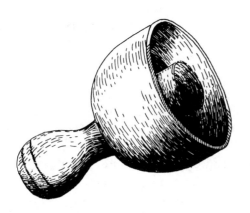

1 recipe of Basic Sweet Dough (page 191)
3 cups vegetable oil
½ cup confectioners or granulated sugar

After the second rising, knead and roll out the dough ⅓-inch thick on a well-floured board. Cut with a floured 3-inch doughnut cutter. Let rise on the board until almost doubled, approximately 40 minutes, uncovered. Heat the oil in a deep, heavy skillet or pan to 375°F. Gently place the doughnuts in the oil, making sure they do not touch one another. Turn them when golden brown on one side or after about 3 minutes. Drain on paper towels. Place the sugar in a bag and shake the doughnuts in it until covered. If glazing them, use the sugar icing used for hot cross buns on page 144.

YIELD: 3 TO 4 DOZEN DOUGHNUTS

Variations: Crullers: Follow the same instructions as for raised doughnuts, but roll the dough ½-inch thick and cut into strips ½-inch wide and 8 inches long. Twirl or braid two strips together and seal the ends for each cruller. Let rise, then fry as for doughnuts—they may take a bit longer to fry because of the double thickness of the cruller—about 4 minutes on each side. Shake in granulated sugar. Yield: About 2 dozen crullers.
Filled Doughnuts: Follow the same instructions as for raised doughnuts, but instead of cutting the dough into round doughnuts with a hole in the middle, cut the dough in 3-inch squares, prick them with a fork several times on top, let rise, and then fry as for raised doughnuts. Use a pastry tube or cake decorator to fill the centers of the doughnuts after they have fried with Vanilla Cream Pudding (page 175), applebutter (page 198), or your favorite

jelly by piercing the tip of the tube into the side of the doughnut. Fill and shake in granulated sugar. Yield: 3 dozen filled doughnuts.

Fried Dough: Follow the same instructions as for raised doughnuts, but cut the dough into strips ¾ inch wide and 8 inches long. Let rise, then fry as for doughnuts. Serve plain or with sugar and molasses. Yield: 3 dozen strips.

FASTNACHTS

Better known as potato doughnuts, fastnachts are always baked for Shrove Tuesday. A tradition with all the Christian churches, this treat is very important to the Pennsylvania Dutch.

1 cup milk
1 cup cooked mashed potatoes
⅔ cup granulated sugar
½ teaspoon salt
3 tablespoons butter or vegetable shortening
3 tablespoons margarine
2 large or medium-size eggs, lightly beaten
1 package dry granular yeast or 1 yeast cake
¼ cup lukewarm water
6 cups all-purpose flour
Vegetable oil for frying
Granulated or confectioners sugar for coating

Scald the milk and let cool to lukewarm while blending the mashed potatoes, sugar, salt, butter, and margarine in a large bowl. Gradually add the beaten eggs and stir until creamy. Dissolve the yeast in the lukewarm water and add to the potato mixture. Alternate adding in the milk and flour, mixing or kneading with a dough hook until the dough is smooth and elastic, about 4 minutes. Turn into a large greased bowl, turning until all sides are greased. Cover and set in warm, draft-free area. Let rise until double, about 45 minutes. Punch down or knead to remove all bubbles. Divide in half and roll out about ¾ inch thick. Cut dough in 3-inch squares, making a 1-inch diagonal slit with a greased knife. Cover squares and let sit until almost double. Fry them in 3 inches of oil heated to 370°F until they are golden brown on both sides. Drain on paper towels and shake in sugar while still warm.

YIELD: 24 FASTNACHTS

Variation: Cut and serve as regular doughnuts, frying the "holes" separately.

FUNNEL CAKES

One of the oldest snacks or after-school treats, these are becoming popular the world over. Great!

1 cup all-purpose flour
2 teaspoons granulated sugar
1 teaspoon baking powder
½ teaspoon salt
1 large or medium-size egg, lightly beaten
¾ cup milk
Vegetable oil for frying
Confectioners sugar

In a large bowl combine the flour, sugar, baking powder, and salt. Gradually add in the

beaten egg and milk until well blended. Let the mixture stand for 15 minutes. Heat ⅓ inch of vegetable oil in a deep skillet to 390 degrees. When the oil is hot, pour the batter into funnel, drizzling a thin stream of batter into the hot oil. Start in the center of the skillet, circling continuously until pan is filled or the cake is the desired size. Do not stop pouring until the cake is complete. Fry on each side until golden brown. Drain on paper towels and serve warm with confectioners sugar for dipping.

YIELD: 6 LARGE FUNNEL CAKES

Variation: Add ⅓ cup semisweet chocolate minichips or morsels or 3 ounces semisweet grated chocolate to the batter.

CHOCOLATE-COVERED PRETZELS

Always served at Amish weddings and other special occasions, these treats have become popular everywhere. They're fun and easy to make and keep well in airtight containers to send to friends. Again, the secret is in the combination of salty and sweet so familiar to the Pennsylvania Dutch.

1 pound chocolate of your choice (I prefer semisweet or any dark sweet chocolate)
1 pound thin pretzels, any size
Sprinkles (optional)

Melt the chocolate in the top of a double boiler over simmering water. (Do not let any steam or even a drop of water make contact with the chocolate or it will harden and crumble.) Cool chocolate until, when touched to the upper lip, it feels cool. This can be done by stirring the chocolate with a silver spoon or working it on a marble or stainless steel surface by hand. Quickly dip the pretzels in the chocolate and lightly cover with sprinkles while still moist. If you coat the pretzels this way, you do not have to refrigerate them, as it prevents the chocolate from spotting at room temperature.

YIELD: ABOUT 2 POUNDS

Variation: Sprinkle with crushed nuts.

ICE CREAM

There's nothing like churning your own ice cream, adding in all the fresh fruits, and sitting down to a creamy bowl—especially on a hot day!

4 large eggs
2⅔ cups granulated sugar
⅓ teaspoon salt
2 (13-ounce) cans evaporated milk
1½ cups heavy cream
2½ cups milk
1½ tablespoons vanilla extract

Cream the eggs, sugar, and salt together in a large mixing bowl, blending until fluffy. Stir in the evaporated milk, cream, milk, and vanilla. Pour into the can of a 4-quart freezer and cover with the lid. Pack with crushed ice and rock salt, turning until the ice cream is hard. (Using rock salt instead of iodized salt will reduce the turning time.) Add more crushed ice, a bit of water, and salt as the ice melts, keeping the ice to the top of the outside of the freezer but not over the lid. Be careful that the salt does not seep into the ice cream mixture inside the freezer can.

YIELD: 4 QUARTS

Variation: Add 2 cups any type of pureed fruit before you start turning the freezer.

FRIED ICE CREAM

Use any flavor ice cream for this delicious treat.

2 tablespoons vegetable oil
4 Crepes (page 49)
1 1/3 cups ice cream
4 teaspoons butter, melted
4 teaspoons light brown sugar
1/4 cup orange juice
Whipped Cream (page 170) or confectioners sugar for garnish

Heat the vegetable oil in a large skillet over medium-high heat until it quickly fries a cube of fresh bread, about 5 minutes. While heating the skillet, place the crepes on a large serving dish and put 1/3 cup ice cream in the center of each one. Quickly fold up the sides of the crepe into the center. Brush tops of the crepe with 1/2 teaspoon of the butter and sprinkle with 1 teaspoon of the brown sugar and 1 tablespoon of the orange juice. Place the crepes in the heated skillet and fry over medium-high heat until they are golden brown, about 3 minutes. Turn and fry them on the other side until the butter, sugar, and juice caramelize, about 4 minutes. Serve immediately with whipped cream or sprinkled with confectioners sugar, if desired.

YIELD: 4 SERVINGS

Chapter 12

Preserves, Relishes, Pickles, and Vinegars

CANNING OR PROCESSING METHODS
Canning—Cold Pack Method

Home canning is really very simple. Although at first it may seem rather expensive to invest in all those jars and a home canner, which is a deep pot fitted with a rack to hold 7 quart jars or 12 pint jars, remember that you will be using them over and over again for years. You only need to buy new replacement lids each time you fill the jars. The rings, if washed and dried after each use, are usually good for at least 5 years. You can use any big, deep pot and put a rack inside, but the canner is a good investment. It doesn't cost much and you can also use it for cooking corn, steaming clams, or any kind of quantity cooking. The rack has handles, so it is easy to lower or lift the jars.

The technique for canning is simple, once you get used to it. First, sterilize your jars for 15 minutes in boiling water, leaving them in the water with the heat off until you are ready to drain and use them. You can also sterilize them by leaving them in a 250°F oven for 20 to 25 minutes. Be sure the jars are hot when you pack them, as the heat ensures that they seal properly. The best and safest jar to use is the type with a vacuum-seal flat lid and a screw-on ring cover that fits over it. Don't boil the lid, which has a rubber seal around the inside; just pour boiling water over it and leave in the water until ready to use.

Drain, fill, and seal the sterilized jars. Most

197

home-canning booklets tell you to leave ½-inch head space for fruits and relishes, but I find it works best to fill the jars to the neck only. I also like to start the canning from cool water, rather than putting the jars into boiling water, as most booklets recommend. I lower the jars on the rack into the canner, add enough water to come to the neck of the jars, bring this to a boil, and boil for the required time with the cover on. This is known as the cold-pack method.

For transferring fruits or relishes to the jars, use glass or stainless steel measuring cups, slotted enamel, stainless steel, or wooden spoons, or enameled ladles, plus a wide-mouthed funnel for filling jars with liquid.

Fruits are canned in a sugar and water syrup. I like to use a thick syrup made from 1 cup granulated sugar and 1 cup water. You may reduce the sugar by as much as ½ cup or use a sugar substitute, following your own taste. Place it in a saucepan and bring to a boil over high heat. When the sugar is completely dissolved, remove it from the heat, keeping the syrup warm until you are ready to pour it over the fruit. Pack the fruit in the sterilized jars and add enough syrup to fill the jar to the neck. Before sealing, release any air that may be trapped in the liquid by running a long, thin, rubber spatula down between the inside of the jar and the fruit, moving the fruit around slightly to let the air out. Wipe the tops of the jars, seal with vacuum lids and covers, and process by filling the canner with lukewarm water up to the necks of the jars. Bring to a full boil, covered, over medium-high heat. Start timing after the water comes to a full boil. Most fruits require 15 minutes for proper sterilization. Remove the canner from the heat and use metal tongs to secure the jars as they are

removed from the water. If you have a canner, the basket is easily lifted up and rests on the side of the canner, making it very easy to remove the jars. Place the jars on linen towels away from drafts to cool. Let them stand at least 12 hours before storing them. The lid should be indented. If it is not, the fruit inside should be discarded or consumed immediately. Before storing the filled jars, wipe the jars clean and make sure each one is sealed.

Canning—Open Kettle Method

Open kettle canning is usually done for jellies, jams, butters, and small amounts of fruit. The process means boiling the jellies or fruit in the syrup over medium heat until it is finished and ready to jar. When boiling fruit, it should give a bit when pressed. If the fruit is halved, 12 minutes is adequate but if the fruit has pits, such as apricots, they should be cooked 15 minutes. Transfer the fruit into sterilized jars, fill to the neck with the hot syrup and seal with new lids and rings. Let them stand at least 12 hours before storing them. Store away from direct sunlight.

APPLEBUTTER

Traditionally, applebutter was made in a huge copper kettle and was an all-day affair. This recipe has been cut down and adapted to today's kitchen.

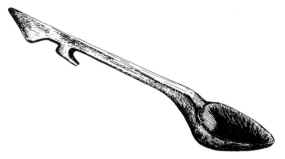

15 pounds tart cooking apples (Winesap,
  Stayman, or Smokehouse varieties are
  best)
2½ cups water
3½ cups granulated sugar
1½ cups cider vinegar
1 teaspoon ground cinnamon
½ teaspoon salt

Wash, peel, core, and quarter the apples. Put apples and water in a large, heavy kettle and cook over low heat until the fruit is soft, about 15 minutes. Drain extra liquid from the apples and puree in a food mill or food processor. Add the sugar, vinegar, cinnamon, and salt to the apple puree. Blend and pour the mixture into a heavy roasting pan. Bake, uncovered, in a preheated 375°F oven for about 2½ hours, stirring every 15 minutes with a wooden spoon to prevent sticking. This also keeps the applebutter color even. It is ready to jar or serve when you can place 2 tablespoons of applebutter on a saucer and turn it upside down without it dropping off. Ladle into hot sterilized jars and seal with new lids and rings.

YIELD: 10 PINTS

Variation: Pear Butter is made by substituting an equal amount of pears for the apples and adding 1 teaspoon ground nutmeg.

SPICED CANTALOUPE

Very delicately flavored, this unusual relish is excellent served with seafood.

2½ pounds firm, ripe cantaloupes (the
  better the fruit, the better the relish)
1 cup granulated sugar
¼ cup water
½ cup cider vinegar
Oil of cinnamon and oil of cloves; use 1
  drop of each per pint
For canning instructions, see pages 197–98

Wash the cantaloupe, and cut it in half to remove the seeds; then cut into 1-inch slices and peel. Cut the slices into 2-inch pieces or place the slices whole into sterilized pint jars. Combine the sugar, water, and vinegar in a small, heavy saucepan and bring to a boil over high heat. Reduce heat to medium and simmer for 2 minutes, then slowly pour some of the syrup over the cantaloupe. Add the drops of oil on top of the cantaloupe, then fill to the neck of the jar with more. Place a new self-sealing lid and cover on each jar and process in a home canner for 15 minutes, timing from the moment the water comes to a full boil.

YIELD: 5 PINTS

Variation: Spiced Peaches: Follow same recipe as spiced cantaloupe, but use peeled peach halves instead of cantaloupe slices.

BRANDIED APRICOTS

There are so many ways to serve this recipe—
let your imagination run wild! My family enjoys them plain. We serve them with warm
pudding or cake and pour the syrup over the
top, sometimes adding extra brandy to flambé.
Try melting your favorite chocolate bars and
pouring it over the apricots right before serving. Fill each apricot half with ice cream or
sherbet or just use them for a fruit salad topped
with whipped cream flavored with 2 tablespoons of its syrup.

2 cups granulated sugar
¾ cup water
¼ teaspoon salt
1½ teaspoons cider vinegar
2 pounds fresh apricots
1 cup brandy

In a large enamel or stainless steel saucepan
combine the sugar, water, salt, and vinegar.
Bring to a boil over high heat and add the
apricots. Reduce heat to medium and simmer
for 10 to 12 minutes, depending on the size of
the apricots. Remove the fruit and let the
syrup boil over medium heat for 8 minutes
more. Remove the pan from the heat, add the
brandy and fruit and blend together. Ladle the
apricots and syrup into hot sterilized jars and
seal with new lids and rings. Do not move the
jars for 12 hours to prevent the seals from
breaking. Store away from direct sunlight for
several weeks at least before serving.

YIELD: 4 PINTS

Variation: Peaches, pears, and plums may be
substituted. Peaches and pears are best when
peeled and plums should be pricked with a fork
several times to prevent the skins from burst-
ing.

BASIC PICKLING SYRUP, SWEET

The Pennsylvania Dutch love their pickles
and relishes sweet, thereby getting the tag line
"Sweets and Sours."

4 cups granulated sugar
2 cups cider vinegar
2 cups water
1 teaspoon salt
1 tablespoon celery seed
1 tablespoon mustard seed
1 tablespoon pickling spices (optional)

Combine all the ingredients in a large saucepan, stir, and bring to a boil. Simmer 5 minutes over medium-high heat, adding any extra spices the pickle recipe calls for. Remove from the heat and pour into sterilized jars. Seal with new lids if you are not using it within a day or two. This syrup will keep for several weeks in the refrigerator.

YIELD: 6 CUPS

Variation: For a semisweet pickling syrup that is somewhat tart, decrease the amount of sugar to 2 cups.

THREE-BEAN RELISH

Many folks add oil and wine vinegar to this to create a beautiful salad served on lettuce with hardboiled eggs.

3 cups green beans
3 cups yellow or wax beans
4 large onions
1/3 cup vegetable oil
6 cups Basic or Semisweet Pickling Syrup (page 200–201)
3 cups canned red kidney beans, rinsed and drained

Cut beans and onions into bite-size pieces. Put beans, onions, oil, and syrup in an 8-quart kettle. Bring to a boil and simmer over medium heat until vegetables are tender but not mushy, about 12 minutes. Add the drained kidney beans and simmer 5 more minutes over me-

dium heat. Ladle into hot sterilized jars, filling to the neck of each jar and seal with new lids and rings. Let jars stand 12 hours before moving to a cool storage area to prevent breaking the seals. Refrigerate after opening.

YIELD: 10 PINTS

DILL BEANS

It takes a long time to pack these beans but they are so good to nibble on and enjoy anywhere, anytime.

4 pounds whole, firm, young, green beans, trimmed
1/2 cup salt
4 fresh tarragon sprigs or 2 teaspoons dried
6 cups white vinegar
4 cups water
2 tablespoons dill seed
2 teaspoons dried dillweed

Soak the beans for 1 hour in a large pot with the salt and enough water to cover. Rinse and cover with fresh cold water. Bring to a boil and cook over medium heat, uncovered, for 2 minutes only. Drain into a colander. When cool enough to handle, pack the trimmed whole beans lengthwise, carefully, into hot, sterilized pint jars. Tuck a sprig of tarragon (or put 1/2 teaspoon dried tarragon) in each jar. Combine the vinegar, water, dill seed, and dillweed in a large saucepan, bring to a boil, and boil 2 minutes over medium heat. Pour over the beans in the jars and seal with new lids and rings. Let stand 24 hours before moving to a cool storage area or shelves to prevent breaking the seals. Refrigerate after opening a jar. They will keep at least 3 weeks if the lid is closed properly.

YIELD: 8 PINTS

CHOW CHOW

One of the most important and colorful of the relishes, chow chow is great served with any meal. The fun in making this relish is to see how many kinds of vegetables you can get in a jar.

1 cup each of lima beans, green beans (cut in 1-inch pieces), yellow beans (cut in 1-inch pieces), drained canned Great Northern beans, drained canned red kidney beans, drained canned navy beans, cauliflower buds, chopped celery, chopped red bell peppers, chopped green bell peppers, carrots (cut in 1/4-inch pieces), corn kernels, pearl onions or chopped onions, grated cabbage, and sliced cucumbers or tiny pickles (1 1/2 inches long)
5 cups Basic or Semisweet Pickling Syrup (page 200–201)
1/2 teaspoon ground turmeric
1/2 teaspoon salt

If frozen vegetables are used, they may be cooked together. For fresh vegetables, cook each vegetable separately in a small amount of water over medium heat until tender but not mushy. Do not cook the canned beans. Drain each and layer in large pan. Gently blend with your hands or a wooden spoon to prevent breaking the vegetables. Drain again. In a large kettle bring the syrup to a boil, add the turmeric, and salt, and gently spoon in the vegetables with a pierced spoon. When vegetables come to a boil, simmer over medium heat for 5 minutes. Ladle into sterilized pint jars, filling to the neck of each jar, and seal with new lids and rings. Let the jars stand for at least 12 hours before moving them to a cool storage area to prevent breaking the seals. Refrigerate after opening.

YIELD: 7 PINTS

CORN RELISH

The cabbage in this relish is what makes the difference.

6 cups Basic Pickling Syrup, using 4 cups white vinegar instead of the cider vinegar and water (page 200–201)
8 cups corn kernels, fresh or frozen
2 cups chopped cabbage
1 cup chopped onion
1/2 cup chopped green bell pepper
1/2 cup chopped red bell pepper (substitute extra green pepper if red unavailable)

Place everything in an 8-quart kettle. Bring to a boil and simmer over medium heat for 10 minutes. Ladle into hot sterilized jars, filling to the neck of each jar, and seal with new lids and rings. Let stand for 12 hours before moving them to a cool storage area to prevent breaking the seals. Refrigerate after opening.

YIELD: 8 PINTS

RED PEPPER RELISH

Colorful, versatile, and tasty.

1 teaspoon salt
½ teaspoon dry mustard
4 cups Basic or Semisweet Pickling Syrup
  (page 200–201)
9 large red bell peppers, cored, seeded, and
  chopped
3 large onions, chopped
1 stem celery, chopped

Add the salt and dry mustard to the pickling syrup in 4-quart kettle. Stir and bring to a boil. Add the peppers, onions, and celery, and bring to a boil. Simmer over medium heat for 10 minutes. Ladle into hot sterilized jars, filling to the neck of each jar, and seal with new lids and rings. Let stand 12 hours before moving to a cool storage area to prevent breaking the seals. Refrigerate after opening.

YIELD: 6 PINTS

Variation: Green bell peppers may be substituted for the red. Add ½ teaspoon of cayenne pepper or Tabasco sauce if you like it hot.

WATERMELON RIND PICKLES

So beautiful to serve, but truly an act of love to make, these are gifts of food that are treasured with every bite.

¼ cup salt
4½ cups water
2½ pounds watermelon rind, peeled (leave
  ¼ inch of the pink flesh for color) and
  cut into 2-inch pieces
2½ cups granulated sugar
1 cup cider vinegar
1 cup water
⅛ teaspoon oil of cinnamon
⅛ teaspoon oil of cloves
  (The oils prevent the fruit from getting
  dark. If the oils are not available, use 1
  teaspoon each of whole cloves and broken
  cinnamon sticks, placed in tea infusers.)

Mix the salt and 4 cups of the water until dissolved and pour over the rind in an enamel, plastic, or stainless steel container. Cover and soak overnight. Next day drain and rinse the rind in cold water. Drain again. Cook over high heat in enough fresh water to cover the rind until rind is tender and translucent, about 30 minutes. Drain. Combine the sugar, vinegar, 1/2 cup water, and oils in a large enamel or stainless steel kettle and bring to a full boil. Remove from the heat and add the rind. Let stand, lightly covered, overnight. Next day, drain the syrup into a large saucepan and bring to a boil. Simmer over medium heat for several minutes and pour over the rind again. Repeat this process for 3 days to make the rind clear. On the last day, cook the rind and syrup together over high heat for 3 minutes. Ladle into hot sterilized jars and seal with new lids and rings. Let jars stand for 12 hours before moving to a cool storage area to prevent breaking the seals. Refrigerate after opening.

YIELD: 6 PINTS

Variation: Add 1/2 teaspoon peeled, sliced ginger root for added flavor.

DILL PICKLES

These are so tasty, easy to prepare, and beautiful in the jars, it is certainly worth the few minutes it takes to prepare them.

3 large cucumbers
1 1/2 teaspoons dill seed
1/2 teaspoon dried dillweed
3/4 teaspoon mustard seed
1/2 teaspoon minced garlic

1/2 cup cider vinegar
6 tablespoons water
2 1/4 teaspoons salt

Wash cucumbers and cut into quarters lengthwise. If they have wax on the shell, run hot water over them until you can wipe it off with paper towels. Arrange in sterilized pint jars and add the dill seed and dillweed, mustard seed, and garlic. In a large enamel or stainless steel kettle, combine the vinegar, water, and salt, and bring to a boil over medium-high heat. Pour over the cucumbers. Seal jars with new lids, cover with rings, and process in a canner for 5 to 6 minutes, timing from the moment the water comes to a boil.

YIELD: 3 TO 4 PINTS, DEPENDING ON THE SIZE OF THE CUCUMBERS

BREAD-AND-BUTTER PICKLES

These are the old standby because they go with everything—no hamburger should be without them, sliced razor thin.

4 large, unwaxed cucumbers, sliced 1/4 inch
   thick
3 large onions, sliced 1/4 inch thick
1/2 large green bell pepper, chopped
1/2 large red bell pepper, chopped
2 tablespoons salt
4 cups ice cubes
3 cups Basic or Semisweet Pickling Syrup
   (page 200–201)
1/2 teaspoon ground turmeric
1/4 teaspoon dried dillweed

Toss the cucumbers, onions, and peppers with the salt in a large bowl. Cover with the ice cubes and let stand three to four hours. Add the turmeric and dillweed to the pickling syrup and bring to a boil over high heat in a large enamel or stainless steel kettle. Rinse the vegetables in cold water and add to the boiling syrup. Boil over medium heat for 3 minutes. Ladle into sterilized pint jars, filling to the neck of the jar, and seal.

YIELD: 5 PINTS

SEVEN-DAY PICKLES

These pickles are so good, they definitely are worth the effort.

5 pounds medium-size cucumbers, 3 to 4
  inches long
4 cups cider vinegar
4 cups granulated sugar
1 cup water
1 tablespoon salt
4½ teaspoons mixed whole pickling spices
Several drops of green food coloring
  (optional)

Wash the cucumbers, holding them under hot water if they are waxed until you can wipe the wax off with a paper towel. Put them in a large stock pot. Cover them with boiling water, cover with a lid and allow to stand for 1 day. Drain and repeat the process every day for four days, using fresh boiling water each time. On the fifth day slice or quarter the cucumbers. Combine the vinegar, sugar, water, salt, and spices in a large enamel or stainless steel kettle. Bring to a boil over high heat and add the cucumbers. Remove from the heat and let stand, covered, till the next day, then drain off the syrup, add the coloring, and bring the syrup to a boil in a large saucepan. Pour over the cucumbers in the kettle and bring to a full boil. Pack in hot, sterilized, pint jars and seal. For canning instructions see "open kettle" method on page 198.

YIELD: 6 PINTS

Variation: Two-day Sweet Pickles: Dissolve 1 cup salt in 16 cups cold water. Let the cucumbers stand in the salt water brine for 24 hours. Drain and puncture each cucumber several times with a fork. Bring the vinegar, sugar, water, salt, and spices to a boil in a large enamel or stainless steel kettle, add the cucumbers, and simmer over medium heat for 30 minutes. Remove from the heat and let stand, covered, for 1 day. Drain the syrup into a large saucepan and add 1 cup vinegar and 1 cup granulated sugar. Stir until dissolved, then simmer over medium heat for 5 minutes. Pour over the whole cucumbers in the kettle and bring to a full boil. Arrange the cucumbers in hot, sterilized pint jars and seal, using new seals. Process according to the "open kettle" canning method, explained on page 198.

YIELD: 6 PINTS

HERB VINEGAR

Use any fresh herb, blossom and all. If you like to combine herbs, put a sprig of tarragon with a sprig of thyme. Chives and chive blossoms look and taste nice with parsley. Rosemary is best with mint. A sprig of oregano or basil with its blossoms is delightful, or combine them for a full-flavored vinegar. You can use small bottles as long as you can find corks that fit them—and don't forget to label them!

Handful of the fresh herbs of your choice
2 cups cider vinegar
2 cups white vinegar
1 tablespoon granulated sugar

Wash the herbs and place several sprigs in each sterilized bottle. Bring the vinegars and sugar to a boil in a large saucepan and pour over the herbs. Cork tightly. Store at room temperature away from direct sunlight. Refrigerate after opening.

YIELD: 2 PINTS

CELERY VINEGAR

Mild and wonderful with fresh cutting lettuce.

1 large bunch fresh celery with leaves,
  chopped
2 tablespoons celery seed
2 cups cider vinegar
3 cups white vinegar
1 teaspoon salt
1½ tablespoons granulated sugar

Place the celery in a gallon jar or crock and add the celery seed. Bring the vinegars to boil in a medium-size saucepan, add the salt and sugar and stir until dissolved. Pour over the chopped celery and cover. Let stand in a cool place for at least two weeks. Strain through a double thickness of cheesecloth, let stand, covered, overnight and bottle in sterilized containers. Cork tightly. Store away from direct sunlight. Refrigerate after opening.

YIELD: 3 TO 4 PINTS

cloth, bottle in sterilized containers, and cork. Store away from direct sunlight. Refrigerate after opening.

YIELD: 3 TO 4 PINTS

PEPPER VINEGAR

A splash of this will liven up any recipe that calls for vinegar. It is particularly delicious splashed on raw oysters, crab, or fish.

2 teaspoons whole black peppercorns
2 cups cider vinegar
2 cups white vinegar
½ teaspoon Tabasco sauce
2 tablespoons granulated sugar

Crush the peppercorns with a wooden mallet and place in a crock or glass container. Bring vinegars and Tabasco to a boil. Add the hot vinegar and sugar to the peppercorns, stirring until the sugar is dissolved. Cover and let stand at least two weeks. Strain through a double thickness of cheesecloth and bottle in sterilized containers. Cork tightly. Store away from direct sunlight. Refrigerate after opening.

YIELD: 2 PINTS

ONION VINEGAR

Fun to make for gifts, it looks extra special when a few tiny onions are placed in the bottles before corking. This tastes great on burgers, fish fillets, or in salad dressings!

6 large onions, chopped
1 tablespoon salt
3 cups white vinegar
2 cups cider vinegar
2 tablespoons granulated sugar

Sprinkle the onions with salt and let stand, covered, overnight or at least 5 hours. Put the onions in a gallon crock or glass jar. Bring the vinegars to a boil and stir in the sugar. Pour the vinegar over the onions and cover lightly. This will foam for a few days, so be sure to use a jar that is large enough to prevent exploding. Steep for two weeks in a cool place. Then strain through a double thickness of cheese-

SUPERB VINEGAR

A very old recipe, this proves that light salad dressings always existed. It also makes a wonderful seasoning for gravies, sauces, and stews.

2 teaspoons allspice
1 teaspoon whole black peppercorns
1 tablespoon freshly grated nutmeg
2 tablespoons grated fresh horseradish
Pinch of red (cayenne) pepper
1 tablespoon salt
1 tablespoon granulated sugar
4 cups white vinegar

Crush the allspice and peppercorns with a wooden mallet. Place everything but the vinegar in a large, heavy saucepan. Then pour in the vinegar and bring to a boil. Remove from the heat, pour into a covered container, and let stand for at least two weeks. Strain through a double thickness of cheesecloth and bottle in sterilized containers. Cork tightly. Store away from direct sunlight. Refrigerate after opening.

YIELD: 2 PINTS

Index